The Meanings of Violence

The media often make sense of violence in terms of 'randomness' and 'evil'. But the reality, as the contributors to *The Meanings of Violence* demonstrate, is far more complex. Drawing on the diverse subject matter of the ESRC's Violence Research Programme – from interviews with killers to discussions with children in residential facilities – this volume locates the meaning of violence within social contexts, identities and social divisions. It aims to break open our way of speaking about violence and demonstrate the value in exploring the multiple, contradictory and complex meanings of violence in society. The wide range of topics considered includes:

- prostitute and client violence;
- violence among young people at school and on the streets;
- violence in bars and nightclubs;
- violence in prison;
- racist and homophobic violence.

This book will be fascinating reading for students of criminology and academics working in the field of violent crime.

Elizabeth A. Stanko is Professor of Criminology at Royal Holloway, University of London, and Director of the ESRC Violence Research Programme.

The Meanings of Violence

Edited by Elizabeth A. Stanko

Routledge
Taylor & Francis Group

LONDON AND NEW YORK

First published 2003 by Routledge
2 Park Square, Milton Park, Abingdon, Oxon, OX14 4RN

Simultaneously published in the USA and Canada
by Routledge
270 Madison Ave, New York NY 10016

Routledge is an imprint of the Taylor & Francis Group

Transferred to Digital Printing 2005

Typeset in Goudy by Taylor & Francis Ltd

British Library Cataloguing in Publication Data
A catalogue record for this book is available from the
British Library

Library of Congress Cataloging in Publication Data
A catalog record for this book has been requested

ISBN 0-415-30129-7 (hbk)
ISBN 0-415-30130-0 (pbk)

Contents

List of illustrations

Tables

Figures

Notes on contributors

Dr John Archer is a reader in history at Edge Hill College of Education. He has published extensively on nineteenth-century rural crime and protest and is currently working on violence in the northwest of England.

Dr Rosemary Aris is a lecturer at the University of Warwick.

Marina Barnard is a senior research fellow at the Centre for Drug Misuse Research at Glasgow University. She has published extensively as a qualitative researcher working in the area of drug misuse and prostitution and more recently on the impact of problem drug use on parenting and child welfare.

Christine Barter is a senior NSPCC research fellow with the Faculty of Health Care and Social Studies at Luton University. She has previously worked on a range of projects concerning the experiences of young people, including children who run away, protecting children from racial abuse, independent investigations into allegations of institutional child abuse and peer violence in residential children's homes.

Anne Basten is now employed as a researcher in the Central Services Agency, a public-sector organisation in Belfast, after previously working for C-STAR in the School of Geography at Queen's University, Belfast. Her research interests relate to sectarian geographies as well as wider issues of equality, social inclusion and urban governance.

Susan Batchelor was formerly a research assistant in the Criminology and Socio-Legal Research Unit, University of Glasgow. She is currently researching her PhD on violent young women detained in prison and secure accommodation in Scotland.

Jane Brown is a research fellow in the Department of Sociology and Anthropology at the University of Glasgow. She has a particular interest in researching sensitive topics and research with young people and children. She has recently completed a study of aggression and violence in young children.

Michele Burman teaches courses in criminology and in research methods in the Department of Sociology and Anthropology at the University of Glasgow, where she is also director of the Criminology Research Unit. She has long-standing research interests in gender and violence, and troubled and troublesome girls.

Karen Corteen is a lecturer in the Criminology Department of Edge Hill College. Her areas of research include sexuality and education.

Susan Creighton is senior research officer at the NSPCC, where she has conducted research and written on the epidemiology of child abuse and child deaths where abuse or neglect is implicated.

Dr Kimmett Edgar is Research and Devlopment Manager at the Prison Reform Trust and formerly research officer at the Centre for Criminological Research, University of Oxford.

Julia Field was a research director at the National Centre for Social Research (formerly SCPR) for 25 years. Now retired, she continues to work for the centre as a consultant, retaining a particular interest in quantitative surveys on personally sensitive subjects, including the 1990 and 2000 National Surveys of Sexual Attitudes and Lifestyles.

Steven Finch is research group director in the National Centre for Social Research's Quantitative Research Department. He has managed a wide range of research projects, mostly in the fields of education, the family and socio-legal research.

Dr Deborah Ghate is co-director of the Policy Research Bureau. She has a strong track record in research on parenting and has authored key texts in the field, including *Parenting in Poor Environments* (2002, with N. Hazel). She provides expert advice on parenting policy and is Visiting Professor in Social Policy Research at Royal Holloway, University of London.

Phil Hadfield is a research fellow in the Department of Sociology and Social Policy, University of Durham. In addition to his work for the VRP, he has worked on a variety of projects concerning alcohol-related violence, policing and regulation, including in-depth studies in Manchester and the West End of London.

Dr Gill Hague is the joint coordinator of the Domestic Violence Research Group at the University of Bristol. She has worked on domestic violence issues for more than 25 years and has very many publications on the issue.

Professor Graham Hart is associate director of the MRC Social and Public Health Sciences Unit at the University of Glasgow, where he directs the unit's programme of research on sexual and reproductive health. He has published widely on sexual and drug-related risk behaviour.

Dr Neal Hazel is senior research fellow at the Policy Research Bureau. He specialises in research involving young people, including studies of youth justice and of parenting. His publications include *Parenting in Poor*

Environments (2002, with D. Ghate) and *Fathers and Family Centres* (2000, with D. Ghate and C. Shaw).

Professor Dick Hobbs is Professor of Sociology at the University of Durham, UK. His research interests are deviance, professional and organised crime, policing, entrepreneurship, violence, and ethnography.

Dr Joanne Jones completed her PhD on nineteenth-century male violence and its representations in the Manchester press in 1999 (Lancaster University) and is now the learning and teaching development officer at the University of Essex.

Colin Knox is Professor of Public Policy in the School of Policy Studies at the University of Ulster. His most recent book is *Informal Justice in Divided Societies: Northern Ireland & South Africa* (with R. Monaghan).

Stuart Lister is a research officer at the University of Leeds. He has published a range of work based on the night-time economy, violence and the social organisation of bar and nightclub bouncers.

Dr Karen Lysaght worked as a research fellow on the Violence Research Programme's 'Mapping the Spaces of Fear' project in Northern Ireland. This project was based at the Centre for Spatial, Territorial Analysis and Research at Queen's University, Belfast. She is currently employed as a lecturer in anthropology at the University of Ulster at Coleraine, where she is concentrating on publishing from her doctoral work on loyalism in Northern Ireland.

Carol Martin was a research officer at the Centre for Criminological Research, University of Oxford, during the ESRC study.

Dr Rachel Monaghan is a lecturer in human geography at the University of Ulster. Her research interests include grass-roots/community conflict resolution in comparative contexts (Northern Ireland and South Africa) and political violence undertaken by single-issue groups.

Dr Leslie J. Moran is reader in the School of Law at Birkbeck College, University of London. He has published extensively in the areas of sexuality and the law and hate crime. He is also involved in several gay and lesbian organisations doing work on violence.

Audrey Mullender is Professor of Social Work at the University of Warwick and a member of the Academy of Learned Societies of the Social Sciences. She researches women's and children's voices in domestic violence and tackling the behaviour of perpetrators.

Dr Ian O'Donnell is research fellow at the Institute of Criminology, University College, Dublin.

Larry Ray is Professor of Sociology at the University of Kent, where he is currently head of the School of Social Policy, Sociology and Social Research.

He previously taught at Lancaster University. He has published widely on social theory and social transformations and (with David Smith) on hate crimes and racist violence.

Emma Renold is a lecturer in the School of Social Sciences, Cardiff University. Her research interests and publications include children's gender and sexual identities; gender-based bullying and sexualised harassment in the primary school; the impact of gender and sexuality on children's learner identities; violence between young people in residential children's homes; and researching sensitive topics.

Beverley Skeggs is Professor in the Department of Sociology, University of Manchester. She has written extensively on issues of class, gender and sexuality.

David Smith is Professor of Social Work at Lancaster University, where he has taught and researched since 1976. A former probation officer, he is currently researching the experiences of Black and Asian people on probation. He has published extensively on probation policy, youth justice and social exclusion.

Elizabeth A. Stanko is Professor of Criminology at Royal Holloway, University of London, and Director of the ESRC Violence Research Programme.

Dr Paul Tyrer was research associate on the Violence, Sexuality and Space project from 1998 to 2000. He is currently research manager of the Northwest Forensic Academy Network.

Liz Wastell is a probation officer for the Greater Manchester probation area of the National Probation Service.

Dr Simon Winlow is senior lecturer in criminology at the University of Teesside. He has published a range of work based on the night-time economy, violence and the social organisation of bar and nightclub bouncers.

Notes on research projects

Name of authors: John Archer and Jo Jones
Title of project: Violence in the North West with Special Reference to Liverpool and Manchester, 1850–1914

This project investigated crimes of interpersonal violence in the northwest between 1850 and 1914. This region epitomised the new industrial society of the nineteenth century, in which all the attendant social problems of urban growth were evident. In addition, Liverpool and Manchester returned some of the highest recorded crime statistics in Britain during this period. The project, through newspapers and other contemporary evidence, investigated everyday interpersonal violence with a view to gauging public attitudes towards violence, perceptions of fear, the role of the police in combating violence and the location of offences by neighbourhood. Violence in the home, pub, street and workplace have also been examined.

Name of authors: Graham Hart and Marina Barnard
Title of project: Client Violence against Prostitutes Working from Street and Off-Street Locations: A Three-City Comparison

This study offered a unique insight into prostitute-reported experiences of client violence from street and indoor locations in the cities of Glasgow, Edinburgh and Leeds. A total of 240 women provided structured information on client violence, and ninety women participated in semi-structured qualitative interviews exploring the determinants of violence in their working environment. A high proportion of street-working prostitutes were dependent on drugs (62.7 percent), particularly in Glasgow, where 81.3 percent reported injecting heroin. High levels of lifetime client violence were reported (63 percent). In the past six months, 37 percent reported having experienced some form of client violation. Street-working women were the most vulnerable to client violence, which was often sustained and brutal. Indoor workers were more vulnerable to the imposition of coercive working practices. Only 34.2 percent of women (44.1 percent of street-working women compared with 18.6 percent of indoor workers) reported violent incidents to police. Client violence is endemic within prostitution, so its prevention should be a policy and service priority.

Name of authors: Neal Hazel, Deborah Ghate, Susan Creighton, Julia Field and Steven Finch
Title of project: A National Study of Parents, Children and Discipline

The first ever nationally representative survey of British parents' attitudes, beliefs and experiences of disciplining their 0–12-year-old children, including the use of physical force. The study comprised a quantitative survey of 1,250 parents, followed by qualitative in-depth interviews with a sub-sample of parents and (separately) their children. A number of group discussions with children aged 8–12 were also held.

The study established the prevalence and incidence of minor, severe and very severe violence used by parents on their children and the characteristics of the parents and children where violence was most likely to be used. It also explored the context in which the violence occurred. Parental attitudes to the use of physical punishment were examined, as were children's. Community definitions of 'acceptable' and 'unacceptable' physical punishment were established, and the aetiology of violence explored through the parent's own childhood experiences of violence.

Name of authors: Michele Burman, Jane Brown and Susan Batchelor
Title of project: A View from the Girls: Exploring Violence and Violent Behaviour

Very few British studies have directly addressed female violence, or the role played by violence in girls' lives. Yet 'violent girls' are a current cause of concern. Using a combination of self-report questionnaires, focus groups and in-depth interviews, this project examined almost 800 teenage girls' understandings, attitudes and experiences of violence, as both victims and perpetrators. As well as documenting the nature and extent of violence in girls' lives, the contexts and settings in which it takes place, the strategies that girls engage in when confronted with or using violence, and the multiplicity of ways in which different forms of violence and abuse impact on girls' everyday lives, this research also documents the different – and shifting – meanings that violence holds for girls and shows how meaning is inextricably bound up with girls' lived experiences, subjective identities, and intimate and social relationships.

Name of authors: Emma Renold and Christine Barter
Title of project: Physical and Sexual Violence between Children Living in Residential Settings: Exploring Perspectives and Experiences

Renold and Barter's chapter draws upon a three-year investigation into peer violence in residential children's homes (Lawson *et al.* 2001). The research aimed to develop an understanding of children's experiences of peer violence within residential settings by exploring both children's and staff's perceptions of the meanings and effects of violence, children's coping strategies and the extent to which children and staff had shared reference systems for understanding and dealing with violence. The research was conducted in fourteen residential units from the local authority, voluntary and private sectors. Semi-structured qualitative interviews (including the use of vignettes) were held with seventy-one children and seventy-four staff in which they could freely explore, identify and contextualise their own personal experiences and management of violence. A central aim of the project is to enable children's own definitions and experiences to inform policy and practice, rather than simply reflect adult interpretations, realities and solutions.

Name of authors: Larry Ray, David Smith and Liz Wastell
Title of project: Racist Violence in Greater Manchester

The research consisted of interviews with perpetrators of racist violence, identified through the probation service, and of observation, discussion groups and interviews with criminal justice system and other personnel, and local residents, in areas that appeared to generate a disproportionately high incidence of racist violence. From the interviews with offenders it was clear that stranger violence was unusual: the perpetrator and victim usually knew each other, although not well. Offences were rarely premeditated and thus did not conform to the classic image of 'hate crimes'; and it was rare for offenders to justify racism in political terms. They tended to deny or minimise the racist element in their offences, while not minimising the violence. They tended to live in poor, outlying, virtually all-white neighbourhoods, in which racist sentiments were widely shared and where violence was a routine means of problem solving among young men and occasionally young women. Many offenders expressed a sense of grievance, resentment and shame as they compared their life experiences with what they took to be the economic success and social solidarity of their South Asian victims. Racist violence should be understood not as a single, unitary phenomenon but as expressing multiple cultures of violence, resentment and exclusion.

Name of authors: Leslie J. Moran, Beverley Skeggs, Paul Tyrer and Karen Corteen
Title of project: Violence, Sexuality and Space

Using two different social locations (Manchester and Lancaster), our study aims to understand how safer public space is produced and sustained by and for three different constituent groups (gay men, lesbians and heterosexual women). The study draws a comparison between a 'safer gay space' through policy, policing, community and business initiatives and another location that has paid scant attention to issues of safety for groups subject to violence. We employed a multi-method approach (census survey, key informant interviews, focus groups, representational analysis, participant observation and citizen's inquiries) and an interdisciplinary approach. The study is theoretically informed by the insights drawn from legal studies, criminology, social policy, feminism, and cultural and social theory. Please see website: *www.les1.man.ac.uk/sociology/vssrp*.

Name of authors: Rosemary Aris, Gill Hague and Audrey Mullender
Title of project: Abused Women's Perspectives: The Responsiveness of Domestic Violence Provision and Inter-agency Initiatives

The Abused Women's Perspectives Project was led by the Domestic Violence Research Group at the University of Bristol and conducted jointly with the Centre for the Study of Safety and Wellbeing at the University of Warwick. It looked at how much the voices and views of women who have experienced domestic violence inform policy and the development of services in the field. The research included a mapping study of projects nationally, in terms of how much they consult abused women, and detailed fieldwork in selected areas to examine the complex issues involved and to analyse examples of good practice. There was much commitment to consultation with service users among inter-agency domestic violence forums and other projects, but few had any idea of how to go about it. Refuge and outreach organisations had a better record of consultation, although this had decreased somewhat in recent years.

The project has produced a guidebook on how to consult women survivors of violence and will shortly be publishing a book on service user accountability with Routledge.

Name of authors: Simon Winlow, Dick Hobbs, Stuart Lister and Phillip Hadfield
Title of project: The Art and Economics of Intimidation: Bouncers, Violence and the Night-time Economy

Our research project started out with the aim of investigating the social organisation of bar and nightclub doormen, or bouncers. From this starting point, we have researched and published on a range of associated issues, but our dominant concern has always been the meaning and structure of violence in the night-time economy.

Name of authors: Colin Knox and Rachel Monaghan
Title of project: Informal Criminal Justice Systems in Northern Ireland

The main aim of this project was to contribute to an understanding of paramilitary policing within Northern Ireland in areas where state agencies, particularly the police and criminal justice system, are perceived to have no legitimacy or control. Specifically, the project examined paramilitary-style attacks, commonly referred to as 'punishment' beatings and shootings, from a number of perspectives – their nature and extent, reasons for their prevalence, the response of communities and voluntary and statutory agencies, and possible strategies for their reduction. Comparative work was undertaken in South Africa, particularly on community policing initiatives and restorative justice processes, with a view to reciprocal policy learning in two countries that have emerged from a legacy of violent conflict and the practice of self-policing.

Name of authors: Kimmett Edgar, Carol Martin and Ian O'Donnell
Title of project: Conflicts and Violence in Prison

Conflicts and Violence in Prison brought an original approach to the problem of prison violence. Violent incidents were investigated in terms of the interests that divided the antagonists, the prisoners' methods of handling disputes, the purposes of the use of force, and the contests of power that escalated disputes.

Name of authors: Karen Lysaght and Anne Basten
Title of project: Mapping the Spaces of Fear: Socio-spatial Causes and Effects of Violence in Northern Ireland

What impact does fear of sectarian violence have on people's everyday lives in the divided city of Belfast? How do residents who face complex time–space configurations of sectarian threat and fear negotiate their daily spatial movements? How do service providers respond to concerns about the safety of their clients and their own staff? How do they manage the 'spaces of fear' or provide services within them? What light does a comparison of fear of homophobic violence cast upon the dynamics at work within these two forms of stranger-directed violence?

In seeking to provide answers to the questions posed, the project adopted a multi-method, multi-level research design. Quantitative and qualitative methods were used on a range of material (such as census data, crime figures, in-depth and focus group interviews, participant observation) with a focus on detailed qualitative work in a sector of working-class, inner-city study areas in Belfast. The views and experiences of over 150 respondents were consulted. In addition to study area interviewees, the respondents included individuals who are gay, lesbian, bisexual or transgender (GLBT), and managers and service providers operating across the Belfast urban area.

Introduction

Conceptualising the meanings of violence

Elizabeth A. Stanko

Attempts to theorise interpersonal violence inevitably lead scholars to speculate about the causes or explanations for a presumed universal phenomenon: 'violence'. Text after text follows this approach, almost to the level of orthodoxy. In general, theorising about violence coalesces around individual violent offenders. Explanations are grouped by discipline, with each 'cause' critiqued by author after author, who demonstrates the (small) proportion of interpersonal violence in so-called advanced, civilised societies that these theories might explain (and by implication that proportion of violence which cannot be explained):

- Biological explanations lead to research into the causes of violence that inquires, for instance, into the genetic make-up, chemical levels in the brain or the hormone levels of identified violent males or females.
- Psychological theories scrutinise, for example, the differential impact of anxieties or aggression fuelled by inconsistent, harsh or neglectful parenting, loss of significant adults or childhood experiences of physical or sexual abuse in the personal histories of identified violent perpetrators.
- Sociological theories probe the social relations of violent individuals, querying the links between interpersonal violence and supportive social features found within class relations, gender relations or interpersonal relations such as the (lack of) or (over)attachment of violent individuals to a (presumed) peaceful, civil community.

The Economic and Social Research Council, the UK's premier social science funding body, commissioned a research programme on violence in 1997. Over five years, twenty research projects exploring a wide range of topics were funded. Intentionally interdisciplinary, studies examined the impact and consequences of violence on the person. Each project generated new and innovative information. Using eclectic social science methodologies – ethnography, documentary analysis, experimentation, interviews, case studies, focus groups – and teams of researchers from across disciplines and geographically from across the UK, the Violence Research Programme aimed to stimulate academic debate on a neglected topic in UK social science and to inform and inspire front-line practitioners and social policy makers to work creatively with violence, its aftermath and its prevention.

This volume, stemming from the debates from within the Violence Research Programme over these years, chooses a different approach to traditional thinking about interpersonal violence. Its logic is underpinned by a refusal to adopt one perspective or meaning for violence. Through the interdisciplinary reflections of researchers who participated in the programme, this collection looks at the meanings of interpersonal violence as understood through the lives of a diversity of people and the policies and practices of institutions. Conventional criminological literature categorises studies of violence through its constituent subjects: offenders, victims, the arbiters of justice, the suppliers of sympathy, support and care, or even the general public's attitudes towards and fear of violence. Although many assume that each of the constituents mentioned above might have differing views on violence and its impact, these essays ponder meanings through research findings. Projects funded under the Violence Research Programme simultaneously examined very different contexts and institutional settings: prisons, schools, doctors' offices, vicarages, sex massage parlours, dance clubs and hospitals are but a few of these. Although the UK is an economically developed, 'first world' country, it is a country that has experienced bloody internal conflict. Northern Ireland, a country that has experienced intense sectarian violence for the past thirty years, is a setting within the UK where the study of violence is highly contested on a day-to-day basis. The Northern Ireland conflict spans the Irish Sea. Mainland Britain has experienced the aftermath of bombings, shootings and other dangers associated with the 'troubles' too. Racist violence erupted in a number of northern English cities in the summer of 2001. Alongside terrorism and racism, the UK's persistent media attention regularly spotlights the potential dangers of random violence in public space. The death of a child killed by a paedophile in 2000 led to demonstrations and attacks on the homes of suspected paedophiles. The racist murder of a young black teenager led to a sea-change in policing in the late 1990s. Domestic harmony has also been queried with the growing recognition of the prevalence of domestic violence in UK households. Finally, at the time of writing this chapter (May 2002) there is a passionate debate about the steep rise in 'muggings' in some parts of Britain, raising persistent questions about the safety of the streets.

The Violence Research Programme showed that many different forms of violence are indeed ever-present in the UK, while the media demonstrated the popularity of this topic on an almost daily basis. Acting as prisms for our awareness, these diverse contexts and forms of violence – together with the projects' assorted physical and social locations – freed the researchers to reach beyond conventional ways of thinking about violence as tied to some 'universal' phenomenon and to search for how, where and why meanings of interpersonal violence arise. Despite an assumed, almost self-evident core, 'violence' as a term is ambiguous and its usage is in many ways moulded by different people as well as by different social scientists to describe a whole range of events, feelings and harm. In an essay exploring ethnic and nationalist violence, Brubaker and Laitin found a similar problem and state:

> The problem [of defining violence] is not that there is no agreement on *how* things are to be explained; it is that there is no agreement on *what* is to be explained, or *whether* there is a single set of phenomena to be explained.
>
> (1998: 427, emphasis in original)

In order to advance our thinking, I suggest that what violence *means* is and will always be fluid, not fixed; it is mutable. This is why it is crucial that a programme on violence *not* be framed through definitions of violence as found in the criminal statutes. As crime surveys tell us time and time again, most people eschew involvement with the police (and subsequently the criminal justice system) as an active choice following a violent incident. Moreover, there is a strong presumption (counter to all our criminological evidence) that an offender is different from a victim. Victims can be (and sometimes are) offenders, and vice versa. An arbiter of justice may also be an offender or a victim. A victim or an offender may be an arbiter of justice. Social institutions may confront or ignore violence within their midst. And so forth.

Through an approach that does not assume a standard definition, violence – as a phenomenon – can no longer be conceptualised as fixed, understood and inevitable. I would even go so far as to suggest that it is only through fluidity of definition that we can think creatively about disrupting violence as a social phenomenon. Violence, I argue, could and should be considered in many instances as preventable. Within the chapters of this collection, there may be some essays that calibrate their meanings of violence against or in the context of legal statutes. But there is no set and agreed definition among the researchers of what violence is. Bullying, verbal abuse, physical harm, threats, intimidation and killing all feature. Sometimes the law and its arbiters of justice appear. Indeed, there was considerable disagreement among programme participants about what could or should constitute a 'hierarchy' of violent harm. We never reached a consensus. Can one quantify or diminish the impact of verbal abuse on schoolchildren if one places it next to damage caused by a killing? Does this naming and constructing hierarchies of harm or of impact and consequences diminish, for instance, children's sensibilities of their worlds? Clearly some children, most especially in Northern Ireland, live with verbal humiliation and killings. But does this give us the right as researchers to privilege the impact of physical and sexual harm above that of emotional indignity for all children? These questions arose continuously as the studies progressed. Researchers found that different participants within the individual projects and among the twenty studies used the term 'violence' differently.

That said, these studies of violence in distinct settings led to sometimes divergent but often convergent problems in grappling with these meanings of violence. Not only did the researchers explore in an open and participatory way the meaning of violence with those they 'studied'. They also did so with each other and between the various projects. At the same time, many of the researchers were all too aware that symbolic discourses about violence existed around them. How can one explain people's knowledge about potential (or actual) threat and intimidation without a firm grasp of the cultural and symbolic legacies of social power? Similarly, researchers (and many of the people they spoke to) were acutely aware of the popularised notion of violence and its ever-present, symbolic threat, which feature prominently in British politics and media. This popularised notion includes two prominent players – one an evil perpetrator, the other an innocent victim. Their presence worried the researchers, as the research programme set out to challenge them. Yet the imagery about the parties in violence continued to lurk, and it was sustained simply because the media kept a steady watch on the programme and our findings. Furthermore, the media were keen and quick to sensationalise the research results using these imaginary parties, as if the meaning of violence is self-evident and is found exclusively in the make-up of the perpetrator and the victim. It is important to remind researchers that the media will inevitably lurk somewhere in the background or foreground of social science study of violence. The meanings of violence are multiple, complex and often contradictory. The Violence Research Programme helped me to understand how essential it is, as a researcher, to come to terms with how this presence censors or distorts the findings of social science research on violence.

Domestic violence, racist violence, homophobic violence, abuse of the elderly, sexualised violence, leisure violence and violence towards and maltreatment of children are but a few of the social concerns that highlight the diminished rights of victims. Studies of violence in the past ten years were an important mechanism for bringing many groups' experiences of discrimination and vulnerability to public attention. Voices of diversity – and demands that different forms of violence be taken seriously – are a demonstration that people are less tolerant of what they are expected to put up with as people living in a complex world. Violence against refugees or those with learning disabilities demonstrates to campaigners and others that some victims are especially harmed by inequalities. Campaigns to heighten awareness of discrimination have gained in prominence and given rise to studies of the impact of violence. There is a contradictory assumption that violence as a social phenomenon is a break from the presumed civilising progression of modernity. It may be that our growing intolerance of violence is an intolerance of inequality. The pace set by legislation in the UK, outlawing, for instance, forms of terrorism, stalking and racist violence, quickened during the 1980s and continues with even greater speed in the twenty-first century (see Stanko and O'Beirne 2002). Somehow, though, I cannot help feeling that we prefer to pass laws than to look carefully at how violence is so much welded to (often unequal) social relations. Action against forms of discrimination and inequality then is action against violence. Threats, as we will see, have power above and beyond law. Intimidation does not have to be verbal or physical to achieve its ends. This does not mean that legislation outlawing forms of violence is misguided. Indeed, it is necessary for the prosecution of some kinds of violence for legal definitions to be more precise. However, prosecution is still the least travelled route following an incident of violence. More often than not, people find a way of coming to terms with 'what happened' outside of the law.

It is my hope that this collection challenges us to move beyond traditional approaches to thinking about violence. It consciously brings together issues that rarely sit alongside each other in text. Racist offenders, battered women, children living apart from families, bouncers, girls, prison inmates and sex workers – to name only a few of our participants – are among those who spoke to researchers about violence. All considered the meanings of violence as they lived and experienced them. Four themes provide the threads for these twelve chapters.

The first part of the collection takes us into considerations of how we actually conceptualise the meaning of violence. Where else should we start but with history? John Archer and Jo Jones take us back to the mid-1800s, when the reporting of crime was dramatically affected by the development of printing technology. This technology enabled daily news to be printed cheaply and quickly. What better story was there than account after account of violence. Moral tales, social commentary, and graphic and gripping details of horror provided ample copy and scope to remark on social relations, roles, rules and social privilege. Archer and Jones found many differences in how violence was portrayed. What are made apparent in these stories are the divergent rules of engagement for violence. Men could fight men, women fight women, sailors stab each other or immigrants (or the Irish) pile into a pub brawl, all reported with amusement, sometimes disgust, sometimes dismay, but always pictured as categories of violence left to the 'less civil'. Of course, the newspapers were quick to pounce on examples of violence that crossed the boundaries of acceptability: random attacks on the railway or the brutal killing of a 'faithful' wife. But what the chapter should provoke is a more sceptical view of today's press, which uses the same techniques to draw lines between acceptable and unacceptable violence. These moral dilemmas continue to be debated in the press. However, what Archer and Jones remind us is that the anguish about violence – are we becoming more or less violent – will always be with us. Perhaps what we do experience in the UK is less tolerance of some of the bolder expressions of, for example, race hatred or homophobia (although these seem to be firmly entrenched in social life).

Ambivalence about the levels of violence that sex workers face and the implications of this for our understanding of the meaning of violence is exemplified by the findings of the next chapter. Graham Hart and Marina Barnard demonstrate that the meanings of violence are embedded in the very fabric of sexual negotiations between prostitute and client. Female sex workers describe the way they attempt to avoid violence by managing the sexual encounter for their own safety. The levels of violence that sex workers face are extraordinarily high. Negotiating sex and performing sex are processes that take into account ways of minimising client violence. How the women agree the price of sex, the handover of payment, the kind of sexual act, the sexual position of the act and venue for the act are but some of the aspects of the sale of sex that take account of potential violence. For sex workers, violence is ubiquitous. The best way of dealing with its probability is to anticipate the dangers that they may face (or have faced) during sexual encounters. Precautionary strategies make good sense in terms of business and in terms of their own health, yet the data indicate that despite these intricate strategies, they do not guarantee safety. Selling sex is risky, and especially dangerous if this is done on the street. The comparison between indoor and street sex workers' experiences of danger shows that street work is far more risky. Violence experienced by sex workers is essentially tolerated. The UK gives no legal protection to sex workers. Its illegality breeds exploitation, conclude the researchers. But our failure to see how ubiquitous violence is to the lives of sex workers enables us to confine the meaning of violence to the protection of the 'law-abiding'. Any debate about violence in general takes no account of those who manage violence on a daily basis and eschews the question of whether violence is acceptable or unacceptable in the purchase of sexual services. Instead, the women interviewed in this study treated violence as 'part of the job', and their approach to violence is one of constant precaution and minimisation.

Ambivalence about the acceptability or unacceptability of violence is addressed in the third chapter of this section. Neal Hazel and his colleagues conducted the UK's first national study of parental discipline and attitudes to disciplining children in the home. The starting point for this research was heavily steeped in sharp divides in moral opinion and legal challenge. Children are the only group in Britain where physical force against them can be argued as acceptable. Within an ongoing and often heated legal and moral debate, the study is the only national evidence addressing the use of physical force by adults in disciplinary relationships with children. The chapter carefully unpicks the complexities of meanings and nuances in this evidence. The meanings associated with 'smacking' children range from 'doing good' to children to 'doing harm' to children. Hazel and his colleagues found that over half of parents reported having used minor physical punishment against their children in the past year. Nearly three in four parents reported having done so at some point in their relationship with their child. One in eleven parents reported using more severe forms of physical harm in the past year. However, smacking is not just one form of physical 'discipline'. These findings, Hazel and his colleagues state, must be carefully analysed for the way in which parents reject many forms of child discipline: the use of implements or the shaking of children, for instance, were considered by the overwhelming majority to be unacceptable. It is in the detail of this analysis that the meanings – to parent and to child (the team spoke to children as well) – become clearer and understood as embedded in the context of parental responsibility to teach the child responsibility, keep the child from harm or manage what may often be emotionally tense periods in the lives of parents and children.

This first section opens a debate about violence that takes it away from law and moves it towards thinking about our social relations, social expectations and social power. The next part of this collection takes four aspects of the study of violence as they intersect with parts of our identities: gender, age, race and sexuality. Each of these chapters argues that identities matter for lived experiences of violence. This is not to say that gender or race alone is a universal feature of a person's experiences with and understanding of violence. What was clear about these projects was that the researchers were conscious of the fact that the research addressed girls, children living in residential homes, racist offenders or people's sexualities. These features of a person's identity are key in locating the perspective from which individuals build their own meanings of and for violence. Such identities inform the way in which we locate ourselves in the world, and whether the way in which we are treated constitutes a harm, and that harm is named as violence. As we shall see, this does not assume that the person is a victim or an offender. Both speak here (at times simultaneously).

The study that attracted the most interest from the media, for instance, was the study of girls and violence. Throughout the duration of the programme, the media so dearly hoped to uncover definitive evidence of the growing savagery of Scotland's female population that Michele Burman, Jane Brown and Susan Batchelor had to be on their guard to counteract the distortion of their project and findings. Steadfast, the team was determined to enable girls to set their own agendas about the definitions and conceptualisation of violence. The team found that girls were not just willing to speak about the ubiquitous nature of violence in their lives, they were eager to speak about it to the team. The project found that girls themselves named verbal abuse as a common expression that triggered feelings of violation. The girls spoke of verbal abuse as 'violence'. (This finding led to lively discussions within the programme meetings. Some colleagues were eager to exclude these conceptualisations from the terminology 'violence'.) These girls also told of witnessing physical assaults: 98.5 percent of the girls reported witnessing a fight. Girls had knowledge about what they felt were the acceptable rules of engagement for some forms of violence, and, like the parents in the above study, distinguished between acceptable and unacceptable use of physical force. By far the highest levels of violence that these girls experienced were from siblings in the home. Yet, similar to the findings of countless other studies on gender and safety, the girls admitted to being fearful in public spaces. Young women clearly recognised that as women they felt more at risk than their male counterparts.

In the chapter following, Emma Renold and Christine Barter extend the debate begun by Burman and her colleagues. This chapter explores the meanings of aggression that children living in residential homes experience. Much peer violence – named as violating and distressing by the above research – is often normalised in settings where children live apart from families (children placed by the state for a variety of reasons in residential homes). What the Scottish girls above named as harmful may be addressed in some form through school programmes on bullying. In residential homes, however, the same forms of behaviour may be overlooked, the authors argue. One of the main aims of the study was to enable children to set their own definition of the harm of 'bullying' and to comment on the effect of these experiences on their lives. The researchers found that residential homes differed, and the rules of engagement differed in different homes. This meant that the children had to negotiate their own space and place, and to find ways to avoid or to use violence for their own day-to-day survival. Situating the experiences of violence within children's cultures was a fundamental step in understanding the processes whereby violence became routine. Accepting 'pecking orders', 'aggressive masculinity' and 'bitching matches' rendered the recognition of the destructive side of gendered identities, deserving retaliation and climates of intimidation invisible. The researchers unfold a challenging analysis, clearly demanding that the meanings of violence must be understood from children's perspectives in order to promote safe interventions and safe residential spaces. In this way, children can be seen to contribute to their own safety and can define how they – as children 'looked after' in England – should be entitled to live.

Entitlement as a social privilege is one pervasive theme throughout the interviews with racist offenders. Larry Ray, David Smith and Liz Wastell explored offenders' own accounts of themselves and their offences. What they found was that the context of social change in Greater Manchester situated the offenders in local contexts where employment and personal success is difficult to find. The acute sense of grievance against non-white residents, who were perceived as being given advantages by the government in terms of housing, schooling and jobs, legitimised the violence against these non-white neighbours. The wider cultural legitimisation of this resentment was indeed supported by other residents. Offenders readily denied that their violence was racially motivated. Instead, offenders spoke of themselves as victims: of economic decline, of lack of achievement, of broken homes and relationships. What the authors suggest is that these offenders feel wronged and therefore feel entitled to act out their anger – festered through economic decline or feelings of emasculation. This research was conducted just before racist riots burned down parts of this northern conurbation near Manchester. Ray and his colleagues argue that acts of racist violence can be understood as situationally specific expressions of the convergence of racism, grievances about economic decline and the use of violence to settle such grievances. Racist violence here is committed mostly by young men who have no commitment to the politics of race *per se*. Such violence is nonetheless heavily imbued with racist assumptions that have a long history in Britain and have had a particular impact in areas that have suffered marked change through deindustrialisation in the past twenty years.

The importance of space and place for identity is also explored in the next chapter. Leslie Moran, Beverley Skeggs, Paul Tyrer and Karen Corteen examined how lesbians, gay men and heterosexual women produced safer leisure space. The debate around homophobic violence, the overarching issue for this research, often focuses on the experiences of physical and sexual assault but tends to overlook that much of people's own experience is of 'fear'. The project explored how people's sexualities intersected with public leisure and the use of bars and clubs in what has come to be known as the 'gay village' in Manchester. The team contrasted this highly visible 'gay scene' (and heralded tourist attraction by Manchester City Council) with the much less visible public gay life in a small town in the northwest of England. Their research found that of those who frequented the gay village, lesbians reported feeling safer than gay men, who felt least safe. This is in contrast to most crime surveys, which find that women are most likely to report feeling worried about their own safety. In contrast, gay men from outside Manchester felt the most safe! The researchers work through these findings, examining the contributions of local knowledge, social knowledge and knowledge about sexualities to feelings of safety.

This second part of the collection highlights the crucial role that social relations, social identities and social contexts play in the meaning of violence. The third section pauses to think about social context through studies of bouncers, battered women and violence in political contexts: punishment beatings in Northern Ireland and vigilantism in South Africa. Rosemary Aris, Gill Hague and Audrey Mullender link the concerns of these two sections of the collection through a discussion of battered women and their interaction with professionals whom the women approach to assist them. Aris and her colleagues pose an important question for those who are concerned with the hidden nature of many forms of violence. As much of the literature on domestic violence suggests, many battered women avoid contact with 'officials'. Women may enlist the support of family or friends, but they are keen to avoid professionals unless they really need them. Battered women, not surprisingly, wish to avoid being labelled 'battered women'. In effect, they eschew the category that may (hopefully) assist them to gain help to minimise the violence they face. Silent or censored, women who experience domestic violence find themselves struggling for their own voice when seeking help. The researchers even go so far as to suggest that the failure of communication between women seeking help for violence and the professionals who label and treat them as 'battered' is a major impediment to improvements in service provision for domestic violence. This is a serious challenge to moving forward from awareness about the extent and damage of domestic violence into action.

In the next chapter, Simon Winlow, Dick Hobbs, Stuart Lister and Phil Hadfield take the debates about violence in the night-time economy further by centring on the discussion of 'class' – a context that seems to be forgotten in sociological debates in the twenty-first century. The mostly male bouncers that Winlow and his colleagues observed and interviewed over a two-year period were 'occupational' specialists in violence. In many respects, their lives were strongly linked to working-class culture, and as such the context of their occupational responsibilities drew upon cultural boundaries of providing physical 'protection', albeit for a wage while employed at a club or pub. These cultural boundaries provided the rules of engagement for violence – the boundaries between acceptable and unacceptable use of force. Bouncers are in effect 'paid to be hard', as the researchers suggest. The work requires them to control crowds, anticipate danger and manage the disorder of inebriated crowds. Such skills are acquired not in school but, more than likely, on the street or growing up in neighbourhoods where one learned how to 'take care of oneself'. Lived experiences then provide the knowledge upon which bouncers draw for insight into how to 'break up fights', 'prevent or diffuse a brawl' or turn away the 'wrong' customer.

The next chapter brings the context and power of lived experience home. Colin Knox and Rachel Monaghan locate the ability to envision meaning with the wider political contexts of Northern Ireland and South Africa. How is it possible to make sense of phenomena such as punishment beatings in Northern Ireland and vigilante attacks in South Africa without a sense of the history of violent political conflict? Punishments in Northern Ireland, for instance, include exile, threats or warnings, public humiliation, curfews, beatings and shootings. Violations of community 'rules' or 'norms' such as petty criminality, car theft, muggings or drug dealing may be punished through action by paramilitaries. Such punishments perpetrate brutal violence on their own communities, their neighbours. Such action, the paramilitary contends, is necessary because the police are so mistrusted. In South Africa, the endemic nature of violence, especially in black townships, has led some members of the townships to take brutal revenge on offenders. Such brutality can only make sense in the context of legacies of intense political conflict, where brutality against some communities took place over many decades and generations. Challenging so-called informal justice and naming it as brutal is risky, but it is one way of demanding that these forms of violence not be silently condoned, either by the community or by the state. Knox and Monaghan set the stage for the final part of this collection, for they query the nature of institutionalised violence.

In the final part of the collection, two chapters address the institutional context of violence. Kimmet Edgar, Carol Martin and Ian O'Donnell discuss their study of conflicts in prison. To many people, violent conflict in prison is felt to be inevitable. Eruptions over seemingly minor events happen regularly. That violence is endemic in prison is in some respects taken for granted. This study questions this truism. Indeed, violence in prison certainly exists, the researchers conclude, but it is not inevitable. A careful walk through the findings demonstrates how conflicts erupt, how they have meaning for the participants, and how action, different action, or inaction might have disrupted the event and altered the nature of the confrontation. Violence in prison serves different purposes: revenge, enforcement of the repayment (or avoidance of) debt, personal animosity, or a form of bullying. The inmates interviewed could trace their steps in a conflict and begin to be aware of how their perceptions led from one step or escalation of the confrontation to another.

Finally, we return to the lessons from Northern Ireland. In this chapter, Karen Lysaght and Anne Basten remind us of the lived context of life in Belfast. For some (some might say many) in Belfast, concern about sectarian violence is ever-present. Such concern is likened to the air that residents breath – it is necessary for life, taken for granted, and often polluted with legacies of conflict. The chapter goes beyond the features of the previous chapters in many respects.

The authors acknowledge the contribution of complex identities, subjective perceptions of danger, and daily negotiations for many residents, who have to go from here to there in a city steeped in a history of violence. Routines such as grocery shopping or visiting a library take on a very different dimension if one cannot 'enter' the space of the other. Catholics and Protestants have ritualised ways to walk, take public transport (and especially taxis), and go to school, work or pursue leisure activities. Knowing that there are 'hostile' territories close by, adults and children become specialists in avoiding (as much as is possible) threat and violence.

Concluding thoughts

One overall lesson from the Violence Research Programme is that it is essential for researchers, policy makers and front-line workers to take the context of violence seriously. Understanding the context of violence means that we specify what happened, when, where and between whom as the beginning in our search to challenge the use of violence. Four elements are crucial in grappling with the meanings of violence: (1) the act itself; (2) the relationship of the participants to each other; (3) the location of the act; and (4) the outcome or the resultant damage. All of these elements combine to create a message from the meaning of violence. Not everyone will hear the message in the same way – and the message may be the spark for a challenge. Nonetheless, it is critical in thinking about the meanings of violence to ponder simultaneously the messages that violence sends to others. Thinking about these elements, I would like to close this introduction by emphasising two points.

The first concerns the way in which the meaning of violence can be viewed via its 'rules of engagement'. Participants in many of the funded studies reporting here spoke in detail about the 'rules of engagement' for violence. These rules take their parameters from social knowledge, cultural legacies or institutional support – often in the form of the unspoken and the unwritten – for social engagement in a place and space, and among particular kinds of individuals. Histories, identities, social power, psychological ambivalence and the ability to name and challenge the impact of violence converge here. Most of the incidents of violence under scrutiny occurred in settings that participants live in and know as largely familiar, sometimes intimate spaces, usually within close geographical locations to work, school and home. So, for example, in a prison setting, violence may be used to sort out problems, to intimidate, to get even or to punish. Those around the fighting inmates might quickly understand the meaning as well as the message of the violence. What violence means is embedded within its context. What messages violence gives are also gleaned from the context, but they are understood in terms of the interpreter's age, gender, sexual orientation, identities and personal history. The outcome of violence, whether it is physical or emotional damage, is thus legitimised or condemned, enabling further support for the use of intimidation or punishment or fostering resistance to its resources for legitimacy. If an inmate uses violence 'indiscriminately' or outside the 'rules of engagement' in the prison setting, the inmate may be labelled as untrustworthy, unpredictable and perhaps even as dangerous. However, if the violence is used as a form of conflict resolution that many understand and agree with, then the use of violence may be condoned.

Participants, bystanders and the assessors who may be brought in to judge violence all hear the meaning, and they may also form an opinion about the messages of violence. Bystanders may choose to allow a man to beat a woman, perhaps because they assume that a couple can sort out differences even if the form of the 'sorting out' involves threat and physical/sexual acts. Another group of bystanders may intervene because they believe that there is no justification for assault between a man and a woman regardless of the relationship. It is therefore at the juncture of act, meaning, message and outcome where views about violence are contested, debated, legislated and acted upon. Not all violence is condemned; not all forms of violence are punished; not all forms of violence receive widespread disapproval. Within every society, there is bound to be disagreement. How disagreement is negotiated within a society tells us a great deal about democracy, social power and the voices of those who have been advantaged and disadvantaged over time. What does seem to have changed in the discourse about violence, as historians have shown, is the attitude towards some of its forms. So-called street violence – where stranger attacks stranger – still elicits widespread condemnation and fuels fear. However, the growing intolerance of violence towards children and within intimate relationships demonstrates that attitudes have indeed changed. The UK legislation that recognised racist violence as a 'special' form of aggravation in an offence is another illustration that tolerance is now different from before. There are some normative features in how agreement is reached and how disagreement is voiced about the impact of violence on groups of people. In some ways, the willingness to make 'ordinary' violence visible heightens awareness about the damage of violence, and this is a good thing. It demonstrates that we are now in a position to challenge the impact of violence for groups of people where before, such violence was 'tolerated' as a condition of living in the world. Now, there are even debates about the rules of engagement for war. International tribunals and courts are beginning to address violations in war that were previously understood as routine damage of our ordinary wars.

This brings me to my second point. The fact that the rules of engagement for violence are known to many participants, and this knowledge is either accepted or challenged, leads me to wonder how long it will take us to realise that we must intervene in the lives of children who experience violence first and foremost. Children cannot alter their environments and homes easily. Children may experience frightening abuse at home – and realise that other children do not suffer the way they do. Some children clearly know that in their home violence is rife but have little understanding about how to challenge these conditions of their personal lives. It is within these environments that young people learn that there are different rules for the use of violence in different settings. Other institutions in children's lives are also important. Not all schools tolerate bullying among their pupils. And where children live also sets the stage for how they understand the usefulness (or not) of violence. Some neighbourhoods may be rife with bullying and abuse among children and young people – sometimes with little intervention by the adult world in challenging the use of violence as a resource in dispute or for respect. As children mature, many already understand that different rules apply in different situations. In other words, divergent experiences inform the way that many people think (differently) about violence.

These divergent experiences sit alongside diversity in the levels of tolerance towards the use of violence in different situations and among different participants. Let me end this commentary by returning to a question: how do we explain the virtual acceptance among sex workers of the ubiquity of violence? Such acceptance comes from a long legacy of denial of the harm of this work. Sex workers are treated with great ambivalence in the UK. Sex workers who sell sex on the street meet so much hostility and intolerance of their situations that much of the violence they confront is taken as 'just part of the job'. Occasionally, when a punter crosses the threshold of unacceptable (acceptable) violence, others may be enlisted to intervene – other street workers, health workers or even the police. But what kinds of change must take place before sex workers no longer have to negotiate every 'sale' as a potentially violent one? Such changes address a level of respect accorded – and deserved – by each person, regardless of who they are or what they do. Non-violence is an aspiration, but its achievement is very much dependent on our collective responsibility for the safety of us all. Imagining non-violence may be the first step in taking on board this collective responsibility. If violence 'has meaning', then those meanings can be challenged. My hope is that the essays in the collection help to stimulate this challenge.

References

Brubaker, R. and Laitin, D.D. (1998) 'Ethnic and nationalist violence', *Annual Review of Sociology* 24: 423–52.

Stanko, B. and O'Beirne, M. (2002) 'Taking stock: what do we know about interpersonal violence', ESRC Violence Research Programme [http://www1.rhul.ac.uk/sociopolitical-science/vrp/realhome.htm].

Part I

Conceptualising the meanings of violence

1 Headlines from history

Violence in the press, 1850–1914

John Archer and Jo Jones[1]

Every historical era has experienced some form of crime-generated social anxiety, and it would be both foolish and unwise for contemporary commentators to view present-day crimes of violence as either novel, unique or representative of 'the decline of society'. For every child-on-child murder, paedophile outrage or serial killer that shocks present-day society, historians can point to incidents and figures from the past. Some are notorious, like Jack the Ripper; others are almost forgotten, like 'Sweet Fanny Adams', the details of whose brutal murder lie forgotten in the columns of Victorian newspapers but whose name has lived on and even been abbreviated into the euphemistic phrase 'sweet FA'.[2]

However, the manner in which we are made aware of crimes of violence is, to a large extent, of recent heritage. The Victorian press served an ever-widening readership and therefore adopted a popular language, tone and layout in which sensation and fact intertwined to generate and arouse interest, fear and concern in equal measure. The main difference between now and then is the current use of pictorial images to portray the victim, the scene of the crime and the perpetrator. Victorian newspapers, by contrast, only occasionally resorted to crude pictorial etchings of a trial and the defendant, preferring instead to describe in highly explicit detail the killing, the victim's wounds and the character and behaviour of the killer. In so doing they set the agenda for the representation and reportage of crimes of violence that is still largely with us. Violent incidents that contained a human interest story were highlighted or amplified because they suggested wider social threats such as the danger posed by strangers to unaccompanied women, or described the helpless child victim. Such news items continue to make particularly sensational and emotionally charged copy. Crimes of violence came to be defined as social problems and indicative of a wider social malaise. History has therefore an important role to play in establishing how violence is portrayed, represented and interpreted both now and 150 years ago.

The press, since the mid-1850s, has been the most important medium for creating the public's awareness and perception of violent crime. Murders, assaults and other crimes against the person have literally made headline news, and as such these news stories and their associated headlines have provided historians with a rich seam of evidence. This chapter intends to investigate the possible significance, meanings and representations of violence through the newspaper headline. Questions concerning the perceived level of crime and the general threat and fear of violent crime, which were implicitly or explicitly addressed within the wording and language of the headline, are also discussed. It will be argued that during the second half of the nineteenth century the presentation if not the language of headlines about violence evolved and became recognisably modern.

Many of the headlines and news stories that appear in this chapter have been taken from the Liverpool and Manchester press between 1850 and 1914. Regional newspapers have proved an invaluable source of nineteenth-century interpersonal violence for our study. Our project has examined reports relating to violent incidents, from common assault to murder, which appeared in what the press at the time referred to as 'police intelligence' or 'local news' columns. The timespan of the period covered by our research, over sixty years, enabled us to note changes in the layout and presentation of news within the regional weekly and daily papers.[3]

The growth of crime reporting

News of the kind that we read on a daily basis is a nineteenth-century creation (Brown 1985: 1). More particularly, the arrival of the modern newspaper can be dated fairly precisely as coming in the 1850s. Many contributory factors, both legal and technical, came together during that decade to allow both the national and provincial press to expand exponentially. Prior to the mid-nineteenth century, newspapers were still relatively expensive, having to bear the weight of the stamp duty – branded as a 'tax on knowledge' – and a tax on the paper used for newsprint. Before the 1850s, with a few notable exceptions such as *The Times*, newspapers were often weekly and contained news that could be many days, even weeks, old. They also failed to highlight to any great extent crime news within a specialised column. Anyone who has had to research county newspapers from the 1830s, for example, will know of the problems of searching the tightly packed stories within the column headed 'Local News' for items relating to crime. Such stories would appear in no particular order and could be juxtaposed with innocuous items concerning local charitable donations. From the mid-nineteenth century, however, many provincial papers began to carry, as one of their main news items, a police intelligence or police court column. In addition, individual news stories of recent crimes, both local and national, were regularly featured.

Early nineteenth-century readers who wanted to learn more about a particularly notorious crime would have normally bought a penny broadside, which would have concentrated solely on the event. Such broadsides, which sold in vast numbers, particularly on the days of executions, offered the reader a potted history of the crime, the trial and the almost formulaic redemption of the accused in the condemned cell (Chassaigne 1999). Also popular, especially in

London, were the *Newgate Calendars*, which gave descriptions of the crime, the criminal and the trial in far more detail (Pelham 1886). In spite of their moralising tone, both calendars and broadsides constituted reasonably accurate and popular crime reportage.

The coming of what is termed 'new journalism' in the 1850s changed the face of crime reporting for ever. The following figures, taken from Jones (1996: 23), show just how fast and large this expansion of newspaper titles was both in London and throughout the provinces. Between 1800 and 1830, 126 papers were established; from 1830 to 1855, the number of titles rose to 415 before mushrooming still further to 492 in the seven years between 1855 and 1861. During this mid-century expansion, 123 towns in England gained a local newspaper for the first time.

The repeal of the advertisement duty in 1853, followed by the abolition of stamp duty two years later and the paper duty in 1861, helped to increase the number of newspaper titles, the size of the newspapers and their frequency of publication. In addition, where expense had been one of the key issues in dictating layout in early nineteenth-century newspapers, small typefaces and dense columns had, as a result, been deployed in order to pack in as much news as possible. All this became less important after 1860, although columns remained traditionally packed for a while longer. However, as the century drew to a close layouts changed, more white space appeared, and news items in some cases became smaller while headlines became larger. The expansion of the press was also aided by other developments, not least the continued expansion of the railway network, cheaper imported newsprint, the penny post, printing machine developments and telegraphy. All these factors combined to make the period from the 1870s to 1914 the 'golden age' (Brown 1985: 32) for major provincial newspapers such as *The Yorkshire Post* and *The Manchester Guardian*. These regional papers could receive and print telegraphed news from London along with their local provincial news before the arrival of the London trains in the morning.

In addition, there was another development wholly unconnected with newspapers but which came to have a symbiotic relationship with the press, namely the advent of the popular 'sensation' novel in the 1860s. Unlike the earlier popular literary genre of the Gothic novel, in which things supernatural often intervened in the plot, the 'sensation' novels were thrillers or mysteries in which human failings, by way of criminal or sexual misbehaviour, played a significant part in the storyline and plot. Thus the popular appetite, mainly middle- and lower middle-class, came to be thrilled by the sensation of exciting details concerning murder and, to modern eyes, heavily disguised passion. Crime, and crimes of violence in particular, came to offer the reading public both fictional narratives that thrilled and titillated and courtroom dramas that brought equal entertainment value. In fact, the reports of some news stories took on the hallmarks of fiction, deploying narrative, melodrama and plot in which the forces of good and evil were played out to a reading public who may have had little direct experience of interpersonal violence. In this way, a newspaper journalist could attract the interest of the reader. Thus language, content, narrative form and the initial eye-catcher of the story – the headline – which used such keywords as 'tragedy' or 'mystery', came to be important.

The use of headlines: historical and contemporary parallels and contrasts

The headline had and still has many important functions, being among other things a tone setter, story precis and signpost. In these functions it has become an enduring feature of crime reportage, so much so that in the case of murders the headline can become the label or title by which the incident is referred to thereafter by both the police and other newspapers (Soothill 1991: 39). Nineteenth-century murders, more often than not, were identified by their location, such as the 'The Whitechapel Murders' or 'the East End Murders', which we now know as the 'Jack the Ripper Murders'. In the beginning, headlines, especially those appearing within the police court or police intelligence columns, were often short, single words even, and were, by modern standards, mundane and prosaic. Such common headlines as 'ASSAULT', 'THE USE OF THE KNIFE' and 'ASSAULTS ON POLICE' served the simple function of alerting readers to violent crime having taken place in their town. Another common headline, 'THE KNIFE AGAIN', goes a step further by implying that stabbing, for which Liverpool was especially renowned, was becoming a problem. Many headlines in the early years of the period under review were of this simple and stark kind. However, with the passing of time there evolved genres of headlines that related to different types of interpersonal violence. Many of these were, as will be seen, fuller, more sensational and even moralising and judgemental in tone. The headline could, in short, concisely convey, promote and emphasise value systems that the newspaper regarded as respectable, worthwhile and healthy.

On 15 December 1999, newspapers in the UK reported former Home Secretary Michael Howard's view of the murder of James Bulger, a two-year-old toddler who had been taken from Bootle Strand shopping centre by two 10-year-old boys and then walked and dragged two and a half miles to the side of a railway line in Liverpool, where he was battered to death with bricks. It was, he said, 'a uniquely and unparalleled evil and barbarous act' (*The Guardian*). Turning to the newspaper headlines of 1993, when the murder was committed, the language and size of type would appear to bear him out. The *Daily Mirror* (22 February 1993), for example, ran a headline above a photo of a carpet of flowers placed near the spot where Bulger's body was found: 'JAMES BULGER: born 16 March 1990, killed 12 February 1993'. Below the photo ran the emotionally charged quote in bold type: 'Goodnight little one. Nobody can ever hurt you again'. A day later, in what it termed a 'News Special', the *Daily Mirror* ran across the top of two inside pages, which were encased within a barbed wire border, a videoprinter-style heading 'BRITAIN UNDER SIEGE + + BRITAIN UNDER SIEGE + + ...'. The murder, it reported, signified a wider crisis afflicting British society in which poor parenting and video 'nasties' were contributing to the rise of a generation of children devoid of moral sense.

While the degree of coverage for this crime may have been unique in the 1990s, the actual killing of a young child by two older boys was not. Ironically, just such a case occurred in Liverpool in 1855, when 7-year-old James Fleeson was killed by two 10-year-old boys, who bricked him unconscious then threw him into the Leeds–Liverpool canal. Among the headlines that the incident attracted were 'THE EXTRAORDINARY CASE OF A BOY KILLED BY A BOY' (*Liverpool Daily Post*, 21 July 1855) and the more emotive 'A LITTLE BOY MURDERED BY TWO OF HIS PLAYMATES' (*Liverpool Mercury*, 24 July 1855). The former, while getting an important fact wrong in that there were two culprits, emphasises the unusual nature of the crime. In the latter, the choice of 'little' and 'playmates' render the story more shocking and can arguably be read in two ways. Such language can suggest a certain poignancy, while a more critical reading can lend it sinister overtones in which playmates have played at murder. However, the subsequent tone of both articles lacked the shocked outrage of the reportage on the Bulger case; in fact, one of the articles refers to the killing as 'a sad case'. The nineteenth-century press does not appear to have projected wider fears about the threats posed by dangerous children; nor was the murder portrayed as a society in crisis in the manner that James Bulger's killing was interpreted. One of the deepest contrasts between the two killings lay in the fact that James Bulger's disappearance was seen by us all on the CCTV tape in which he is caught, hand in hand, walking away with two older children. That haunting image both reinforced and fed the newspapers' headlines and coverage.

More recently, some elements of the English tabloid press have orchestrated widespread panic concerning paedophiles in the wake of the murder of 8-year-old Sarah Payne in rural West Sussex in the summer of 2000 (*The Guardian*, 4 July 2000). Social anxieties concerning paedophiles reached such a pitch that lone adult males and families were driven from their homes during a naming and shaming campaign against alleged child sex offenders (*The Guardian*, 11 August 2000). In 1876, a Blackburn barber, William Fish, sexually assaulted, murdered and dismembered a young girl. This crime, headlined as either 'THE BLACKBURN MURDER' or 'THE BLACKBURN TRAGEDY' in the regional press, like the more recent case excited universal condemnation. It was regarded as 'one of the most diabolical outrages of modern times', and the *Liverpool Mercury* reported (15 August 1876) that special trains were laid on to transport people from all parts of Lancashire to the trial in Liverpool, where 'persons in all walks of life' clamoured for tickets for admission to the court. Yet this case failed to generate wider fears about the safety of children. This was in part due to the fact that the crime was considered so unusual and that the culprit, Fish, who had been captured quickly, was himself regarded as distinctly singular in terms of his upbringing and his physical appearance. He had, it was reported, fallen 40 feet from an aqueduct as a child, leaving a permanent indentation in his skull. He was perceived to be different, if not monstrous, and his very appearance almost explained the monstrosity of the crime, a fact confirmed by the subheading of a report on his and another's execution, 'PHRENOLOG-ICAL CHARACTERISTICS OF FISH AND THOMPSON'. The description that followed not only helped the reader to visualise Fish, it also confirmed his criminality by describing the converging negative attributes of poor upbringing and mental and physical deformity. For those readers who had been unable to catch a glimpse of the defendant during the trial, the Liverpool Waxworks had a model of Fish on display before his execution (*Liverpool Mercury*, 7 August 1876). In contrast to contemporary fears relating to the ever-present dangers of predatory paedophiles, Fish represented, particularly in his death by execution and the waxwork model, the defeat of the 'bogeyman'. He was regarded as a 'one off' whom the criminal justice system was able to overcome. Once dead, the threat no longer existed in the column inches of the press or in the minds of the newspaper-reading public.

Domestic and family violence: headlines as social commentary

News stories and court reports frequently referred to cases of domestic violence, especially from the 1860s onwards. The headline in such reports could in many ways act as a signpost for the reader, but this signpost could be pointing in one of many different directions. Whether as a summary of an event or as a direct quotation from the main report, the headline offered an indication of the news contained in the body of the report, and in so doing it could shift the focus away from the actual violence towards the interpretation of that violence. The news reports of these cases of domestic violence often sought to explain these crimes. Many went beyond the simple recitation of names of defendants and victims, of addresses and brief descriptions of the injuries. The reports frequently made some comment, variously describing the defendant's behaviour as 'brutal', 'monstrous' or 'cowardly'. Conversely, the victim, in some reports, was portrayed in a very unfavourable light and had, by implication, provoked the assault upon herself. The headlines in all these cases were signposting accountability or were asking the reader to feel outrage or shock with one or other of the couple. Occasionally, headlines and the subsequent reports of domestic violence fulfilled a different function. By locating the violence within a poor home, where alcoholism was a problem with both partners, the headlines might emphasise instead the deviant lifestyle of the husband and wife.

Where the behaviour of the husband or male partner was being condemned, the headline clearly signposted the fact: 'A BRUTAL WIFE BEATER' (*Liverpool Mercury*, 24 February 1875); 'A COWARDLY WIFE BEATER' (*Liverpool Mercury*, 27 July 1870); 'INHUMAN TREATMENT OF A WIFE' (*Manchester Weekly Post*, 3 January 1880); or 'A FIENDISH HUSBAND' (*Manchester Evening Mail*, 12 July 1876). In these headlines, emphasis has been placed on the deviancy of the man; moreover, through the use of such words as 'brutal', 'fiendish' and 'cowardly', the man's behaviour as a husband has been castigated. The reader would not in fact have needed to read the report to know that the man had failed to fulfil the role of a loving and protecting partner. In the report headed 'A COWARDLY WIFE BEATER', the husband, Patrick Doran, had been discharged from prison 'only yesterday' and had been met on his release by his wife carrying a babe in arms. Moreover, she gave him money, 'nearly all she had', to buy drink. Not long after, Doran, it was reported, returned for more money, which she refused to hand over as she needed to buy food for the child. There followed a fight in which he knocked the child out of her arms and beat the mother. At the subsequent court hearing, the stipendiary magistrate belittled Doran's masculinity by saying that 'those fellows who struck women were those who dared not exercise their fists upon men'. 'It made his blood boil', the report continued, 'to hear these cases day after day of such brutes as the prisoner who had women in their power'. In another case, headed 'AN UNFEELING HUSBAND' (*Liverpool Mercury*, 21 February 1877), the report represented the woman as fulfilling all the archetypal feminine and maternal roles of having been married for 14 years, bearing five children and being of respectable appearance. Moreover, it was reported that although suffering from consumption for the past four years she had been able to maintain herself and her family. The husband, on the other hand, was 'frequently very violent', neglected his children, when in work spent all his wages on drink, and threatened to murder the entire family, 'sometimes three or four times a day'. This catalogue of neglect and violence was compounded by the implication that he was also unfaithful.

In some headlines the victim's deviancy, rather than the defendant's, is indicated. Although not condemning the violence, such reports imply that the wife had somehow brought the violence upon herself through her own actions and failings. Nowhere is this more clearly stated than in the following: 'KILLING AN UNFAITHFUL WIFE' (*Manchester Weekly Post*, 12 February 1881). Her alleged infidelity in this case suggests a rational explanation for the husband's actions, which simultaneously seems to lessen his guilt. Just occasionally, both the headline and the report prefer to concentrate on the joint deviancy of the couple and emphasise both their poor relationship with one another and their mutual responsibility for the violence. This is usually done by concentrating on their heavy drinking, thriftlessness and low living. Stories headed 'A TROUBLESOME TWELVE MONTHS MATRIMONY' (*Liverpool Mercury*, 24 September 1901) and 'AN UNHAPPY COUPLE SEPARATED' (*Liverpool Mercury*, 27 February 1883) introduce reports in which both husband and wife are regarded as contributing to their domestic disorder.

The headlines, in addition to attributing blame or passing judgement on one or both of the warring partners, sometimes take the violence of the event as their news handle. In 'CUTTING AND CARVING A WIFE' (*Liverpool Mercury*, 18 October 1875), the husband's use of the knife is graphically emphasised. However, in 'A PERSIAN BASTINADOING HIS WIFE IN LIVERPOOL' (*Liverpool Mercury*, 7 May 1878), one suspects that the headline served a dual function, allowing the reporter or sub-editor to show off his knowledge of vocabulary as well as highlighting an exotic form of violent behaviour that readers would not normally associate with Liverpool. In consulting a dictionary the reader would have discovered that bastinadoing was a form of punishment or torture in which the soles of the feet were beaten with a stick. In those news stories in which methods of brutality were emphasised, particularly gruesome headlines could be the result. In 'ROASTING A WIFE LIKE A HERRING – HORRIBLE CASE IN LIVERPOOL – A MONSTER IN HUMAN FORM' (*Liverpool Mercury*, 10 February 1883), the defendant's behaviour in setting his wife alight and then callously refusing to extinguish the flames as they enveloped her is sensationalised as being almost beyond human agency.

If reports of spousal violence are set to one side, news stories that covered violence between relatives often produced a very different set of headlines. When sons, for example, were involved in violent incidents, the tone and language of the headlines focused on the transgressive son, whose behaviour was deemed to be unnatural. 'A MOTHER BEATER' (*Liverpool Mercury*, 17 December 1868) simply echoes the wife-beater style headlines, but 'AN UNFILIAL BRUTE' (*Liverpool Mercury*, 2 March 1870) describes how a son not only beat his mother but also stole from her. Even more explicit was the following: 'A VIOLENT SON AND LOVING MOTHER' (*Liverpool Mercury*, 2 March 1870), in which the juxtaposition of the descriptors 'violent son' and 'loving mother' ought to have aroused in the reader feelings of compassion for the latter and anger at the former's actions. The headline 'DRUNKEN SAVAGE MOTHER BEATER' (*Liverpool Mercury*, 29 March 1870) introduces the wrongdoing of excessive drinking as well as the imagery of the uncivilised. Intra-family violence extended far beyond sons attacking their mothers to encompass most familial variations from fathers attacking their offspring to sibling rivalries. In many of these cases of family violence, headlines contain adjectives such as 'heartless', 'unnatural' and 'inhuman', as in 'A HEARTLESS PARENT' (*Liverpool Mercury*, 24 April 1882), 'AN INHUMAN FATHER' (*Liverpool Mercury*, 3 October 1884) and 'AN UNNATURAL MOTHER' (*Manchester Chronicle*, 23 May 1859). Mothers who were thought to have displayed insufficient maternal feelings and were lacking in womanly behaviour were singled out. 'A DRUNKEN MOTHER'S NEGLECT' (*Liverpool Mercury*, 29 July 1896) neatly encapsulates for the reader two failings, drunkenness and neglect, which invite scorn and heavy punishment. In a similar case from 1901, 'A DRUNKEN, VIOLENT AND CRUEL MOTHER' (*Liverpool Mercury*, 13 September 1901), the headline condemns the woman by emphasising the absence of both maternal feeling and womanly decorum. It concisely establishes how this particular woman represented the very antithesis of domestic woman-hood that was popular at the turn of the century.

Graphic accounts: violence as spectacle

While being highlighted in the headlines, the brutality of many violent inci-dents and assaults was also dwelt upon within the body of the news reports. Incidents in which 'blood spurted', 'brains were battered out', stomachs were jumped upon and heads were kicked in were described graphically and at length. In what were often highly charged pieces, one senses or suspects that readers pruriently 'enjoyed' a set of ambivalent feelings when reading such detailed descriptions. Acting almost in the role of spectator, or voyeur even, they were enabled by such detailed reports to watch the drama unfold, to view the victim as she fell down the stairs or was knocked senseless to the floor by a poker. This detailed description was sensational in so far as it evoked sensations of both horror and disgust as well as a morbid fascination with pain not far removed from what Halttunen (1995: 312) has described as a growing obsession within nineteenth-century literature. Readers, she has argued, wanted to be 'shocked and thrilled', but only from the safe distance of their parlour or drawing room.

In the newspaper reports of murders and the more extreme cases of domestic violence, the descriptions of the events are usually followed by detailed expositions of the injuries, in which the length and depth of cuts and wounds were measured to the nearest half-inch and reported on by medical witnesses. One could argue that 'expert' medical opinion both lent the reports a legitimation for the earlier description of the injuries and offered evidence that extreme violence had been used on the victim. The reader was thus justified in feeling a sense of revulsion and outrage. It is perhaps also worth recalling that as the law prohibiting aggravated assaults on women and children was passed only in 1853, the reports of wife beating were also fulfilling an educational function in which readers were being civilised by acknowledging that wife beating was wrong, cruel and unacceptable. Certainly, such headlines as 'WIFE BEATERS BEWARE' (*Liverpool Mercury*, 14 April 1876), in which a heavy prison sentence was meted out to the defendant, would suggest such a function. In order to achieve this, the reports had to dwell on the detail of the suffering and pain, which in turn aroused a sense of horror and disgust in the reader. For pain to be considered obscene and unacceptable, it had to be described in detail and acknowledged as wrongful and criminal behaviour.

Type set and setting a type: the technology of moral panics

We are familiar nowadays with the deployment of large headlines, which contribute to the build-up to scares and moral panics with regard to violent crime. Exaggeration and over-emphasis of events can be achieved in a number of ways and by various techniques: for example through the size of typeface and language of the headline, or by the repetition of the same or similar stories over a number of consecutive days and weeks. In the nineteenth century, the press could and did choose to run with scares relating to particular types of violent crime, which created moral panics and folk devils, people who were perceived to threaten society and who were branded as antisocial and criminal in their behaviour (Cohen 1972). The most manufactured scare of the century was probably the 1862 garotting panic, which dated from 17 July 1862, when Hugh Pilkington, MP for Blackburn, was attacked and robbed in the street on his way home from a late sitting of the House of Commons (Davis 1980; Sindall 1990). Earlier garotting incidents, particularly in the early and mid-1850s in Manchester, had failed to energise the press, although Sindall has argued that the garotting panic of 1856 was probably 'the first moral panic with the press acting as moral entrepreneurs' (1990: 47). The 1862 panic was far more intense and was to all intents and purposes a new journalistic phenomenon that could only have been started in the second half of the nineteenth century with the advent of cheap newspapers and new journalism. Garotting was not the only media scare. There was the closely related ticket-of-leave panic, which exaggerated the dangers of returned convicts released back into the community.[4]

There occurred another scare that the press did much to develop and one that has attracted surprisingly little historical attention, namely the possibility of being attacked on a railway train. The headline that set the panic off is, to modern eyes, lacking in sensational language or impact; 'MURDER IN A FIRST CLASS CARRIAGE ON THE NORTH LONDON RAILWAY' (*The Times*, 11 July 1864). Apart from locating the violent event in London and on a train, the headline would have been particularly pertinent to affluent commuters for the important detail of the murder having taken place in a first-class compartment. Many middle-class readers would have, until this date, regarded a first-class compartment as a privileged and secure space that protected its occupiers from the threats and dangers of the criminal classes. The provincial press in both Manchester and Liverpool ran with the murder for fourteen consecutive days, and *The Times* had over sixty stories relating to the murder and other railway assaults between July and September 1864. What began as a unique and intriguing mystery of the murder of a senior city bank clerk soon took on more ominous meanings, especially for unaccompanied women travellers. The murder coincided with another widely reported assault on a young woman travelling by train. The headlines 'THE ASSAULT ON A FEMALE IN A RAILWAY CARRIAGE' (*Manchester Courier*, 22 July 1864) and 'THE PERILOUS RAILWAY JOURNEY' (*Manchester Courier*, 13 July 1864) helped to transform the initial scare into a wider and more specific fear for women travellers. An editorial headed 'LADIES IN DANGER' (*Daily Post*, 21 July 1864) left women in no doubt as to the dangers of travel by both rail and foot.

Brutes, roughs and hooligans: labelling violent offenders in the nineteenth century

Throughout much of the second half of the nineteenth century, young men who lived their lives on the city streets became the leading folk devils of the period. In Manchester and Salford, juvenile gangs were identified as a menace (Davies 1998), whereas in Liverpool the threat came from a slightly older age cohort of men. Headlines featuring 'cornermen' came to signify and symbolise male lawlessness and aggression. Such men formerly went under the labels of 'brutes' or 'roughs' in the 1860s and early 1870s. In fact, the nomenclature 'rough' became a keyword to northern readers, signifying men lacking in education who were idle, unemployed, poor and threatening and who had the ability to intimidate the more law-abiding members of the community. They were regarded as an underclass of violent criminal types, usually male, who personified many social problems, not least violence and heavy drinking. The street rough, while remaining in the headlines through to the outbreak of the First World War, was relabelled more frequently as a cornerman from 1874. In that year, a group of young men kicked a working man to death in a busy Liverpool thoroughfare in what became known as the Tithebarn Street murder. The alliterative (the Victorian newspapers were fond of alliteration) 'COWARDLY CORNERMEN' (*Liverpool Mercury*, 22 December 1893) and the more alarmist 'THE ROUGH TERROR' (*The Times*, 24 September 1874) clearly and explicitly portray these supposedly new figures of fear. The association of cowardice with this group of men had become common by the 1890s, when headlines like 'COWARDS OF THE WORST TYPE' (*Liverpool Mercury*, 13 March 1894) and 'COWARDLY SCOUNDRELS' (*Liverpool Mercury*, 14 March 1894) belittled their masculinity and physical strength. These headlines would appear to be trying to suggest that male repute should not be based on the capacity to beat other men, usually with their favoured weapons of heavy boots or clogs. The cowardice label also pertained to their preference for working in groups, thus giving them an unfair advantage over individual victims. The fact that cornermen preferred to rely on their footwear as weapons instead of the manly pair of fists provided editors with further damning copy and headlines such as 'AN ENGLISHMAN AND HIS KICKS' (*Liverpool Mercury*, 26 August 1890). By the early twentieth century, when widespread industrial action peaked shortly before the 1914 war, these groups of poor under and unemployed men were rebranded as politically dangerous men. 'HOOLIGAN REVELS RUINING A CITY, THE IRON HAND NEEDED FOR IRRESPONSIBLE RIOTERS IN MANCHESTER' (*Manchester Evening News*, 5 July 1911) warned of the dangers of slum terror over-throwing civil society. These same men and the scenes described in the newspaper article are precisely those described by Robert Roberts, son of a Salford shopkeeper, but in very different terms and language in *The Classic Slum* and, as such, offer a useful and instructive contrast, as the following extract shows:

> Men rushed yelling and cursing into the alley-ways. A score ran towards us, their clogs clattering over the setts, pursued by mounted police. A child, standing terrified by the door, I saw an officer lean forward on his horse and hit a neighbour with his truncheon above the eyes, heard the blow like the thump of wood on a swede turnip. The man ran crouching, hands to his face, into a wall and collapsed .... For half a lifetime afterwards the same man stayed among us, but did little work after. Something about him seemed absent.
>
> (Roberts 1973: 94)

The use of the word 'hooligan' in the context of labour strife shows how rapidly it had changed its meaning. Pearson, in his influential study *Hooligan: A History of Respectable Fears*, notes that the London press used the term to describe London youth street gangs as late as 1898 during the media panic surrounding their violence on the capital's thoroughfares (1983: 75). By rebranding or rechristening striking labourers as hooligans, newspapers were inviting readers to associate them with brutal, uncivilised and un-English violence. By labelling them in this way, the authorities would have met with relatively little dissent when it came to repressing them with troops and mounted police.

Women were rarely classed as roughs, although just occasionally headlines allude to women who were thought to belong to this group, as in 'FEMALE ROUGHS AT WARRINGTON. SONG AND DANCE IN A POLICE COURT' (*Liverpool Mercury*, 13 November 1890). More commonly, violent women attracted headlines that carried either classical allusions to 'viragos' and 'amazons' or cannibalism and savagery. In 'FEMALE SAVAGES IN CIRCUS STREET' (*Liverpool Mercury*, 27 August 1874) and 'A FEMALE CANNIBAL' (*Liverpool Mercury*, 12 June 1877), the women's behaviour, through the language of the headlines, is portrayed as unfeminine, uncivilised and dangerous. The reference to cannibalism is an allusion to the popular conception of how women fought. It was believed that women not only fought differently from men, they also fought in a more unrestrained and violent manner. 'BITING AN EAR OFF AND EATING IT' (*Liverpool Mercury*, 10 January 1873) and 'CHAWING MEN'S EARS' (*Liverpool Mercury*, 24 August 1879) amply illustrate male prejudices about the underhand methods that women employed in fighting.

To the middle-class outsider, the slum neighbourhoods of Victorian towns and cities must have appeared alien, threatening, dangerous and criminal. Newspapers, through their use of headlines, did much to label specific areas. These could range from the ironic 'A NICE NEIGHBOURHOOD' (*Liverpool Mercury*, 18 August 1876) to identifying specific streets, as in 'THE ROUGHS OF SCOTLAND ROAD, COWARDLY ASSAULT UPON A CONSTABLE' (*Liverpool Mercury*, 2 January 1872), to the highly emotive and alliterative 'BRUTAL BOOTLE – LUCKY TO GET OUT ALIVE' (*Liverpool Review*, 27 June 1889). Very little would appear to have changed, for in a recent edition of *The Liverpool Echo* (16 March 2001), the paper proclaimed 'YOB MAP TARGETS STREETS OF CRIME' in bold type on its front page. The same story, based on the computer analysis of incidents reported to the police over a number of years, was continued on an inside page with the headlined question 'IS YOUR STREET A CRIME HOT SPOT?'

While headlines from local newspapers often identified and continued to brand certain streets or areas within their own cities as dangerous, national newspapers did much to label regions or cities as criminal. In recent years, Manchester has gone under the unfortunate and damaging sobriquet of 'Gunchester', whereas in the nineteenth century, 'CRIME IN LIVERPOOL' (*The Times*, 25 December 1874) and 'LAWLESSNESS IN LIVERPOOL' (*The Times*, 7 January 1875) would have confirmed and reinforced London readers' preconceived perceptions of northern criminality and brutality. Such labelling for Liverpool, and to a lesser extent Manchester, has stuck and has been repeatedly built on up to the present day.

Violence and humour

It would be erroneous to believe that sub-editors or whoever prepared the copy were altogether lacking in humour. Victorians were fond of riddles, puns and word play, and nowhere is this more apparent than in the wording of headlines. Only in a city like Liverpool, with its deep sectarian and political divisions, could the headline 'A HOME RULER' (*Liverpool Mercury*, 13 March 1874) relate not to the campaign for Irish autonomy, as the headline suggests, but to the story of the prosecution of a young man who fought the rest of his family. In a similar vein, 'LYNCH LAW' (*Liverpool Mercury*, 2 April 1873) plays on the surname of the defendant. This theme of mocking the Irish can be seen in the more explicit 'AN IRISH PROSECUTION' (*Liverpool Mercury*, 3 April 1880), in which the court case is reported as a music hall comedy. Direct speech is reported in an Irish brogue: 'Ah, shure, that's what I want to know myself', during which the reported sequence of events is interspersed with laughter from the court and the prosecutor seemingly playing to the gallery, while the defendant countered with a contradictory and opposing set of events. Whereas some headlines, as in 'BURYING A WIFE ON FRIDAY AND COURTING ON SATURDAY, "STRIKING" SCENE AT A WEDDING PARTY' (*Liverpool Mercury*, 11 March 1870) not only contain word play, in the use of 'striking', but also tell a story that makes a social comment on how the lower orders lived. In the case of 'A REAL ETHOPIAN MINSTREL' (*Liverpool Mercury*, 26 April 1876), the word 'Ethopian' was used to signpost to the reader the colour of the defendant's skin. The theme of blackness was then pursued rather unusually through the report, which contained references to the assault weapon being 'a black bottle' and the trigger for the assault being the singing of 'nigger songs'. In other examples, the juxtaposition of seemingly unrelated topics allowed for social commentary and ironic humour. 'BRICKS AND BEER' (*Liverpool Mercury*, 12 October 1875), for example, refers to a drunken fight in which bricks were thrown; 'KICKING AND CUDDLING FOR THREE HOURS' (*Liverpool Mercury* 28 December 1874) emphasises the highs and lows of a stormy relationship; while 'A GOOD TEMPLAR AND BAD TIPPLER' (*Liverpool Mercury*, 29 August 1879) mocks the failings of someone who had signed the pledge of abstinence from alcohol.

Conclusion

The style and content of the headline, while fluctuating from the mundane, prosaic and factual to the emotionally charged and judgementally condemnatory, could serve many functions beyond simply signposting a story or catching the reader's eye. Through its construction and language, the headline was able to convey social comment on how the poor lived or raise fears concerning the prevalence of particular violent crimes like garotting or railway assaults. They could also identify and highlight the perpetrators of violence, the roughs and their female equivalents and in doing so implicitly and explicitly compare the middle-class readers' superior values with those of the 'brutes'. The language of the headline became more varied over time, reflecting in part the growth and popularity of sensational fiction, so that they could almost, at times, read like the precis of fictional narratives themselves and thus invite the reader to read on.

Notes

1   This chapter is based on material drawn from a project on 'Violence in the north west with special reference to Liverpool and Manchester 1850–1914' funded by the Economic and Social Research Council (award number: L133251004) as part of the Violence Research Programme. We wish to extend out thanks to Andrew Davies for his helpful advice and comments.
2   Fanny Adams was sexually assaulted, killed and dismembered in the Hampshire town of Alton in the summer of 1867. A solicitor's clerk, Frederick Baker, was found guilty and sentenced to death at the Winchester winter assizes (*Liverpool Mercury*, 27 August and 7 December 1867). Her murder coincided with the introduction of tinned meat in the Royal Navy, and it was thought that naval ratings when asked about the quality of the food said that it looked and tasted like 'sweet Fanny Adams'.
3   The project has examined approximately three months of newspapers per year for the period 1850–1914. Newspapers are a particularly valuable source for historians as they provide details that surviving court registers do not. The language of the reports also provides insights; see Jones (1999). However, press reports must be treated with care; see D'Cruze (1998) and, for more recent cases, Chibnall (1976).
4   Garotting was the Victorian equivalent of mugging – violent street robbery. It usually involved three individuals, one to choke the victim from behind, one to act as a look-out and one to rifle through the victim's pockets. It was claimed at the time that ex-convicts, who had in former times been punished with transportation but who were now serving relatively short sentences in penal servitude before being released back into society, were responsible for much serious crime in Britain in the early 1860s.

References

Boyle, T. (1989) *Black Swine in the Sewers of Hampstead: Beneath the Surface of Victorian Sensationalism*. New York: Viking.

Brown, L. (1985) *Victorian News and Newspapers*. Oxford: Clarendon Press.

Chassaigne, P. (1999) 'Popular representations of crime: the crime broadside – a subculture of violence in Victorian Britain?' *Crime, Histoire et Sociétés* 3(2): 23–56.

Chibnall, S. (1976) *Law – and – Order News: An Analysis of Crime Reporting in the British Press*. London: Tavistock Press.

Cohen, S. (1972) *Folk Devils and Moral Panics: The Creation of Mods and Rockers*. London: Paladin.

Davies, A. (1998) 'Youth gangs, masculinity and violence in late Victorian Manchester and Salford', *Journal of Social History* 32(2): 349–69.

Davis, J. (1980) 'The London garotting panic of 1862: a moral panic and the creation of a criminal class in mid-Victorian England', in V.A.C. Gatrell, B. Lenman and G. Parker (eds) *Crime and the Law: A Social History of Crime in Western Europe since*

1500. London: Europa.

D'Cruze, S. (1998) *Crimes of Outrage: Sex, Violence and Victorian Working Women.* London: UCL Press.

Halttunen, K. (1995) 'Humanitarianism and the pornography of pain in Anglo-American culture', *American Historical Review* 2 (April): 303–34.

Jones, A. (1996) *Powers of the Press: Newspapers, Power and the Public.* Aldershot: Scolar Press.

Jones, J. (1999) 'Male violence directed at women as reported in the Manchester press, 1870–1900', unpublished PhD thesis, University of Lancaster.

Pearson, G. (1983) *Hooligan: A History of Respectable Fears.* London: Macmillan.

Pelham, C. (1886) *The Chronicles of Crime or, The New Newgate Calendar.* London: Reeves & Turner.

Roberts, R. (1973) *The Classic Slum: Salford Life in the First Quarter of the Century.* Harmondsworth: Penguin.

Sindall, R. (1990) *Street Violence in the Nineteenth Century: Media Panic or Real Danger?* Leicester: Leicester University Press.

Soothill, K. and Walby, S. (1991) *Sex Crime in the News.* London: Routledge.

2 'Jump on top, get the job done'

Strategies employed by female prostitutes to reduce the risk of client violence

Graham Hart and Marina Barnard

Introduction

In the last two decades of the twentieth century, public concern over prostitution has most often focused on the sexual transmission of infection, particularly HIV. In our own work during the 1980s and 1990s, we certainly studied prostitution in relation to drug use as a means of understanding better the possible onward transmission of HIV (Hart *et al.* 1989; McKeganey and Barnard 1992; McKeganey *et al.* 1991). Other researchers also adopted this approach (Day 1988; Faugier *et al.* 1992; Ward *et al.* 1993), but during the 1990s there was increasing interest in the other risks faced by prostitute women, with client violence a key concern (Barnard 1993; Whitaker and Hart 1996; Ward *et al.* 1999). It was clear that street-based prostitution afforded the greatest degree of risk, with women routinely confronting clients whose behaviour ranges in severity from minor abuse to serious physical assault (Barnard 1993; Lowman and Frazer 1995; Silbert 1981).

However, our study of client violence against prostitutes, under the aegis of the ESRC Violence Research Programme, is the first in the UK to provide prevalence data on client violence against female prostitutes working in both street and indoor settings, such as flats and saunas. This demonstrates exceptionally high levels of violence in both situations, although street-based work is significantly more dangerous (Church *et al.* 2001). Previous work indicates that the client–prostitute encounter is replete with potential for conflict and tension, particularly where both parties hold conflicting views of who is in control of the encounter (Barnard 1993). Tensions are likely to coalesce around such specifics as money, whether condoms are to be used, the type of location where sex will be provided and the type of sex to be provided (Lowman and Frazer 1995). Vanwesenbeck (1997), reviewing work she had undertaken on the prostitute–client encounter in the Netherlands (Vanwesenbeck *et al.* 1994, 1995), identified absence of control as a factor associated with women she described as 'risk takers'. This risk taking was primarily in relation to non-use of condoms with clients, but Vanwesenbeck also found that a reduced level of control was associated with increased exposure to violence, 'unhealthy' coping responses (e.g. drug use) and a combination of features that represented power-lessness in the face of aggression. Women who had control over the sexual encounter were also more likely to work in less dangerous, off-street locations. A London study found that women working from flats, supported by a 'maid', were able to formulate and execute strategies to prevent or reduce the impact of violence (Whitaker and Hart 1996).

However, despite this range of studies, we have found no research that reports specifically on the strategies employed and identified by women prostitutes themselves to control the sexual encounter and thereby reduce their risks of exposure to violence. One promising avenue for investigation in this area is offered by recent work in the sociology of health risk, particularly in relation to HIV. Risk behaviour in this paradigm is understood as the outcome of a complex interplay between individual and social factors, interpersonal relationships and situations (Bloor 1995). Such an approach has relevance in the development of a theory of risk, control over the sexual encounter and violence. To date, such theorisation has primarily been constructed in terms of HIV risk behaviour such as needle sharing (McKeganey and Barnard 1992; Rhodes 1995) or non-commercial sexual relations (Hart and Flowers 1996). The commercial sex encounter has not been analysed using this approach, although it is the product of social action – the interaction between client and prostitute, the situation within which the interaction takes place and the broader economic, institutional and social context of commercial sex (Kane 1992). The potential for violence between prostitute and client has to be seen as embedded within this complex interplay of individual, interpersonal and social factors, and women's strategies for control of the encounter could prove to be a key mechanism for reducing the risk of client violence.

In this chapter, we describe a study of women working in the commercial sex industry, from both on-street and off-street locations, and focus on the strategies they used to organise and manage men, most of whom are strangers, in the execution of paid-for, intimate sexual acts. We believe that this is the first description of the means employed by sex workers to control sexual encounters while ensuring the delivery of a professional, safe and efficient sexual service to men. We use women's own accounts of their experiences to elucidate the means by which they seek to reduce the physical risks involved in this kind of work.

Methods and analysis

Three cities were selected in which to undertake the fieldwork: Glasgow, Edinburgh and Leeds.[1] These cities were chosen because prostitution in Glasgow is more frequently street-based, whereas in Edinburgh it is associated with indoor work (in saunas); in Leeds, prostitution occurs in both street and indoor settings, including flats. Street workers were defined as those women who reported that the street was their primary means of contacting clients in the month prior to interview; indoor workers were those whose primary means of contacting clients was through working in a sauna/massage parlour or working in a private flat in the month prior to interview (usually contacting clients by advertising in national or local newspapers).

A structured questionnaire was used to interview 240 women; 115 working on the street (75 in Glasgow; 40 in Leeds) and 125 women working indoors in saunas or flats (75 in Edinurgh; 50 in Leeds). We also undertook semi-structured interviews with a sample of these women: 45 with street workers (25 in Glasgow; 20 in Leeds) and 45 with indoor workers (25 in Edinburgh; 20 in Leeds). The data gathered included demographic characteristics, drug and alcohol use in the last six months, working patterns and the organisation of work, experiences (type and frequency) of client violence throughout the time worked and within the last six months, and whether they had ever reported an incident of client violence to the police. Interviews were under-taken between October 1998 and December 1999 and either took place in the respondent's place of work (in the case of sauna workers), in drop-in centres for street-working prostitutes and, less frequently, in the respondent's home, or in cafes. All interviews were carried out by experienced female interviewers.

Interviews were tape-recorded and transcribed verbatim, coded using the qualitative data package WINMAX and analysed using the method described by Glaser and Strauss (1968) as grounded theory, in which external categories are not imposed upon the data, but emerging and recurrent themes are identi-fied, and views according with or opposing these are juxtaposed to determine the extent to which given themes are present or absent in the accounts of participants in other settings. The transcripts were read by both authors, coding was undertaken by a research assistant and further analysis was undertaken by the lead author; his interpretations, and selection of themes were confirmed in discussions with the co-author. The aim, as with much qualitative research, was to achieve full representation of a range of opinion from respondents from given social categories (street-working women; women working in saunas and flats).

In the following sections, women's names, whether professional or private, have been changed, and any other potentially identifying features have been removed to maintain anonymity.

Results

Violence – an ever-present risk

The first point to note is that all street-working women, and most of those who worked indoors, were aware that the potential for client violence is ever-present in their work. Although this chapter is primarily concerned with the means by which women sought to control the sexual encounter to ensure that risk of violence was minimised, the strategies employed were not always successful. The following examples suggest the contingent nature of the work, and the circumstances in which, quite unexpectedly, violence can occur.

BARBARA: Anyway I says, 'Are you looking for business?' He says, 'Yes, get in'. And I took him down to this car park, and I got money off him, started doing business, but ... then he started getting me mad and things, asking daft questions ... Like saying, 'Do you like it?' You know, just being really fucking weird. And I was trying to keep my calm and like get inside and go. Anyway, I started doing the business with him, and he started being proper aggressive while I was doing the business ... Anyway, I said, 'Your time's up', and he just fucking grabs me and starts going all mad, started going off his head.

INTERVIEWER: Was he hitting you?

BARBARA: Yes, he were on top of me on t'seat. I were laid back, and I slided up and I got the back door open and turn on to my side, you know struggling, and he put his hand over me mouth. I tried to wriggle up to t'back, because the front seat were laid down passenger seat. I tried to wriggle up and out t'back door, and he's ... half of me hanging out back door and he was on top of me, and covering me mouth, fucking suffocating. I went dizzy and I come round, and I fought him like ... but he had his hand over me mouth, I come round, still fucking choking me, I just bit his hand, and then he let go for a split second and I wriggled free. And I flew over car park and he chased me. Then he went back and got in his car.

(Leeds, street worker)

Although the literature cited earlier identifies points at which violence may occur (e.g. with regard to disputes over the service offered, or cost), this type of apparently random and unprovoked attack is understood to be a constant threat. This is an example from a sauna worker of such an instance:

INTERVIEWER: Have you done [sold sex to] him more than once?

ALISON: I have done him about four times, like this were t'fifth time maybe and it were just, we had done the business and he had had a shower afterwards. I got sorted out, got dressed, saying nice to see you again, blah blah blah, the next thing he just fucking attacked me.

INTERVIEWER: How did he do that?

ALISON: All of a sudden he says 'it would be good to see you again' all of a sudden it were just like he ... just like total change – he just punched me, just straight in my mouth.

INTERVIEWER: There was no warning?

ALISON: There was no warning at all, he just did it, he just did it ... I was that shocked because I was on the floor then, like my God what's going on ... by this time he was kicking hell out of me. He started kicking my body. I was on the floor, he was kicking me in the head, in my face. I mean the time he finished with me there was lumps all over me head. The whole attack must have lasted I would say 30–40 seconds.

(Leeds, sauna worker)

In the following sections, we focus on the strategies employed by women in an attempt to ensure their safety, but it is salutary to remember these examples of violence and the propensity of many clients to introduce violence into the paid sexual encounter. We identified four strategies employed by women to gain control over and, where necessary, wrest control from clients, and otherwise manage the exchange of sex for money. These were confidence in relating to clients, acting the part, use of sexual position to ensure control, and achieving spatial control for safety.

Confidence in relating to clients

As with any personal service, selling sex for money has its own etiquette and rules, which both parties to the exchange are expected to follow. The sex worker is clearly most experienced in this interaction as, no matter how frequently men use the paid sexual services of women, they are unlikely to have had as many episodes of paid sex as the sex worker. The knowledge and experience of the sex worker is such that, if the man is unused to paying for sex, he will be guided through the process by the prostitute. However, those men who are very experienced in this interaction are also expected to follow the rules, and they will be reminded of this more or less forcefully – depending on the approach of the woman involved – if he departs from a well-established *modus operandi*. The most frequently described means by which women sought to secure control over the situation was through an active display of confidence throughout the encounter. The strategies employed to effect this varied between women, but they share a number of features. Some women had learned from others how to achieve this:

INTERVIEWER: You talk about ... being in control with the client. Has anybody ever spoken to you about how to do that kind of thing?.

JOANNE: Just from girls that you know I've worked with that have done it a long time ... I've watched how they've sort of handled customers and ... if you do a double you know and Julie ... she's often with me and 'cos she's done it a long time I've done a few with her ... She's always in control as you've seen ... she's very dominant and I like it ... A lot of the customers like it – they like being told what to do.

(Leeds, sauna worker)

However, many more women had learned from experience that confidence in relating to clients was an appropriate strategy to adopt, and it was important to establish this early in the encounter:

SARAH: Ah mean from the minute they come over or like it's usually ah go over to them, ah wouldn't act in any way nervous because ah don't think it gives a good impression. Ah don't want anyone t'think that ah don't know, they could take advantage really. Ah don't … ah think if you act confident then they're less likely to try anythin'.

(Leeds, street worker)

GEMMA: Ah just don't really tend to give them much chance to say anythin', ah just sort of like get straight in there and go for it, don't really give them much of a chance ….

INTERVIEWER: So … what do you do when you walk through that door?.

GEMMA: Ah feel really confident, ah walk in, straight away take ma clothes off, right, get ma bed down: 'Do you prefer oil or talc?' and … ah like spread their legs apart and ah massage them from like between their legs and that and they just sort of … ah don't know, it's just the way ah am, ah'm quite forceful ah suppose with them.

INTERVIEWER: Right. So you just kind of take charge ….

GEMMA: Take charge straight away.

(Leeds, sauna worker)

'Taking charge straight away' is a key element of many women's accounts of how they control the interaction, and this directiveness is pursued throughout the encounter. In the last example, the respondent describes being 'quite forceful' with clients, and in the next account it is again evident that women seek to follow a regular, unchanging series of actions to ensure an efficient and, if possible, rapid progress to the completion of the sexual exchange.

BLAIR: See when yer through there [indicates room] workin', right, yer given them a massage, right, and yer askin' questions but it's jist standard questions, right, and ye go through, ye do their back, ye do their front, give it [penis] a wee rub, get it hard, get the condom on, jump on top, get the job done, get off and jist get them ready and … out the door … And that's it, simple.

(Edinburgh, flat worker)

Confidence in relating to clients can help to realise the two goals of greatest importance to the sex worker: processing men with a speed that allows them to feel they have gained satisfaction from the encounter, while not inconveniencing the woman temporally (it is quick), or affecting her physically (it is painless) and mentally (she is left untouched psychologically by the experience). In this way, confidence and assurance throughout the sexual encounter may contribute to the reduction of some of the health and social risks attached to sex work.

Acting the part

In many ways, confidence in relating to clients involves presenting a public face of assurance – of acting the part of self-controlled, well-organised and experienced sexual agent. Women frequently referred to the dramaturgical element of their work directly, as Sarah, the Leeds street worker, did above, making it clear that a set script is followed: that a positive 'persona' or character must be presented to the customer.

TINA: It's all part of the act ... As soon as that door shuts, it's like 'On we go', you know, 'Lie doon sweetheart. What huv ye been daen the day? Is this you goin' for a pint?'... It's usually when they're gettin' undressed but then again ah tend tae find ah'll say tae them 'Right, I'll pop the shower on for ye an ah'll go and get ma oil', and ah'll leave them tae get undressed.

(Edinburgh, sauna worker)

The use of commonplace enquiries and 'normal' (non-sexual) conversation is the means by which this woman asserts control, making it clear to the client that this is a routine activity for her, one that she is used to directing and managing. However, this was not the limit of the acting skills required. One of the main ways in which women sought to control the encounter was to ensure that it was as brief as possible. This usually involves arousing the man to a level of excitement that results in ejaculation soon after the start of any sexual act. Sexual arousal was stage-managed by the women, often pretending that they were deriving some sexual pleasure themselves in order to hasten the client's orgasm.

JADE: It's ... straight[forward] acting.
INTERVIEWER: Do you think some of them actually think that you're really enjoying it? ... That they're coming here and giving you pleasure?.
JADE: Yeah, yeah. And you give them lines to make them feel good like 'Ah've never had it that good before', 'Me boyfriend doesn't do it that good'. Ye know, ye just give 'em a few lines.
INTERVIEWER: ... Is it hard to do that, the acting thing?.
JADE: Sometimes when ... you're tired, like today and [you've got] PMT and ya just can't be arsed. But some days it's fun, ye think 'Oh, yer gullible!'.

(Leeds, sauna worker)

For some women, and particularly those working on the street, this display of sexual pleasure on their part would be seen as beyond the call of duty, and unnecessary. Indeed, it could be dangerous, as pretending to have an orgasm may be disempowering, making the client feel that he has control over the interaction. However, in saunas this appeared to be less of a problem and was simply another technique in the armoury of means to achieve a good result – a rapid end to the sex.

NICKY: Some clients ... [say] 'I want you to enjoy it', ye know, and you're like 'Fuck, how am ah supposed to enjoy it? ... Ye're just payin' me!' ... So you've got tae kid on [pretend]. Ye've got tae make all the orgasm noises, [but] when yer doin' it, yer thinkin' 'Yes! Ah've got forty pound, ah can go and get ma messages [shopping]', ye know [laughs] ... He's probably thinkin' 'Are you enjoying this?' 'Ah'm lovin' it baby', ye know what ah mean?.

INTERVIEWER: Have you ever enjoyed it?.

NICKY: No ... Ah've never actually thought about it, ye know.

(Edinburgh, sauna worker)

This is a further example of a woman, even as she mimics the sounds suggestive of sexual arousal, who is left untouched emotionally or physically by the experience. However, most women, even in saunas, would never pretend that they had achieved orgasm and were happier using compliments and flattery to realise their goal.

JESS: Some of them say, 'Oh, is my penis too big for you?' ... 'cos they really think they're men. And then I'll boost their egos ... I'll play their game. That's what they want. That's what they come here for ... I'll say, 'It's the hardest I've ever seen', or 'The biggest I've ever seen' or whatever ... Oh they're such idiots, they really are. Every time I do a massage ... I always find something nice ... usually I use the skin, 'Your skin is so soft and beautiful' ... 'Oh you've got a beautiful back' ... because that's what men want, they want their egos boosted. A man needs his ego to be stroked at all times, so I stroke their egos.

(Leeds, sauna worker)

Acting could also mean allowing men to feel that they were in control, although this has the same potential for loss of control that pretending to orgasm may have. However, in the case of this respondent, this could never be a possibility:

ROMA: Well, like that guy that was just in. ... He was only like ten minutes or so, but that was ... because I wanted [it] to be ten minutes. If I ever wanted it to be longer or whatever I'd make it longer, but it's all ... controlled by me. That's the way I see it, it's all controlled by me, and as long as they know that then there's not a problem. There is ones that do try to come in and do try to take over, but I don't let that happen.

(Edinburgh, flat worker)

This indicates that most clients are themselves fully aware of the parameters of the paid sexual encounter, and of the rules surrounding it. This is certainly the case for those men who pay for a particular sexual fantasy to be played out (with them as a naughty schoolboy, or the sex worker as dominatrix or sadistic mistress), because an explicit dramaturgical narrative is central to the action: the script is very clearly established prior to the act. It follows a recognised storyline and culminates in previously agreed words or actions that result in orgasm for the man. However, for most men it appeared – from the perspectives of these women at least – that the act was either 'successful' (i.e. they were persuaded that the woman was having an orgasm/enjoying the experience/ admired their body) or sufficiently persuasive to bring the interaction to an appropriate conclusion.

Use of sexual position to ensure control

Confidence in relating to clients and acting the part may succeed for some women in starting the interaction, and getting the man into a (social) position whereby he understands that the sex is being directed by the other party, but for many women the sexual position she adopts constitutes the main focus of her management of the situation. Choice by her of the physical position taken during sexual intercourse was a key strategy employed to ensure that the sexual act was completed quickly, with minimal risk and requiring the exercise of the least possible emotional and physical effort. Jane suggests that being taken by the man from behind frees her from having to think about the sex act at all:

JANE: If you [have] it from behind, 'cos it's easier, you don't have to look at them and you can sit there thinking 'Jesus, where's my nail file?' It happens all the time [laughs] … Ah love it from behind … it's the way you take the lead. Ah suppose that's the way you don't get scared because once you lose that element of control then you're the victim …. Ah have no hang-up on what ah do and ah think that's because ah stay in control.

(Leeds, sauna worker)

For Lisa, working either in a house or from the street, the context determines her choice of sexual position, and how relaxed she is about this.

LISA: If I'm in somebody's house I'll always … let them start off doing it that way [him on top] and … just let them do it that way 'cos it's easier … but in the car I always get on top of them and I just get them to stay in the driver's seat … I don't get in the back or let them on top of me 'cos then I can do it … get off them, and get my clothes back on.

Many women chose to be 'on top' during sex as this seemed to serve as both a physical and psychological demonstration of their control. This is evidenced most clearly by Blair, who explicitly makes the connection between sexual position and dominating the situation.

BLAIR: You just don't let them get the upper hand and the majority of the time if they're wanting a full service … when ah'm havin' sex with them, ah'm on top o' them.
INTERVIEWER: Right.

BLAIR: Ah mean ah'm by far the more dominant person in the room, right? and ah think if ye keep yourself in that situation, yer gonnae keep yersel' out o' trouble.

INTERVIEWER: So what if they want someone who's a bit submissive?.

BLAIR: Then they're fucked. They're no gonnae get that frae me.

(Edinburgh, flat worker)

An unusual example of the use of sexual position to achieve control is reported by Amelia, a street worker in Glasgow. It is quite difficult to envisage precisely how she achieves this in practical terms, but according to her, this is what she 'always' does:

AMELIA: See if yer underneath in the car ... Ah'm lucky, ah've got big long legs, ah always put ma feet ... ah don't lean them on the dashboard, ah put them right up against their windae 'cos if they start, their windscreen's goin' oot first an' foremost ... That way somebody can hear me.

(Glasgow, street worker)

Often, choice of sexual position is used to hasten the act to a conclusion, and many women were flexible about the position chosen if this resulted in more rapid male orgasm. This, along with other features of sauna culture ('reverse massage' is defined as allowing the client to rub or touch the sex worker), is described by Jess, the Leeds sauna worker cited earlier:

JESS: He had [penetrative] sex and oral [sex] but then I finished with the oral and I said 'OK, what position would you like?' ... And he said, 'No, I'll play with you for a while'. So I said to him, 'My love, that's £50 – that's reverse massage'. He ... played with my boobs a bit, and then there's a mirror on the one wall, so I said to him – I could see he was watching himself in the mirror, one of these arseholes – so I said to him, 'You know, I think we can do doggy style, like this, so you can see yourself in the mirror'. And that was exciting to him, so ....

INTERVIEWER: So you managed to get him done?.

JESS: Yeah, yeah, or else he was going to take longer massaging my boobs and irritating the shit out of me, so give him the more exciting option .... You try to manipulate them.

(Leeds, sauna worker)

This very confident respondent – quickly adding £50 to the bill because of the 'extra' service requested by the man – demonstrates how she took the opportunity afforded by the man's narcissistic interest in what was happening in the mirror to speed the interaction to a close. It may appear that by allowing the man to enter from behind the woman is in fact in a more vulnerable position, as he would be able to grab her neck and head from behind. However, women felt that this was less risky than a man being on top and able to grab her from the front.

There were other elements of control in this situation, particularly in saunas, where women would ensure that a man never brought a bag into the room where the sex took place, or at least a bag would be searched beforehand (to prevent him bringing in a rope, or knife), and they would make certain that the man was naked before starting sex, again to obviate any attempt to conceal anything about his person. Thus, a man's only weapons in these circumstances would be his hands and, as we have seen, many women felt in greater control if the client entered from behind.

Achieving spatial control for safety

Although sexual position is one example of what might be described as micro-spatial control, arranging limbs and bodies to achieve power over the situation, even if this has the goal orientation of rapid progression to orgasm, other more evidently spatial strategies were employed by women in their attempts to reduce the physical and other risks to their persons. For most women working in saunas, this spatial issue was of less concern, as one of the attractions of 'indoor' work such as this is that safety is assumed to be a defining feature of sauna work. Within saunas the organisation of the working space often meant that several women would be sitting in an open area, with sofas and chairs, near the front of the building, from which it is then possible to access private rooms. Clients must walk through this public area prior to and immediately after the provision of the service, and this serves to discourage violent activity and to prevent situations of clients refusing to pay. However, for non-sauna workers, it is necessary to identify other means of ensuring that risk of violence is kept to a minimum.

CHERRY: We do escorts from here. ... If a customer rings up and he wants an escort ... I never visit a private house, I never visit houses ... I [ask the] number of the hotel, room number and [their] name and I'll ring [them] back. So when you ring them back you know that they're actually genuine. They are at that room, at that name and in that hotel.

INTERVIEWER: So you feel safer?.

CHERRY: Yeah. So then you ring them back and you talk to them; you come to an agreement over the phone; you go and meet them. You go upstairs, he can't kick off [argue, fight] in a hotel because if he kicks off ... if he refuses to pay, you [can] kick off. ... Is it really worth his reputation to be shown up like that in the middle of a hotel?.

INTERVIEWER: You don't feel scared because it's just you and him?.

CHERRY: No. Because I mean a hotel is a busy place, in't it? ... If he kicks off, you know, you kick off plus the fact you always leave the number and the name of the person, the room number with somebody that you know. So then after say about an hour if you don't ring them for the time that is agreed they know to ring the hotel. 'Put me through to room such and such'. So you let the customer know that. You say to the customer 'There is a friend and she knows I'm here, she knows your name and she knows your room number and if I don't ring her in an hour she will be ringing you with that – O.K?' And they're happy with that, they're happy with that.

(Leeds, sauna worker and escort)

This long quotation is cited because it illustrates clearly a number of strategies employed by escorts to ensure safety, notably the choice of the relatively public location in which the sex takes place (hotel), alongside the specific security measures taken (prior confirmation that the client is actually in the room given, by returning his call; telling the client that a friend is aware of the location and length of the meeting). However, for street workers, spatial strategies are most important if they are to ensure control and safety, represented very clearly in this account:

NICKY: There's a residential area that I go [to] – just down at the riverside flats there's a car park there, because it's all lit up in there ... if you're screaming someone's bound to stick their head out of the windows. If you go somewhere like industrial, and it's fucking pitch black ... and you end up getting a client that turned on you, you're fucked aren't you? ... He could get out and chase you. ... If you're in the city centre and you're right next to the city centre, you get out of the car – he's not going to chase you. Because you only have to get out t'car and there's all these people about.

(Leeds, street worker)

The choice of a residential area or city centre in which to carry out her business allows this street worker to feel confident in interactions with clients because she knows that these relatively public spaces afford her some protection, in comparison with unpopulated industrial areas. Indeed, as Collean suggests below, if a client expresses a strong wish to have sex in a location of his choice, this could be indicative of bad faith on his part and in itself be seen as a cause for sufficient concern to put an end to the interaction:

COLLEAN: If they say they do want business when you are in't car and if they refuse to go to certain places ... if they are adamant that you go to a place where they want to go ....
INTERVIEWER: And would you go?.
COLLEAN: If they were like 'No ... you have got to come to where I want to go to', I say 'No I'm not coming'.
INTERVIEWER: They have to go where you want to go?.
COLLEAN: Yeah, if they won't come where I want to go to then it doesn't happen.

(Leeds, street worker)

As we have seen, determining the location of sex is very important to ensure safety for both escorts and street workers, with the latter in particular using the same locations on a regular basis because this gives them confidence that, should a client be violent or physically threatening, they would be able to summon help, or at least escape quickly. However, even among sauna workers, location and the spatial organisation of work were seen to serve a psychological function in terms of restraint, as clients were not on 'home turf' and would therefore think twice before causing trouble. This, combined with many of the other features reported in relation to confidence with clients, acting the part and sexual position, served to increase the confidence of this sauna worker that her own physical safety could be ensured:

INTERVIEWER: Right, what do you think is the most important thing that keeps you safe at work. It could be anything – it could be something physical, something about you …?.

JULIE: Um it's a combination, it's like with the door upstairs it's wrought iron and the camera [CCTV] and they are on our territory … and they are naked and the acting bit, the character bit you know it's character versus character who is going to win, and I always win. … It's everything all combined. See out on the street you don't have that control. You're not on your own territory, you are on no man's land.

INTERVIEWER: Or in their car?.

JULIE: Or in their car – well, that's their territory, you are vulnerable then.

(Leeds, sauna worker)

This respondent contrasts the relative safety of sauna work with that of the street, primarily in terms of its spatial organisation, and the reduced confidence of clients when not on 'their territory'; her explicit reference to the vulnerability of street-working women is couched in these spatial terms and once again argues for the centrality of control over the sexual encounter, with location being one of a number of elements through which this is achieved.

Conclusion

Most women were able to report some strategy or combination of strategies by means of which they sought to control the sexual interaction, and much of this was seen in terms of a battle of wills, with every effort expended to ensure that clients were always at a disadvantage. Confidence with clients, acting the part, using sexual positions to ensure control and employing spatial control for safety were all examples of such strategies, and although individual women had their own specific techniques, there were commonalities between them, as we have seen from the quotations used. It was exceptional to find a respondent who did not subscribe to the view that control over the sexual encounter was a vital determinant of how safely and successfully it would progress, so this account is therefore very unusual:

EMMA: Well, we're not really [in control], are we? 'cos I mean, they've paid us
so, really, they can do it because they've paid. ... You can't really be in
control with your client, tell them not to do this and not to do that ....
INTERVIEWER: So do you feel that they're more in control of the situation than
you are?
EMMA: Um, yeah.

(Leeds, street worker)

However, for most women, there was no doubt that it was their primary aim,
early in the interaction, to gain control over and, where necessary, wrest control
from, clients, and otherwise structure the exchange of sex for money in a manner
that was most beneficial for them. This meant getting sex over as quickly as
possible, at least in the case of non-regular clients ('regulars' were often afforded
more care and consideration), and with the least amount of inconvenience to
the sex worker, including the avoidance of physical and mental harm.

Whereas street workers' control is limited to whether sex takes place in a car,
and where it takes place, sauna and other indoor women have to navigate
clients through a social and sexual topography of sauna etiquette and space.
This allows, indeed requires, them to consider carefully the specific moments at
which, and sites where, the exercise of control is necessary during the sex
worker–client encounter. 'Confidence with clients' and 'acting the part' were
vital to this, and although these issues are not entirely unimportant to street
women, there is less scope for the exercise of complex strategies of control over
the sexual interaction. In great part this accounts for the relatively little weight
placed on this issue by street workers.

Much of the recent work in the sociology of health risk has emphasised the role
of the micro-social context in influencing risk behaviour. There has been research
that has investigated the drug and sexual risk taking of injecting drug users
(Rhodes 1995), and studies have focused particularly on the gendered nature of
power within heterosexual relationships of drug users, including that of MacRae
and Aalto (2000), which found that male partners injected their female partners
as part of what the women considered to be a loving relationship. However, in
relation to the sexual encounter, research has mostly been concerned with the
negotiation of safer sex between young women and their male partners (Holland
et al. 1991; Waldby *et al.* 1993), and there has been little work on the negotiation
of sexual encounters by prostitutes with their clients. An exception to this is the
work of Bloor *et al.* (1990) and Barnard (1993), which demonstrated that female
prostitutes were more skilled than male prostitutes in ensuring that payment for
sex was agreed prior to the act, so that female prostitutes suffered few of the problems of their male counterparts in terms of definitions of the situation (an
exchange of sex for money, rather than unpaid consensual sexual relations).
However, we believe that the current study is the first to report on the detail of
prostitute–client encounters in terms of actual and potential violence, and the
response to this through attempts to control the sexual interaction, the course the
encounter takes and its management by the sex worker.

The perspective of the sociology of health risk is useful to the study of paid sexual encounters in that it can alert us to the macro-structural (at the level of societies, e.g. the legal position of prostitution), meso-structural (the organisational level) and micro-social contexts of sex work (Hart and Carter 2000; Hart and Flowers 1996). We have seen how, at the meso-social level, the organisation of sex work in saunas or flats facilitates increased control over the sexual encounter between prostitute and client, whereas there is less opportunity for this in relation to street work. At the micro-social level, women's strategies and techniques can be interrogated, and the social interaction involved in the meeting of sex worker and client can be unpacked. All of this takes place in a particular historical moment of gendered power relations, in a society in which most of the activities surrounding the sale of sex for money are illegal, so the macro-social structural features of the situation impose themselves in a way that ensures that these strategies and techniques take a particular form, and have to be established by the women early in the interaction.

The focus of this chapter has been the reportedly successful exercise of control by female prostitutes over their clients, but we noted earlier how violence can occur unpredictably and despite the strategic efforts of the sex worker. We propose in future to describe how such strategies are challenged by clients, and that their very employment can result in violence against women. The policy implications of this work are also at the macro-, meso- and micro-social structural levels. Every effort should be directed towards the prevention of prostitution, mainly by offering women drug treatment, employment and other opportunities to avoid the social exclusion that is often a precursor to sex work, but if commercial sex continues to occur, women could be helped by a number of policy and practical changes. The decriminalisation of many of the activities surrounding the exchange of money is necessary if there are to be improvements in the social organisation of prostitution, and changes introduced that would facilitate increased control on the part of female prostitutes. This could contribute significantly to improved health and safety at work. At the micro-social level, it would be advisable to encourage some form of mentoring, with more experienced women providing training for new entrants to the work, rather than young women learning from their mistakes, as currently occurs, and thereby risking exposure to violence. The techniques of relating to clients, managing and securing control over the sexual encounter are vital to risk reduction and harm minimisation in commercial sex work. These issues have not been accorded sufficient thought or consideration in relation to the occupational health and safety of female sex workers, and this is an important first step if we are to see reductions in the number of violent attacks against sex workers in this country.

Acknowledgements

We would like to thank Stephanie Church and Catherine Benson for their work on this study, and to express our gratitude to all of the women who agreed to participate in the research.

Note

1 Ethical permission to undertake the study was sought from and granted by the University of Glasgow Ethics Committee for Non-Clinical Research on Human Subjects.

References

Barnard, M.A. (1993) 'Violence and vulnerability: conditions of work for streetworking prostitutes', *Sociology of Health and Illness* 15(5): 683–705.

Bloor, M.J. (1995) *The Sociology of HIV Transmission*. London: Sage.

Bloor, M.J., McKeganey, N.P. and Barnard, M.A. (1990) 'An ethnographic study of HIV-related practices among Glasgow rent boys and their clients: a report of a pilot study', *AIDS Care* 2: 17–24.

Church, S., Henderson, M., Barnard, M. and Hart, G. (2001) 'Violence by clients towards female prostitutes in different work settings: questionnaire survey', *British Medical Journal* 322: 524–5.

Day, S. (1988) 'Prostitute women and AIDS: anthropology', *AIDS* 2: 421–8.

Faugier, J., Hayes, C. and Butterworth, C. (1992) 'Drug-using prostitutes, their health care needs and their clients', London: Department of Health.

Glaser, B. and Strauss, A. (1968) *The Discovery of Grounded Theory*. London: Weidenfeld & Nicolson.

Hart, G. and Carter, S. (2000) 'Drug consumption and risk: developing a sociology of HIV risk behaviour', in J. Gabe, S. Williams and M. Calnan (eds) *Theorising Medicine, Health and Society*. London: Sage.

Hart, G. and Flowers, P. (1996) 'Recent developments in the sociology of HIV risk behaviour', *Risk, Decision and Policy* 1: 153–65.

Hart, G.J., Sonnex, C., Petherick, A., Johnson, A.M., Feinmann, C. and Adler, M.W. (1989) 'Risk behaviours for HIV infection among injecting drug users attending a drug dependency clinic', *British Medical Journal* 298: 1081–3.

Holland, J., Ramazanoglu, C., Scott, S., Sharpe, S. and Thomson, R. (1991) *Between Embarrassment and Trust: Young Women and the Diversity of Condom Use*. Lewes: Falmer Press.

Kane, S.C. (1992) 'Prostitution and the military: planning AIDS intervention in Belize', *Social Science and Medicine* 36: 965–79.

Lowman, J. and Frazer, L. (1995) 'Violence against persons who prostitute: the experience in British Columbia', Vancouver: Simon Frazer University.

MacRae, R. and Aalto, E. (2000) 'Gendered power dynamics and HIV risk in drug-using sexual relationships', *AIDS Care* 12(4): 505–15.

McKeganey, N. and Barnard, M. (1992) *AIDS, Drugs and Sexual Risk*. Buckingham: Open University Press.

McKeganey, N.P., Barnard, M.A., Bloor, M.J. and Leyland, A. (1991) 'Injecting drug use and female streetworking prostitution in Glasgow', *AIDS* 4: 1153–5.

Rhodes, T. (1995) 'Theorising and researching "risk": notes on the social relations of risk in heroin users' lifestyles', in P. Aggleton, P. Davies and G. Hart (eds) *AIDS: Safety, Sexuality and Risk*. London: Taylor & Francis.

Silbert, M. (1981) *Sexual Assault of Prostitutes*. San Francisco: Delancey Street Foundation.

Vanwesenbeck, I. (1997) 'The context of women's power(lessness) in heterosexual interactions', in L. Segal (ed.) *New Sexual Agendas*. London: Macmillan.

Vanwesenbeck, I., van Zessen, G., de Graaf, R. and Straver, C.J. (1994) 'Contextual and interactional factors influencing condom use in heterosexual prostitution contacts', *Patient Education and Counselling* 24: 307–22.

Vanwesenbeck, I., de Graaf, R., van Zessen, G., Straver, C.J. and Visser, J.H. (1995) 'Professional HIV risk-taking, levels of victimisation and well-being in female prostitutes in the Netherlands', *Archives of Sexual Behavior* 24(5): 503–15.

Waldby, C., Kippax, S. and Crawford, J. (1993) '*Cordon sanitaire*: "clean" and "unclean" women in the AIDS discourse of young heterosexual men', in P. Aggleton, G. Hart and P. Davies (eds) *AIDS: Facing the Second Decade*. Basingstoke: Falmer Press.

Ward, H., Day, S., Mezzone, J., Dunlop, L., Donegan, C. *et al.* (1993) 'Prostitution and risk of HIV: female prostitutes in London', *British Medical Journal* 307: 356–8.

Ward, H., Day, S. and Weber, J. (1999) 'Risky business: health and safety in the sex industry over a 9 year period', *Sexually Transmitted Infections* 75: 340–3.

Whitaker, D. and Hart, G. (1996) 'Managing risks: the social organisation of indoor sex work', *Sociology of Health and Illness* 18: 399–414.

3 Violence against children

Thresholds of acceptance for physical punishment in a normative study of parents, children and discipline

Neal Hazel, Deborah Ghate, Susan Creighton, Julia Field and Steven Finch

Physical punishment as a focus of debate

The use of physical force by adults in disciplinary relationships with children is currently the subject of major debates in the United Kingdom, Europe and beyond. Crudely, the debates question whether 'smacking' (or 'spanking') is, on the one hand, a necessary and legitimate part of responsible child rearing or, on the other hand, yet another type of interpersonal violence that should be outlawed. We can note not only the large 'international controversy' on this topic in the scientific research community (Rohner *et al.* 1996: 842; Ghate 2000) and among social care professionals (Cloke 1997: 276) but also considerable disagreement on an international scale in legal and political arenas. The subject of physical punishment has been seen as having important implications for children now, for their longer-term development and for the future of society as a whole. Consequently, issues and concerns regarding physical punishment of children, together with the possibility of restricting such actions, have been 'firmly placed on the political agenda in many countries in recent years' (Overton 1993: 76).

Moreover, issues surrounding physical punishment have clearly captured the interest of the media and wider public. The British media regularly devotes many column inches to court cases and pronouncements involving smacking by parents. Recent press headlines include 'Teacher who smacked daughter overturns classroom ban' (*The Times*, 2 November 2001) and 'Scot convicted of belting daughter' (BBCI, 10 September 1999). Newspapers frequently run columns and editorials supporting or attacking physical punishment (e.g. *The Telegraph*, 8 September 2001; *The Observer*, 11 November 2001), and the tabloids have devoted letters pages to the public 'outrage' over the jailing of parents in cases involving physical chastisement (*The Sun*, 9 May 2000). In addition, the press has run feature articles on whether a whole range of famous personalities from novelists to bishops have ever hit, or sympathised with those who hit, their children (e.g. *Sunday Telegraph*, 27 October 1996). Even the Prime Minister's wife, human rights lawyer Cherie Booth, has described this subject in a newspaper as 'a fascinating one' (*The Independent*, 3 October 2001). It is a fascination that has been echoed around the world.

The long-established legal position in Britain has been that 'moderate and reasonable' physical chastisement is an acceptable part of responsible parenting. This has been repeatedly used by parents as a flexible defence against charges of assaulting their children. The precedent was set in common law over 125 years ago, when Chief Justice Cockburn judged that parents (and their delegates): 'By the law of England ... may for the purpose of correcting what is evil in the child, inflict moderate and reasonable corporal punishment' (R v. Hopley 1860; see Smith 1999 for a useful legal summary). The position was underlined by legislation in the 1930s that specifically ensured the protection of parents' and teachers' rights to physically chastise children (Children and Young Persons Act 1933 (England and Wales); Children and Young Persons (Scotland) Act 1937) and was specifically not amended as part of the sweeping changes in the Children Acts of recent years (England and Wales 1989; Scotland 1995). Although this defence has generally been removed in schools and professional child-care situations, parents (and their childminders) are still permitted to use physical punishment. In contrast, there are currently ten European countries that have effectively outlawed physical punishment by parents.[1]

Following a ruling in the European Court of Human Rights (A v. United Kingdom 1998), the government was required to review this defence of 'reasonable chastisement'. The case had been taken to the European Court after an English jury in 1994 found that repeated caning of a 9-year-old boy by his stepfather was 'moderate and reasonable' rather than actual bodily harm. The European Commission and Court deemed that the English legal system had failed to protect the boy from 'inhuman or degrading treatment', prohibited under Article 3 of the European Convention on Human Rights. The high profile that the government review would take was clear by the day following the court's judgment (24 September 1998), when at least four national newspapers ran editorials on the issue (*The Express*; *The Mirror*; *The Times*; *Daily Mail*). Subsequent consultation documents, introduced separately in Scotland, Northern Ireland and England and Wales, were met with renewed and immediate interest by media and campaigners alike. Newspapers ran with emotive headlines such as 'Parents will face prison for smacking' (*The Independent*, 18 January 2000). In the end, both the Department of Health and the Scottish Executive decided against moving to a complete ban. In England and Wales, it was concluded that the Human Rights Act 1998, which incorporated European Court judgments into UK law, would suffice. Scotland would make moves towards legislation more explicitly outlawing physical punishment in certain contexts, including the use of implements, and with children under 3 years old.

These conclusions still leave children in a unique legal position. Children are the only group in Britain where physical force against them can be argued as acceptable. Children are the only people who, in their everyday lives, can be struck by others and the law does not regard it as an assault. Campaigners have argued that it should be seen as 'no more acceptable to hit a child than anyone else' and that a ban on physical punishment by parents and carers would simply bring children's rights into line with 'the rest of us' (EPOCH 1991). Lawyers in the recent European Court case outlined their aim as trying to achieve a recognition that children should be afforded the same legal rights as adults (*The Times*, 15 June 1998). If a parent should strike their partner, this would generally be labelled domestic violence, yet it can be defended as appropriate between parent and child. This apparent anomaly is allowed to exist because, unlike in other contexts, there seems to be no consensus that this type of interpersonal conflict is wrong or unacceptable, let alone violent. In law, and in wider policy discussions, violence is not necessarily understood to 'mean' or refer to physical chastisement by parents.

Some in the scientific, practice, policy and legal debates have made it quite clear that they do see physical punishment as both unacceptable and violent. Labelling all acts of physical force on children as 'violence' has enabled abolitionists to relate lawful physical punishment to more extreme images on a continuum of 'violence' that includes 'serious physical and sexual abuse, pornography and prostitution, the murder of street children and the effects of armed conflict' (Newell 1995: 215). Acts of physical punishment have either been described as discrete types of violence (e.g. Straus and Gelles 1988; Graziano *et al.* 1991; Gelles 1997) or as shades along a continuous spectrum of violence (e.g. Payne 1989; Graziano and Namaste 1990; Hemenway *et al.* 1994; UNICEF 1997): 'All action intended to cause a child physical pain – from a "little smack" to a fatal beating – is on one continuum of violence' (EPOCH 1990: 3).

Moreover, the term 'violence', like 'abuse' and 'inhuman', is given specific emphasis in the debate because of legal references in, for instance, the European Convention on Human Rights and the UN Convention on the Rights of the Child (Scottish Law Commission 1992: 27). The UN Committee on the Rights of the Child has argued that physical chastisement is incompatible with Article 19 of the UN Convention on the Rights of the Child, which prohibits all forms of 'violence' (UNICEF 1997: 6).

In contrast, others in the debate have been clear that they do not consider physical punishment *per se* as violence, inappropriate or unacceptable. Proponents of physical punishment have argued vehemently that associating physical force in disciplinary situations with violence is 'not helpful' (Greenway, House of Commons, Education Bill (Lords) debate, 22 July 1986: 237; see also Scottish Law Commission 1992: 27, 29). Indeed, such acts are often suggested as necessary in order to bring up children responsibly. During the recent legal review, the then Education Secretary, David Blunkett, declared publicly that smacking his sons had 'worked' and was sometimes necessary as 'the only way of getting the message across' (*Metro*, 11 December 2000). It is argued that a reduction in physical punishment has already destroyed parental control in the family and caused a wider breakdown in behaviour that threatens society as a whole (noted in Cloke 1997: 278–9; Maurer and Wallerstein 1987: 1).

Clearly, in addition to the policy dimension of this debate, it must be recognised that physical punishment is a 'very emotive subject' (EPOCH 1991: 3; Fox

Harding 1991: 8; Evans and Fergason 1998: 357). Any challenge to its accept-ability, or attempt to label it inappropriate or violent, seems to strike a raw nerve in policy makers and the media. But how representative are they of parents in Britain? How far does any challenge to physical punishment still question adult–child disciplinary relationships, which are deeply rooted in cultural beliefs and norms (Ortega *et al.* 1997: 11; Loseke 1991: 163)? To what extent did the English jury and defendant in the European Court case really reflect parents across Britain when they considered that repeated caning was 'reasonable chastisement'?

In this chapter, we explore these questions, drawing on findings from a recent study of parents across Britain to examine how parents distinguish between acceptable and unacceptable physical responses in a disciplinary context, and we consider whether there is in fact a clear consensus on where the boundary between the two may lie.

What do we know about attitudes to physical punishment?

Existing research

The media readily quote statistics about the numbers 'smacking' or agreeing with 'smacking'. However, this readiness belies a gap in our knowledge about the way parents across Britain really feel about the acceptability of smacking and the 'meaning' they give to different types of physical chastisement. First, questions put to respondents have tended to concentrate largely on whether specific acts should be legal or illegal. Given the arenas in which the debate on physical punishment has perhaps been most prominent (i.e. the courts and Parliament) this focus is quite understandable. However, there is a limit to how far approaching the topic solely within a legal framework can explore the underlying *meaning* that parents (and others) attach to the use of physical force in discipline. Second, research studies that have at least touched on attitudes to such acts have tended to be smaller community studies focusing on, say, one city, rather than giving a wider and more statistically representative picture of parents in Britain. Third, these studies are now mostly several years, if not generations, old. In an area with such fast-moving legal and political debates and proposals (as well as a regular turnover of parents and children), it is crucial that researchers ensure that figures informing the debates are as current as possible. Fourth, the data often quoted have tended to come from 'market research-style' opinion polls, where the sample may not have been drawn repre-sentatively, or questions may have been asked out of context.

Nevertheless, certain research studies and polls have been innovative or influential with respect to the media or policy debates and are worth recapping here. One often-cited community study of physical punishment, conducted by Marjorie Smith and her colleagues between 1991 and 1993, looked at physical punishment by parents in the southeast of England. Although analysis concen-trated primarily on reported behaviour rather than attitudes, researchers did enquire about parents' views on whether physical chastisement should be made illegal. They found that approximately three in four parents disagreed with any 'anti-smacking law' similar to that imposed in schools, while only a small number would approve of such a law (Smith 1998). A second study was carried out in 1994 with 1,034 adults across Britain (Creighton and Russell 1995). That survey, which focused mainly on childhood experiences, included a few questions on acceptability of punishments. The research found a distinction between 'slapping with an open hand' (79 percent considered justified) and slapping with objects (5–7 percent justified) or hitting with a closed fist (<1 percent justified).

This limited research has been supplemented, often to satisfy the appetite of the media, by opinion polls broaching the topic. The most influential opinion poll in Scotland was carried out for the Scottish Law Commission's Review of Family Law in 1992 ($n = 1,055$). Understandably framed strictly in legal terms, the poll highlighted a public distinction between the legitimacy of smacking with the open hand and the use of implements. The survey found that a large majority of adults considered that smacking 'in a way not likely to cause lasting injury' should remain lawful (83 percent for 3-year-olds, 87 percent for 9-year-olds, 63 percent for 15-year-olds). In contrast, only a minority felt that hitting with an object (same restrictions) should be lawful (3 percent for 3-year-olds, 7 percent for 9-year-olds, 10 percent for 15-year-olds). This opinion poll was taken into consideration during the recent Scottish Executive consultation.

Likewise, the Department of Health in its consultation (2000a) referred to an ONS Omnibus Survey of a sample of adults it commissioned in 1998. Most questions followed the legal framework of the Scottish Law Commission, and it again showed the large majority supportive of smacking, depending upon age (85 percent for the law to allow parents to smack 'a naughty child' over 5 years old, 53 percent for over 2 years old, 13 percent for less than 2 years old). Similarly, there was only minority support for allowing the use of implements (7 percent for a naughty child over 7 years old, 4 percent for a child over 5 years old, 1 percent for a child over 2 years old). Further questions about the 'necessity' of sometimes punishing in different ways found a similar pattern of distinction (88 percent for smacking, 9 percent for using implements).

As a counterbalance to the Department of Health poll, the 'Children are Unbeatable!' anti-smacking campaign group commissioned another poll on the law surrounding physical punishment. In this poll, however, the questions were phrased in terms of children having equal rights of protection with adults, and they contained an assurance that parents would not be prosecuted for 'trivial smacks' or when restraining the child for safety reasons. Consequently, the usual support for smacking was replaced with 73 percent of people supporting equal legal rights for children against being hit. This highlights the importance of exactly how survey questions on physical punishment are framed and underlines the need to obtain as full a picture as possible to understand perceptions on this complex topic. However, most other opinion polls have only tended to ask one or two questions on this topic and have not investigated beyond the more usual pattern above of finding a majority in favour of smacking, or more precisely put, the legal right to smack (e.g. MORI 1999b; ICM 2000).

The national study of parents, children and discipline

The findings outlined below draw on data from the first major national study of parents, children and discipline in Britain, carried out by the Policy Research Bureau, the NSPCC and the National Centre for Social Research.[2] In spring 2000, face-to-face interviews were conducted with a representative sample of 1,250 parents of children under 13 years old across England, Wales and Scotland. These interviews were completed on laptop computers, the computer being turned around for the respondent to complete, in privacy, the most sensitive sections of the questionnaires. Follow-up qualitative in-depth interviews were carried out with a smaller number of the parents from the larger survey. Although not discussed in this chapter, the research team also conducted in-depth interviews and group discussions with young people aged 8 to 12.

One key focus was the incidence and prevalence of different parental responses to misbehaviour. In summary, the study found that over half (58 percent) of parents reported having used 'minor' physical punishment in the past year (defined as including smacked bottom, slapped arms or legs), and nearly three-quarters (71 percent) reported having done this at some point in time with their child. The overall proportion of parents using more severe forms of physical punishment (including hitting around the face or head, hitting with a hard object, shaking, biting or pinching) was much smaller: 9 percent in the past year, but almost one in six (16 percent) at some point in the child's life. These figures were further analysed in relation to a number of contextual factors known from the previous literature to be associated with child discipline, including the wider parent–child relationship, child behaviour, the health of parent and child, the parent's own childhood, and current problems in the parent's life. The survey also asked about the parent's beliefs and attitudes towards discipline. The remainder of this chapter concentrates on analysis of this last element to try to establish and understand community thresholds and norms.

What physical responses to misbehaviour do parents find acceptable?

An appropriate starting point in the analysis of the meaning and attitudes that parents bring to disciplinary situations with their children is to ascertain general levels of acceptance of physical responses to misbehaviour. It should be noted that the survey questions created for this purpose were deliberately framed in the relatively neutral terms of 'acceptability', or whether the action is 'OK', rather than in terms of legal rights to hit or be protected from being hit. All parents in the study were asked how acceptable they considered a range of disciplinary responses. Figure 3.1 lists the exact question and responses for items that referred specifically to physical responses to misbehaviour.

As the figure shows, not all responses to misbehaviour were considered equally acceptable by parents. The clearest message was that there are certain acts that almost all parents reject as never acceptable. First, almost all parents considered that there were never any circumstances in which shaking a child

Q: Thinking about a child the same age as [your child] is now, would you say these things are always or usually OK; sometimes OK, depending on the circumstances; or never OK?

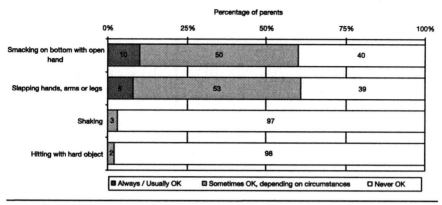

Unweighted base = 1248 (all)

Figure 3.1 Acceptability of different types of physical response to misbehaviour

was acceptable. One could speculate that this strength of feeling may well be associated with recent high-profile court cases involving children's deaths from shaking (e.g. *au pair* Louise Woodward's trial in the USA). In addition, it may point to the success of a number of parent education campaigns in recent years that have highlighted the dangers of shaking younger children.

Second, there was an almost universal rejection of the use of implements as a response to children's misbehaviour. Indeed, the figure of 98 percent considering it never acceptable to hit with an object was even higher than that obtained in most other polls and research, however their questions were phrased. Furthermore, this rejection was echoed very clearly in the study's qualitative in-depth interviews with parents. Respondents stressed that using implements was an 'old-fashioned' practice, unacceptable in present society: 'It's not considered normal now. It's well out of order. It's outdated. It doesn't prove anything apart from what a small person you are' (mother of 9-year-old boy).

Again, we could speculate about the extent to which the association of implements with a bygone age is related to the ban on the common use of such punishments in state schools (enforced in 1987). Certainly, the concern repeatedly voiced by parents in interviews that using objects carries an unacceptable risk of injury concurs with concern expressed in the Department of Health consultation document, if not in subsequent policy: 'The risk in the scale of injuries will be significantly higher if parents use implements' (Health Minister John Hutton, *The Independent*, 18 January 2000).

However, attitudes to smacking children's bottoms and slapping their limbs with the open hand were more divided. Only a minority of parents rejected these punishments outright. This follows the usual pattern in previous research and polls in that, unlike the use of implements, the majority of parents are disinclined to show complete disapproval of more 'minor' forms of physical punishment. However, it should be noted that this minority considering that smacking was 'never OK' was more sizeable than the percentage rejecting phys-ical punishment in previous research and polls. Nevertheless, most parents still showed at least some tolerance of both smacking the bottom and slapping the limbs of children. However, it is important to note that, even among those who did not reject the physical punishments outright, very few parents were prepared to accept that such actions were 'always' or 'usually' acceptable. For both types of minor physical punishment, when acceptance was voiced, the majority of parents gave it only conditionally (i.e. that these responses to misbe-haviour were only permissible in certain circumstances).

Clearly, then, a simple question requiring a dichotomous answer (yes/no) would find the majority of parents accepting smacking. However, slightly more sophistication indicates that endorsement, when given, is rather more complex. Certainly, acceptance of physical punishment *per se* seems to be more ambiva-lent among parents than the 'overwhelming public support' claimed by governments in recent years (*cf.* Department of Health 2001: 1). But what is behind this ambivalence in parents' acceptance of physical punishment? If physical responses to misbehaviour are only 'sometimes OK, depending upon the circumstances', what then were the contingencies that parents had in mind? In other words, what were parents' conditions of acceptability?

Conditions of acceptability for physical force

It is already clear that, for most parents we interviewed, beliefs about the appro-priateness of physical force in child discipline amounted to more than simple acceptance or rejection of physical punishment. Parents indicated that they were more ambivalent, with acceptance of a physical response to a child's misbehaviour dependent upon the circumstances in which it takes place. To understand these beliefs more fully, then, it was necessary to understand the conditions on which this acceptance would depend.

A number of contextual factors influencing acceptance of physical force were evident from both quantitative and qualitative interviews with parents. For instance, the age of the child being punished was mentioned repeatedly as relevant, corresponding to concerns held in the scientific literature (Socolar *et al.* 1997: 759), previous surveys (e.g. Scottish Law Commission 1992) and legislative developments in Scotland. However, two other factors were consis-tently mentioned by parents in relation to the acceptability of disciplinary actions: the risk of immediate harm to the child; and the 'purpose' behind the parental action (i.e. what the parent was trying to achieve). As such, we will examine both of these areas in some detail here.

Risk of immediate harm to the child

One factor highlighted as relevant to parental concerns about the acceptability of different punishments was the risk of immediate harm to the child. As when gauging parental support for the different types of response to misbehaviour, parents were questioned on their acceptance in relation to two possible physical effects of punishment on a child. These were designed to capture different levels of severity of visible injuries to the child that might be sustained in a conflict situation. A 'red mark' was intended to represent a relatively less severe and more temporary injury, whereas a 'bruising or a cut' represented a more severe and longer-lasting injury. Parental responses to these possible outcomes are listed in Figure 3.2.

Parents very clearly rejected both causing a red mark and causing a bruise or a cut as never acceptable, no matter what the circumstances. No level of immediate physical harm to the child was considered appropriate. Indeed, for the more serious outcome of bruising or causing a cut, only six parents out of 1,247 who responded considered it acceptable. This picture corresponded very closely with what parents told us during qualitative interviews. Respondents stressed that hurting their child was incompatible with their idea of 'child care': 'As a human being, I don't have the right to inflict hurt and injury on another human being to that level. As I say, it's more of a shock thing than [wanting to] physically [hurt them]' (father of 8-year-old girl).

These findings show parents to be more firmly against marking a child than was suggested in the recent Department of Health opinion poll (see existing research, cited above). That survey found a majority of only 60 percent who thought that no punishment was 'reasonable' if it left any mark on a child. Our finding, that parents consider that no mark should ever be left on the child, indicates that they did considered that any negative physical effects should not last beyond the 'moment' of punishment. This particular understanding of physical punishment implies an interesting modern rejection of some more 'traditional'

Q: Thinking about a child the same age as [your child] is now, would you say these things are always or usually OK; sometimes OK, depending on the circumstances; or never OK?

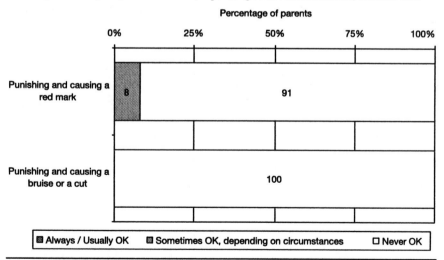

Unweighted base = 1247 (all)

Figure 3.2 Acceptability of marking or bruising/cutting children during physical punishment

parental warnings to children, such as 'you won't be able to sit down' after the event. According to parents, it seems, physical punishment should not be about creating a lasting 'reminder' of the child's correction. In addition, this finding may suggest that a mark on the child could provide a very visible indication for anyone watching, such as child protection professionals, that physical force by parents had gone beyond the normative threshold of acceptability for parents in this country. The risk of harm also seemed to be a common factor in parents deciding that striking a child's head during punishment was unacceptable. In qualitative interviews, the danger of harm was a common theme when considering 'hitting the head' or a 'clip around the ear': 'I don't really like [the idea of hitting] heads because the brain's in there and I think you might do some damage if you hit somebody's head. So, there's no heads' (mother of 11-year-old girl).

Acceptability of reasons for physical force

Another factor highlighted by parents as distinguishing acceptable from unacceptable instances of physical punishment was the precise purpose for which the act was being employed. Figure 3.3 shows how legitimate parents found various possible reasons for the use of physical punishment.

There were clear indications that some reasons why parents might employ physical force in a disciplinary relationship were felt to be more acceptable than others. Moreover, there seemed to be underlying characteristics that distinguish the most acceptable from the least acceptable reasons. The more popular reasons tended to relate to an attempt to deal with the current moment: for example, trying to intervene quickly in a crisis. Indeed, stopping a child doing something

Q: Which of these, if any, do you think are acceptable reasons for parents to use physical punishment?

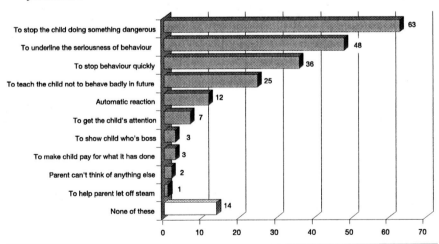

Unweighted base = 1238 (All)

Figure 3.3 Acceptability of reasons for using physical punishment

dangerous was the only reason for using physical force that commanded acceptance from the majority of parents. The more acceptable purposes also tended to
focus on explicit communication with the child: for example, to 'teach' the
child not to behave badly in the future. Communication was also a central
theme in the reasons for smacking given by parents in qualitative interviews:

> The point [is not] to cause them pain, just to smack them to say, 'Oh, pack
> it in. You've pushed me to the edge. Don't do it any more', you know ....
> They know that they're really annoying me if I smack them. They know
> that I'm dead cross with them.
>
> (mother of 10-year-old boy)

Conversely, possible reasons for physical force that were considered unacceptable by the vast majority of parents related to the assertion of power, catharsis or
'letting out stress', and retribution against the child for their misbehaviour. First,
parents' rejection of the use of smacking to assert their power, 'to show the child
who is the boss', in a disciplinary situation is a finding that contradicts both
research with previous generations of parents and a popular theme with proponents of physical punishment. For example, in research in the 1960s, Newson
and Newson reported that parents stressed the need to curb defiance in order to
shape the child's will, because 'he's got to learn who is the master' from a young
age (1963: 111). Furthermore, the idea of enforcing obedience through physical
punishment is stressed heavily by pro-smacking writers and campaigners, who
cite the need to overcome 'deliberate defiance' in children as one of the main
reasons for smacking them (*cf.* Anne Davis, Families for Discipline, cited in
Scotland on Sunday, 26 March 1995: 1; Dobson 1978).

Second, respondents' rejection of the cathartic reason of 'helping the parent
let off steam' is also contrary to both an often-cited justification for smacking (i.e.
that it is a pressure valve to avoid child abuse), and past research. For example,
Gough and Reavey noted that adults framed their discussions of physical force
'with reference to the alleviation of parental needs rather than those of children'
(1997: 426). Third, parents widely rejected retributive intent, 'to make the child
pay for their misbehaviour', as a legitimate reason for using physical chastisement.
This rejection contradicts observations from commentators almost a generation
ago that parents' use of physical punishment for 'judicial' purposes gathers a 'positive and sympathetic response' within our culture (Fine and Holt 1983: 85).
However, it would appear to fit with other themes in parents' responses to our
study, such as the unacceptability of the child suffering hurt or harm for their
misbehaviour and the rejection of more severe types of punishment.

Beliefs underlying the acceptability of physical force

The various conditions that parents placed on the acceptance of physical force
has illustrated that parents approach discipline with a complex set of considerations. They appear to hold clear views on the appropriateness of using force to

punish children in a way that would suggest that they do indeed attribute a 'meaning' to such acts. As such, analysis of parents' understanding of such acts would not be complete without an attempt to explore the beliefs and arguments that underlie these views. What beliefs inform the meaning that parents give to physical force in discipline?

The study examined parents' views in relation to various arguments that have appeared within existing debates surrounding physical punishment, by asking parents to state their agreement or disagreement with a range of statements reflecting 'things that some people have said' about physical punishment. These arguments have been divided here, for the purposes of analysis, into three areas: (1) the risk of harm; (2) parents' and children's rights; and (3) the necessity of punishment in 'proper' child care. In addition, we explored whether agreement with each of the statements meant that parents were significantly more likely to consider physical punishment of any kind acceptable. In total, 74 percent of parents found at least one of the four types of physical response to misbehaviour – smacking bottom, slapping limbs, shaking, hitting with a hard object – acceptable, either outright or conditionally. Did agreement with any particular argument separate the 'accepters' from the 'outright rejecters'?

Beliefs about the harmfulness of physical force

First, a key area of disagreement in the debate over the appropriateness of physical punishment relates to whether or not this type of parental response to misbehaviour carries any risk of 'harm' to the child. We have already noted that parents almost universally rejected physical harm caused to a child by physical punishment as unacceptable. To what extent do parents consider that harm, physical and otherwise, is a risk when employing physical punishment *per se?* The wider policy and scientific debates have suggested that the parent–child relationship can suffer various types of damage, either at the time or as a long-term consequence of physical punishment. Are these concerns shared by parents? Or, conversely, do parents agree with the persistent claim that smacking is essentially a safe activity that 'does not do a child any harm' (Scottish Law Commission 1992: 26–30; Department of Health 1994)?

Four statements were read to parents in order to ascertain their level of agreement[3] with different aspects of this line of concern. These related to harm to children generally: for example, teaching children to use violence, parents hitting harder than intended, and damage to the parent–child relationship in general (Table 3.1).

The only statement that was endorsed by the majority of parents was that parents who use physical punishment risked hitting children harder than they intended. Again, this corresponds directly to the concern previously identified with physical harm and injury. Most parents did not agree with the other three statements, although each one struck a chord with a sizeable minority of parents (between a third and half of the sample). In particular, almost half of parents expressed the concern that physical punishment was in some general way

Table 3.1 Parents' views about harm arising from physical punishment

	Percentage of parents in agreement with statement		
	All	*Parents endorsing physical response*	*Parents rejecting physical response*
Physical punishment is harmful to children	49	41	72*
Parents who use physical punishment risk hitting harder than they mean to	64	60	74*
Smacking teaches children that it is OK to hit other people	38	30	61*
Parents who smack can damage their relationship with the child	41	33	64*

Unweighted bases for items ranged from 1,245 to 1,248 (all)
*p < 0.001

'harmful to children'. The argument that smacking can damage the parental relationship was employed in parent education campaigns after a ban in Sweden (Swedish Department of Justice 1979), and this study suggests that the argument already holds some credence with a sizeable minority of parents here.

Interestingly, as far as parents were concerned, the least persuasive of the arguments relating to harm was that physical punishment taught children that it was acceptable to hit others. Psychologists have long presented theories and evidence of modelling aggression from physical punishment (*cf.* Straus 1996; Maurer and Wallerstein 1987; Fergusson and Lynskey 1997), and commentators have argued that this concept has achieved a 'taken-for-granted status' of acceptance among the general population in the United States (Loseke 1991: 162–3). However, this survey suggests that we cannot conclude this for the majority of parents in this country. Nevertheless, a substantial number still expressed this concern, and qualitative interviews also suggested that this was a theme in parents' considerations:

> My attitude is [that hitting is] going to be passed on 'cos it's something that they think is right. They think, 'Well, we've had it done to us, we do it to whoever'. That's how I think anyway.
>
> (mother of 12-year-old girl)

In addition, the table shows that there were significant differences of opinion between those rejecting all forms of physical punishment and other parents on all questions put to them regarding risk of harm in both the short and longer term ($\Delta^2 - p$ <0.001). Those who found physical punishment acceptable to at least some degree were less likely than other parents to believe that these acts could harm children or the parental relationship.

Beliefs about physical punishment and the rights of parents and children

The second key area of argument about which parents were questioned related to the respective rights of those involved in the disciplinary relationship. Disentangling the relative rights of both parents and children has been a central preoccupation among policy makers and campaigners over the years. Indeed, the Department of Health has made it clear that battling with this issue is central to its concerns about any legislative changes for physical punishment:

> We must recognise both the rights of parents to exercise their parental responsibility and to bring up children safely, and as they think best, without undue interference from the State, while the rights of children remain protected.
>
> (Department of Health 2000b)

In the survey interview, all parents were asked to rate their agreement with two contrasting propositions – one emphasising parents' rights and the other focusing on children's rights (Table 3.2). Again, analysis compared how the level of agreement related to parents' acceptance of physical punishment overall.

The study found more support from parents for the statement advocating parents' right to punish physically than the proposition that children should have the right not to be hit. Overall, getting on for two-thirds of parents felt that they should have the right to use physical punishment if they wished. This was in accordance with previous surveys and polls, which have suggested majority public support for parents' *legal* rights, although it presents a lower percentage in agreement than most figures previously cited (e.g. Scottish Law Commission 1992; Department of Health 2000a). Conversely, the belief that children should have the right not to be punished physically was shared by a minority of parents, albeit a substantial one (two in five). The fact that these questions did not elicit an overwhelming polarisation of support for the rights of

Table 3.2 Parents' views about rights and physical punishment

	Percentage of parents in agreement with statement		
	All	*Parents endorsing physical response*	*Parents rejecting physical response*
Parents should have the right to use physical punishment if they wish	60	68*	38
Children should have the right not to be physically punished	43	35	64*

Unweighted bases for items ranged from 1,245 to 1,247 (all)
*p < 0.001

either party seems to reflect the difficult balance of responsibility and protection voiced by the government in the quotation above. Indeed, parents in qualitative interviews stressed the conflicting concerns about rights that underpinned their thinking about the acceptability of physical punishment. For instance, parents voiced support for children's rights but worried that, in practice, this might undermine and perhaps hinder effective parenting:

> I think anybody should have the right, however old, not to be hit around the head or smacked or physically abused in any way. But I also think that if I need to get through to them and nothing else is working ... I ought to be able to smack them to get the point across. So, yes, it's very contradictory, but I still think both of them, if you know what I mean.
>
> (mother of 10-year-old boy)

Like concerns about risk of harm, Table 3.2 also shows that parents who considered physical punishment acceptable tended to have very different opinions about respective rights from those opposing all physical punishment ($\Delta^2 - p < 0.001$). Those agreeing with physical punishment were significantly more likely (by a ratio of about 2 to 1) to support a parent's right to respond physically to misbehaviour. Conversely, those opposed to physical punishment were significantly more likely (by a similar margin) than others to endorse arguments for children having the right not to be punished in this way.

Beliefs about the necessity of physical punishment

The last area of the physical punishment debate on which parents' views were sought in our study relates to the belief that these types of punishment are in some way unavoidable or necessary as part of appropriate child care. Commentators have noted that this has been a particularly prominent concern of proponents of physical punishment (Cloke 1997: 279), employed for example in legal cases surrounding smacking (*The Times*, 7 July 1993).

Parents were asked about their agreement with five statements, each reflecting themes of argument relating to 'necessity' that have been presented in the wider debate (Table 3.3): that physical punishment is both necessary and good; is needed with younger children; is important as a 'last resort'; and is needed to communicate with a child. Conversely, parents were asked about their agreement with a statement suggesting that physical punishment is not essential to bringing up a properly socialised child.

The clear pattern that emerges from Table 3.3 is that the majority of parents did not believe that physical punishment was a 'necessary' part of discipline. This is an important research finding, because it seems to question opinion poll evidence that has been presented by the government to rule out a ban on physical punishment. The Department of Health consultation document cited 88 percent of people agreeing that 'it is sometimes necessary to smack a naughty

Table 3.3 Parents' views about the necessity of physical punishment

	Percentage of parents in agreement with statement		
	All	Parents endorsing physical response	Parents rejecting physical response
Physical punishment is necessary and good for children	24	29*	10
Physical punishment is necessary with younger children but not so much with older children	24	28*	13
Physical punishment is necessary as a last resort	49	58*	24
Sometimes a smack is the only way to get the message across	40	49*	16
You don't need physical punishment to bring up a well-behaved child	69	62	88*

Unweighted bases for items 1,248 (all)
*p < 0.001

child' (Department of Health 2000a), which is almost double the percentage obtained for any of the measures of 'necessity' used in this national study.

However, the most popular argument for the 'necessity' of physical punishment, supported by almost half of parents, was that the punishment needed to be held in reserve as the 'last resort' in a disciplinary relationship. This belief is in line with the role of physical punishment previously presented by the government, that smacking might be used when parents have not been able to influence a child through 'other powers of persuasion' (Department of Health 1994: 2). Other researchers have noted this belief as underlying parental acceptance of physical punishment (Davis 1996: 301) and, as the previous quotation illustrated, this was reiterated in our qualitative interviews.

Once again, agreement with each of these arguments significantly differentiated those who rejected all physical punishment as unacceptable from other parents. Parents who found physical punishment acceptable were significantly more likely to agree that such acts were necessary and good, more necessary for younger children and necessary as a last resort ($\Delta^2 - p$ <0.001). Conversely, as one might expect, those rejecting physical force as a disciplinary method were significantly more inclined to believe that physical punishment was not needed to bring up a well-behaved child.

Discussion

This chapter has highlighted how parents in Britain have clear thresholds of acceptance for physical punishment in disciplining children. Not all physical punishments were considered equally acceptable. Whereas parents almost universally rejected some forms of punishment, such as shaking and hitting with implements, feelings about more 'minor' forms of physical punishment were far more ambivalent. Although the majority of parents found smacking a child's bottom or limbs with the open hand acceptable, most of these parents were conditional in their acceptance. Contingent factors included the age of the child, any risk of immediate physical harm to the child and the purpose of the punishment. Purposes that were considered more legitimate tended to relate to communicating quickly with the child, particularly in terms of averting danger, whereas unacceptable reasons for smacking related to power assertion, retribution and catharsis for the parent.

In addition, the 'meaning' that parents attribute to acts of physical force in disciplinary situations appears to be informed by a complex set of beliefs about physical punishment. Parents expressed various levels of agreement with a number of prominent arguments in the policy debate on smacking, including the risk of hitting harder than intended, parental rights to use physical punishment, and whether it is possible to bring up a well-behaved child without smacking. Furthermore, agreement or disagreement with such arguments distinguished significantly between those who found physical punishment acceptable and those who rejected all such acts.

In a number of areas examined, the findings in the national study indicated that parents are less favourable towards aspects of physical punishment than previous studies and opinion polls have suggested. It is possible that some of this difference may be due to variations in sample populations. For instance, while this research focused on parents, most polls seek to find the views of the adult electorate. Indeed, there is evidence from other surveys that parents are less in favour of physical punishment than the wider public (e.g. Scottish Law Commission 1992; MORI 1999a).

Nevertheless, it is unlikely that sampling alone would explain all of the differences. We are led to conclude that examining parents' perceptions about physical punishment in this level of contextual detail reveals a far more complex picture than is often suggested by the polls and subsequently presented by policy makers. In particular, the substantial minority of parents who reject all physical punishment and the rather conditional acceptance of the majority questions the assumption of 'overwhelming support' (Department of Health 2001:1) for physical punishment by the 'vast majority' (Scottish Executive 2000) that appears to have underpinned government policy on this issue. Rather, our findings seem to support the anecdotal assertion by some charities and support groups that smacking is not in fact held particularly dear by parents. As a spokesperson for Parentline has been quoted, 'We know from the parents who call us that they don't want to use physical punishment' (*Community Care*, 27 April–3 May 2000: 9). Consequently, it may be that parents in Britain actually look upon smacking more negatively than the government would believe. The chairman of the House of Commons Health Committee, David Hinchliffe, has asserted that 'the public ... is well ahead of the government in its desire to protect children' (*The Guardian*, 19 April 2000). Certainly, the research data suggest that the government might well be pushing a door that is ajar, if not entirely open, if it wishes to move against physical punishment by parents – whether through legislation or education.

Perhaps above all, our study has demonstrated the importance for parents of 'context' when considering these acts of physical force. The stress laid upon 'circumstances', the relevance of the child's age, the rejection of acts causing physical harm and the distinction between legitimate and illegitimate reasons for smacking all begin to reveal the 'whole range of factors' (Creighton and Russell 1995: 28) relevant to parents' assessments of such acts. In essence, this 'contextual' approach to the acceptability of physical punishment is reflected in the ways that both the European courts and legislators in Scotland have tried to tackle cases involving parents' use of physical force. For instance, the European Court of Human Rights has stated that the legality of an act:

> depends on all the circumstances of the case, such as the nature and context of the treatment, its duration, its physical and mental effects and, in some instances, the sex, age and state of health of the victim.
>
> (A v. UK; 23 September 1998, para. 20)

In short, parents have reminded us that whether this debate takes place in the legal, political or scientific arena, we only begin to understand the full picture when physical force in disciplinary relationships is considered as such – within the wider context of *disciplinary relationships*. We may come to the conclusion that physical force against a person in any context is unacceptable, or 'violent', but the context of a parenting relationship cannot be ignored. Whether in terms of the relationship, or the situation, or the characteristics of those involved, the perceived context clearly has an effect on the 'meaning' that people ascribe to acts of interpersonal force.

Notes

1   Sweden (1979), Finland (1983), Denmark (1986), Norway (1987), Austria (1989), Cyprus (1994), Latvia (1998), Croatia (1999), Germany (2000) and Italy (arguably, through case law) (see Newell 1995; EPOCH Worldwide 1996; EPOCH Worldwide 1997).

2   Details of methodology and full findings from this study will appear in our forthcoming publication: D. Ghate, N. Hazel, S. Creighton, J. Field and S. Finch (book in preparation) *Parents, Children and Discipline in Britain*.

3   Parents were asked to rate agreement on a five-point scale (strongly agree, tend to agree, neither agree nor disagree, tend to disagree, strongly disagree). For the purposes of the analysis presented in this section, 'agreement' indicates a reply of either 'strongly agree' or 'tend to agree'.

References

Cloke, C. (1997) 'Forging the circle: the relationship between children, policy and practice in children's rights', in C. Cloke and M. Davies (eds) *Participation and Empowerment in Child Protection* (2nd edition. Chichester: John Wiley & Sons.

Creighton, S.J. and Russell, N. (1995) *Voices from Childhood*. London: NSPCC.

Davis, P.W. (1996) 'Threats of corporal punishment as verbal aggression: a naturalistic study', *Child Abuse & Neglect* 20(4): 289–304.

Department of Health (1994) *The Children Act 1989: Registration of Childminders.* Local Authority Circular LAC(94)23.

Department of Health (2000a) *Protecting Children, Supporting Parents: A Consultation Document on the Physical Punishment of Children.* London: DoH.

Department of Health (2000b) 'Protecting children, supporting parents', press release, 18.1.00.

Department of Health (2001) Responses to 'Protecting children, supporting parents' [*www.doh.gov.uk/scg/pcspresponse/*].

Dobson, J. (1978) *The Strong-willed Child: Birth through Adolescence.* Wheaton, Ill.: Living Books.

EPOCH (1990) *Child Abuse and Physical Punishment.* London: APPROACH.

EPOCH (1991) *Hitting People Is Wrong – and Children Are People too.* London: APPROACH.

EPOCH Worldwide (1996) *Campaign against Physical Punishment of Children.* London: APPROACH.

EPOCH Worldwide (1997) *Legality of Physical Punishment in Council of Europe*, October. London: APPROACH.

Evans, H.H. and Fergason Jr, C.A. (1998) 'Pediatric discourse on corporal punishment: a historical review', *Aggression and Violent Behavior* 3(4): 357–68.

Family Policy Studies Centre (2000) 'Families and the physical punishment of children', *Family Briefing Paper 17.*

Fergusson, D.M. and Lynskey, M.T. (1997) 'Physical punishment / maltreatment during childhood and adjustment in young adulthood', *Child Abuse & Neglect* 21(7): 617–30.

Fine, M.J. and Holt, P. (1983) 'Corporal punishment in the family: a systems perspective', *Psychology in the Schools* 20, January, 85–92.

Fox Harding, L. (1991) *Perspectives in Child Care Policy* (1st edition). London: Longman.

Gelles, R.J. (1997) *Intimate Violence in Families.* Thousand Oaks, Calif.: Sage.

Ghate, D. (2000) 'Family violence and violence against children: a research review', *Children and Society* 14: 395–403.

Gough, B. and Reavey, P. (1997) 'Parental accounts regarding the physical punishment of children', *Child Abuse & Neglect* 21(5): 417–30.

Graziano, A.M. and Namaste, K.A. (1990) 'Parental use of physical force in child discipline', *Journal of Interpersonal Violence* 5(4): 449–63.

Graziano, A.M., Kunce, L.J., Lindquist, C.M. and Munjal, K. (1991) 'Physical punishment in childhood and current attitudes: a comparison of college students in the U.S. and India', *Violence Update* 1: 9.

Hazel, N. (2000) 'British children's views on physical punishment', paper presented to the international conference 'Violence to Children and Youth', University of New Hampshire, USA, June 2000.

Hemenway, D., Solnick, S. and Carter, J. (1994) 'Child-rearing violence', *Child Abuse & Neglect* 18(12): 1011–20.

ICM (2000) The Guardian/ICM Monthly Poll, August 2000 [*http://www.icmresearch.co.uk/reviews/2000/guardian-poll-august-2000.html*].

Loseke, D.R. (1991) 'Reply to Murray A. Straus: readings on "Discipline and Deviance"', *Social Problems* 38(2) (May): 162–5.

Maurer, A. and Wallerstein, J.S. (1987) 'The influence of corporal punishment on crime' [*http://silcon.com/percent7Eptave/maurer1.html*].

MORI (1999a) 'Strong parental support for anti-smacking law' [*http://www.mori.com /polls/1999/smackrel.shtml*].

MORI (1999b) 'Bringing up today's child – Sunday Mirror' [*www.mori.com/polls/ 1999/sm990319.shtml*].

Newell, P. (1995) 'Respecting children's right to physical integrity', in B. Franklin (ed.) *The Handbook of Children's Rights*. London: Routledge.

Newson, J. and Newson, E. (1963) *Infant Care in an Urban Community*. London: George Allen & Unwin.

Ortega, G.J., Gonzalez, J.M.M. and Cabanillas, M.C. (1997) *Spaniards' Attitudes towards Physical Punishment in Children*. Madrid: Ministerio de Trabajo y Asuntos Sociales.

Overton, J. (1993) 'Child abuse, corporal punishment, and the question of discipline: the case of Mount Cashel', *Critical Social Policy* 12(3): 73–95.

Rohner, R.P., Bourque, S.L. and Elordi, C.A. (1996) 'Children's perceptions of corporal punishment, caretaker acceptance and psychological adjustment in a poor biracial Southern community', *Journal of Marriage and the Family* 58 (November): 842–52.

Scottish Executive (2000) 'Consultation paper on the physical punishment of children', press release, 24.2.00.

Scottish Law Commission (1992) *Report on Family Law*. Edinburgh: HMSO.

Smith, M. (1998) 'Children's views on physical punishment, in relation to their parents' views and behaviour', paper presented at International Society for Behavioural Development (ISSBD), XVth biennial meeting, Berne, Switzerland (July).

Smith, R.K.M. (1999) 'To Smack or Not to Smack? A review of A. v. United Kingdom in an international and European context and its potential impact on physical chastisement', *Web Journal of Current Legal Issues* 1: 1–14 [*http://webjcli.ncl.ac.uk/ 1999/issue1/smith1.html*].

Socolar, R.R.S., Amaya-Jackson, L., Eron, L.D., Howard, B., Landsverk, J. and Evans, J. (1997) 'Research on discipline', *Archives Paediatric and Adolescent Medicine* 151 (August): 758–60.

Straus, M.A. (1996) 'Spanking and the making of a violent society', *Pediatrics* 98(4): 837–42.

Straus, M.A. and Gelles, R.J. (1988) 'How violent are American families? Estimates from the National Family Violence Survey and other studies', in G.T. Hotaling, D. Finkelhor, J.T. Kirkpatric and M.A. Straus (eds) *Family Abuse and its Consequences: New Directions in Research*. London: Sage.

Swedish Department of Justice (1979) 'Can you bring up children successfully without smacking and spanking?' Stockholm: Justitiedepartementet.

UNICEF (1997) 'Intrafamilial violence to children', *Innocenti Digest* 2 – Children and violence.

Part II
Violence, meaning and social identities

4 'Taking it to heart'

Girls and the meanings of violence

Michele Burman, Jane Brown and Susan Batchelor

Introduction

This chapter highlights the importance of social and situational context to an understanding of girls' violence (and to girls' understanding of violence). The research study[1] that forms the basis of the chapter commenced, in Scotland, against a backdrop of increasing concern in Britain about violence by, and among, young people. Youth violence is rapidly becoming one of the most contentious issues in current debates about crime and criminal justice policy and, while the main focus has been on the violence of young males, part of the concern has been about the perceived increase in violence as measured by violent offending by girls and young women.[2] In both academic (e.g. Hardy and Howitt 1998) and media accounts (e.g. Brinkworth and Burrell 1994), girls' violence is commonly portrayed as more grave and disquieting than boys' violence, and as presenting more of a problem (Batchelor *et al.* 2001). While there is evidence to support claims that young women are increasingly being drawn into the criminal justice system for violent offences,[3] closer scrutiny of the official figures reveals that, in fact, young women account for a very small percentage of violent crime,[4] and violent crime forms a tiny percentage of young women's offending in general.[5] Moreover, this pattern has remained largely unchanged for the past 20 years.

Despite the high level of interest in 'girl violence' (Stanko 2001), there is a paucity of British literature on girls and violence, as most research on youth violence has focused on boys. Girls' voices are rarely heard. However, the international research literature shows not only that forms of violence and aggression differ between girls and boys but also that girls' violence emerges from experiences that are qualitatively different from those of boys. Girls who use violence have frequently been physically, sexually and emotionally abused, often by close family members (Artz 1998; Baskin and Sommers 1998; Chesney-Lind 2002; Miller 2001; Stewart and Tattersall 2000). This results in girls running away from home and their subsequent drug or alcohol abuse (Belknap and Holsinger 1998). They are also significantly more prone to self-harm and depression (Leschied *et al.* 2000). As a consequence, the behaviour that brings girls to the attention of juvenile justice professionals is often different from that presented by boys. Researching girls and violence, then, demands qualitatively different questions from those concerning boys.

In embarking on this research, our interest was not in establishing whether or not there had been an increase in girls' violent offending but with investigating girls' views about and experiences of violence – as both victims *and* perpetrators. A key aim was to understand the ways in which different forms of violence – physical, sexual, verbal and emotional – impact on girls' lives. This was intended as an exploratory study to open up a discursive space for young women to talk about their experiences and attitudes towards violence. We were interested not only in exploring the nature and extent of violence experienced by girls, through personal accounts of their own involvement in violence and conflict situations, but also in exploring both the symbolic and instrumental meanings that violence holds for them. We took a multi-method approach, using a self-report questionnaire, a series of small-group discussions and in-depth interviews.[6] Girls were drawn from a range of socio-economic backgrounds and diverse communities across Scotland and were located through their membership of youth groups and clubs, through schools, youth out-reach workers and contacts with other girls.[7]

The study started from the assumption that the meaning(s) of violence for those who use it and experience it are inextricably bound up with lived experiences, subjective identities, and intimate and social relationships. In this study, as in several others that have focused on aspects of girls' lives (e.g. Griffiths 1995; Hey 1997; Hudson 1989; Lees 1993), girls demonstrated considerable insight into their own personal, gendered circumstances and the social inequalities underpinning their lives; all were well aware of 'being a girl'. Coming from different social, material, economic, demographic and educational backgrounds, however, they did not constitute a homogeneous group. The ways in which girls subjectively experience violence, and the ways in which they bring these experiences to bear on their definitions and views about violence, are in turn mediated and shaped by factors of class, race and sexuality, and by their place of residence. Furthermore, while there were some broad similarities in terms of girls' experiences of violence,[8] there were also some key differences in terms of using violence. Whereas 30 percent of girls reported ever having hurt someone through the use of physical violence, only 10 percent reported being routinely physically violent. This group of girls also had a disproportionate experience of violence in their own lives; they were able to normalise the impact of violence and showed a high tolerance for the use of physical violence, particularly defensive violence. Yet for others, like Suzanne in the following quote, exposure to physical violence was far outside their own field of experience:

We were near Leicester Square and it was really slow-moving traffic and there were these guys on the pavement and they started a fight. It was actually quite terrifying because I have just never … and it was proper fighting. I haven't ever seen that properly before and it is really, really shocking to see it because it's just amazing the way you suddenly see people really trying to damage each other.

(Interview 9)

'Violence': a continually contested, politically sensitive term

Exploring the nuanced meanings of violence held by girls with such divergent experiences and occupying different social positions was a challenging task. This was exacerbated by the overarching problem of the contested meanings of the term 'violence', which we encountered at a theoretical, methodological and analytical level. Most of the projects in the ESRC Violence Research Programme appear, at some stage, to have encountered and grappled with problems associated with the definition and/or measurement of 'violence', and specifically what sorts of behaviour, action, situation or orientation are meant by the use of the term within the context of each study. Using the word 'violence' implies that we share a common understanding of what it means to be violent, yet the term itself remains imprecise and continually contested (Leibling and Stanko 2001). It is used to denote a *range* of acts, consequences and practices, it has powerful connotations, and it is arguably one of the most confused, emotive and subjective terms in our moral and social language (Norman 1995).

Ordinarily, the word 'violence' is associated with the practice of physical harm inflicted by one person on another. Yet it can also refer to the trauma (emotional or psychological) that comes from being frightened or threatened, or consistently terrorised, and it has also been used to denote not only particular acts or their consequences but also a general climate in which the omnipresence of violent acts creates an atmosphere of fear and demoralisation (Tonry and Moore 1998). The experience of violence is subjective in so far as different people perceive different types of behaviour differently. As Littlechild comments: 'One person may view a situation as violent and threatening, whereas a colleague may not' (1997: 77). Hence an individual witnessing a violent assault may be more distressed than the actual victim of the assault (Bowie 2002). This means that in order to comprehend fully the causes and consequences of violence, it is important to bear in mind the wider meanings that embrace emotional and psychological effects, as well as individual incidents of physical harm.

The competing discourses defining and conceptualising violence draw attention to its socially and *politically* constructed nature. Arriving at a precise, yet inclusive, denotation of violence is much more than a simple definitional issue; it is also an important political and policy issue. Yet it is debatable whether an objective definition of violence could be found. Because its meaning and impact vary for different people, violence researchers must confront the dilemmas of engaging with a field where their research findings become part of a popular discourse that has a special moral mission in contemporary society (Sasson 1995; Sparks 1992).

This moral discourse is steeped in contradictory notions of what kind of crime and violence are normal, acceptable, illegal and abnormal. As researchers we are often in situations where we are to make judgements about behaviour, and decide whether such behaviour is worthy of note.

(Leibling and Stanko 2001: 426)

The words we choose to talk about such behaviour are consequential (Best 1999: 27). They have implications for the way in which violence is explained and responded to, and they affect our capacity for dealing with it.

Following a research agenda examining girls' violence may push a researcher to the 'edges' of mainstream feminist debates (Batchelor 2001a). One of the dangers of researching particular subjects is that by acknowledging their very existence we may contribute to their problematisation. The publicity generated by research into girls and violence may lead to the perception that girls' violence is a growing problem, or that girls are just as bad as, if not worse than, boys (Batchelor 2001c; Tisdall 2002). This ia a key reason why feminists have traditionally ignored female violence, fearing the potentially negative political and social costs for the feminist movement more generally. After all, if energy and resources are expended on addressing *female* violence, the hard-won acknowledgement that sexual and physical violence are gendered crimes may be lost within a 'women blaming' backlash.

The social meaning of girls' violence

Accounts of female violence are almost always framed in a discourse of gender (Batchelor 2001b; Burman 2001). The fact that violence perpetrated by young women is considered worthy of attention at all is related to the fact that hegemonic femininity is commonly perceived as passive, non-aggressive and non-violent. Girls' violence challenges dominant gender codes and is therefore regarded as a 'problem', a threat to the moral fabric of society, and something about which something 'must be done'. In order to keep existing models of femininity intact, female violence has to be portrayed as an aberration (masculinised, pathologised), or redefined as *part of* the natural feminine condition (adolescent girls as emotional, irrational and out of control). Where girls' agency *is* recognised, this is blamed on an erosion of traditional femininity, in turn attributed to feminism and women's liberation. Alternatively, it is blamed on masculinity and patriarchy ('the cycle of abuse').

The tensions and inconsistencies set up by the ways in which girls' violence is commonly conceptualised, and responded to, renders this already thorny and complex issue difficult to address or analyse critically. Mixed messages are conveyed, which increases confusion. Consider the following characterisations. Whereas girl victims of girls' violence are characterised in media accounts by their vulnerability (e.g. physically frail, friendless, loners, not conventionally attractive, etc.), 'violent' girls are presented as fierce and dangerous thugs who get a kick out of inflicting harm and pain, transgressors who have located themselves in opposition to conventional or appropriate femininity. This juxtaposing of the innocent with the dangerous is premised on the construction of difference between girls, and in many ways it echoes the basic conventional stereotypes of 'good' and 'bad' girls found in discourses of adolescent femininity.[9] Yet there is a blurred boundary between girls as perpetrators and girls as victims of violence. As highlighted above, a number of researchers have identified a pattern of violent female offending that begins with their victimisation.

Throughout the various discourses, girls' violence is depicted in oppositional (and highly contradictory) ways. On the one hand, it is portrayed as dangerous, irrational, stemming from a lack of control, a manifestation of individual pathology, and hence largely incomprehensible (Campbell 1993; Motz 2001). On the other hand, violent girls are described as coldly calculating, intentionally targeting, manipulative and scheming (Mitchell 2000). They are depicted as 'just as bad' as boys but simultaneously as 'deadlier than the male'. Their violence is either trivialised, variously presented as unthreatening, amusing, sexy and not as serious as *real* (male) violence (e.g. girls' boxing), or it is constructed as particularly frightening (e.g. girl gangs randomly attacking innocent strangers) and a threat to (patriarchal) society (Batchelor 2001b).

The meaning of violence to girls

It was against this backdrop that we set out to establish girls' *own* definitions and conceptualisations of violence. In doing so, we sought to avoid setting parameters as to what sort of behaviour or actions might be included as 'violent'. Young people's perceptions of what counts as violent do not necessarily mirror normative (adult, legal) conceptions of violence, and ruling out certain kinds of experience because they did not fit a particular paradigm seemed inappropriate to us. At a methodological level, we sought to devise ways to explain the research topic to those who took part and why we were doing it, but without pre-defining 'violence' in any way. This did not prove entirely unproblematic (see Burman *et al.* 2001 for further discussion). At an individual level, what counts as violence is highly subjective and personalised. Furthermore, girls' definitions of violence were unpredictable and seemed at times contradictory. What emerged from girls' accounts of their experiences was a diverse collection of behaviour and actions. Here, the term 'violence' was interpreted widely and loosely as girls used it to describe and categorise a range of incidents. Some, like fights, attacks, hitting or being hit with objects, robberies and some sexual encounters entailed physical action and had particular consequences, but a whole range of other experiences did not involve any physical contact, like threats, name calling, ostracism, gesturing, accusations, harassment, insults, swearing, stalking, 'flashing', and various forms of intimidation.

Additionally, and like others researching violence from the perspective of children and young people, we found that the actual word 'violence' is very rarely used by girls in everyday discourse. Rather, they employ an array of terms to describe a spectrum of unruly and violating behaviour from paradigmatic acts of interpersonal criminal violence to threats, to the kinds of verbal intimidation and aggressive posturing cited above. While some of these colloquial expressions such as 'battering' (beating up), 'giein' the heid' and 'nutting' (both of which mean head butting), 'chibbing' (stabbing), and 'sticking the boot in' (kicking) attract legal censure (and have a more or less equivalent legal definition), others, such as 'slagging' (denigration or vilification), 'perving' (salacious leering or sexualised posturing) and 'growling' (giving dirty looks), do not. Attention to the language employed by and between young people when talking about different incidents is instructive. Not only are the expressions that they use graphically descriptive, they also convey and communicate different messages and meanings about specific practices and behaviour (Burman 2002). Although some expressions are associated with particular regions, this is very much a shared social vocabulary, attention to which can offer insight into the multifaceted nature of violence.

Girls reported very high levels of verbal abuse (or what they called 'slagging' or 'trashing'), a practice that is seen as a common expression of violence: 91 percent of girls reported being verbally intimidated by offensive name calling, threats, insults and the like. This experience crosses economic, ethnic and cultural divides, and it affects girls of all ages. On the other hand, 72 percent of girls reported being verbally abusive themselves – mainly to other girls, but also to boys and adults. Verbal threats, personalised, sexualised and racialised name calling, and intimidation are important precursors to, and in certain situations can spill over into, physical violence. Verbal conflicts are a pervasive feature of girls' everyday lives, and for many they constitute a major source of anxiety. Girls' have a heightened sensitivity towards the emotional costs and long-term impact of verbal abuse, and many considered verbal abuse to be more harmful and damaging than physical violence. This kind of abuse draws on individual girls' perceived sexuality, body shape, demeanour and, frequently, dress style (particularly where the style is distinctive or idiosyncratic or unfashionable; see Nilan 1992), and it frequently involves insulting remarks or insinuations about girls' families, especially their mothers. A key point about this type of abuse is that it is rarely a one-off altercation; rather, it is an ongoing verbal onslaught that can be kept up for long periods. Those who had been subject to sustained verbal abuse were also more likely to report self-harming behaviour, another practice named as 'violent' by many who took part in this study. A sole focus on the physical practice of violence would mask these other forms, and for these reasons, our exploration of the impact of violence in girls' lives could not be confined to physical acts alone. The collection of behaviour and practices that were relayed to us provides an indication of the many forms that violence takes in girls' lives and at the same time reminds us of the nebulous nature of the term as it is used in everyday discourse. Knowing the extent and forms of violence is important, as is documenting its pervasiveness in girls' lives. In order to inform policy and practice in this area, we need to ensure that our definitions and understandings of violence are both grounded in and pertinent to girls' own lived experiences. Yet there are also crucial political, theoretical, policy and practical imperatives to distinguish clearly between different behaviour and orientations. It is for these reasons that, in the rest of this chapter, we differentiate between physical violence and verbal abuse.

The importance of context

The meaning of violence cannot be achieved by solely addressing the motivations of the 'perpetrator'. All of those involved in a particular event – whether as actors socially engaged in it ('victims' and 'perpetrators') or as witnesses to it (such as us as researchers) – have an influence on the meaning of that event. The meaning and significance of a violent act lies in the convergence of a number of interactional, contextual, cultural and social situational factors. It is the interaction of these factors that produces a situational dynamic that can influence the ascription of meaning (Kennedy and Forde 1999). Hence an act can be rendered more or less serious, purposeful or pointless, intentionally harmful, consequential or written off as 'just a laugh' by reference to the particular configuration of a range of social and situational factors that shape and influence that particular social interaction, and the decisions, choices and interpretations of those involved. In other words, the meaning of violence is not inherent in a particular act but emerges and becomes established as a consequence of the actions and interpretations of individuals or groups in particular social, situational and spatial contexts.

Much of the violence research undertaken in North America in recent years has adopted a situational or transactional approach to explain violent events (e.g. Baskin and Sommers 1998; Felson 1993; Polk 1994; Sommers and Baskin 1993). This in turn borrows somewhat from the work of Goffman (1959) on the ways in which individuals learn how to act through situated transactions. In these transactions, the meaning in the situation is drawn from the ways in which people act towards one another. The transactional or situational approach views violent events as interactions involving the convergence of motivations, perceptions, the social and spatial context, the social control attributes (formal and informal) of the immediate setting, and the ascribed meaning attached to the event (Fagan and Wilkinson 1998). An advantage of this approach is that it takes into account both the motivations that bring individuals to violent (or potentially violent) situations and the decision making that takes place within the violent event. There are some elements of this approach that are useful for understanding the (multiple and contradictory) meanings that girls ascribe to certain acts, behaviour or practices, and which we draw on here. The importance of context for understanding violence is well established (e.g. Edgar and Martin 2001; Messerschmidt 1997; Newburn and Stanko 1994; Stanko 2001). While the actual content and form of the violent act and its consequences are important, contextual influences, in particular where the act takes place, the relationship between those involved, who is present and how they respond, the likelihood of intervention, and the availability and prevalence of behavioural norms are important mediators of meaning. In order to see how different meanings can emerge from particular incidents, we need to address not only the incident itself but also what precedes and what follows it. Context is again important here, whether the interaction is public or private, the relationship (and past history) between those involved, and the availability of other means of response. Context provides an important controller on the ways in which decisions are made by individuals in the interaction both prior to and after the event (Kennedy and Forde 1999: 29).

In this next section, we draw on examples from our study to illustrate how the interplay of social, situational and contextual factors shapes and filters the meaning and the impact of different forms of violent and abusive behaviour encountered by girls in their everyday lives.

Friends, families and the private sphere

One of the most established, and significant, gender differences between young people involves the amount of emphasis placed on close interpersonal relationships. Several studies have shown the salience of intimate relationships for girls, especially those with same-sex friends (e.g. Gilligan 1982; Griffiths 1995; Hey 1997). The creation, maintenance and operational style of girls' friendships are substantially different from the friendships held by boys (Hey 1997). In particular, girls' friendships are seen as more expressive of emotions, more confiding, more reciprocal, more mutually supportive, empathetic, nurturing and intimate and more disclosing of personal information than boys (Martin 1997). Girls in our study described their friendships with other girls as *the most important* thing in their lives. Hanging out and talking with friends was a prime social activity. Inclusion in a close network of friends is also an important source of self-confidence and self-esteem (Hey 1997).

Ironically, many conflict situations are played out within the context of intimate relationships. As well as being sources of comfort, well-being and security, girls' friendships are also a key site of conflict. Several researchers have remarked on the normative behavioural codes or 'scripts' that both structure and underpin friendship relationships between girls and the priority afforded to trust, reciprocity and understanding in such relationships (e.g. Griffiths 1995; Hey 1997). Girls place immense emotional investment in their friendships, and 'falling out' with friends can have momentous consequences. Girls' friendships are used both as a method of inclusion and as a mechanism of exclusion. Being excommunicated from a close friendship group is a devastating experience for many girls, particularly if ostracism, ridicule and the disclosure of intimate secrets (the 'worst' form of betrayal) occur in the aftermath. Given that girls' social orientation is relationship-centred and that their friendship groups tend to be solidarity-based, conflict within friendships is sometimes unavoidable. The following is taken from a focus group involving a group of 15- and 16-year-old friends who lived on one of the Scottish islands.

ELSA: Usually, if you have got friends, the girls usually tell their friends every-thing. They don't have any secrets, but the boys don't do that. So the girls know everything about each other so if they do fall out it is over major stuff. It can make you so suicidal. It can make you so depressed.

JENNY: Boys just fight over stupid things, like football and that.

EMMA: Yes, and girls.

ELSA: As I said, girls know everything about each other, and if one was to fall out with the other they would tell everyone else their secrets and the other one would be more hurt and it would cause a big fight.

(Group 9)

Key reasons for 'falling out' were stealing someone's boyfriend, spreading false rumours and malicious gossip, particularly if this was of a sexual nature or if it concerned family members. The inferential significance of sexual reputation and in particular the connotations of being labelled a 'slag' are well known (e.g. Lees 1993). Falling out with friends invariably involves the continued use of various forms of verbal abuse and intimidation. As previously stated, verbal abuse was seen by many girls in this study as a common expression of violence; its impact is strongly compounded when it occurs in the context of 'falling out'. In illustration, being the target for malicious gossip, particularly by 'friends', emerged as a major fear for girls (61 percent), and more than half said they were worried about being verbally bullied or threatened by ex-friends. This is exemplified in a discussion between a group of younger girls (aged 13 and 14) who lived in a predominantly rural area but came together to attend a youth club:

KIKI: [Gossip and bad-mouthing] can break up friendships and that, those that have been together for ages.

ANNE: And that hurts more than getting a punch in the face or something ....

JO: ... and I can tell you a lot about that! [All laugh]

KIKI: It depends who is punching.

JENNA: I think that verbal stuff hurts you longer. Physical violence, well, that is going to go away ....

ANNE: Yeah.

JO: Verbal violence is really gonna, it's really gonna be there for ever. I think verbal abuse is actually worse than physical abuse.

SUE: Yeah, and they just keep on saying it, even when they know it is really hurting you.

(Group 4)

Although relatively little is known about the situational dynamics of girls' involvement in assaultive behaviour, the interactional process suggests three key stages: verbal conflict, in which identities are assailed; threats and/or evasive action; followed by physical attack, in which retaliation plays a crucial motiva-tional role (Baskin and Sommers 1998: 114–24). Verbal abuse has been consistently identified in the international literature as a critical provocative factor in girls' aggression (Leschied *et al.* 2000) and was almost always a precursor to the physically violent events reported in this study. Gossip (especially that impugning sexual character), verbal threats, talking 'behind backs', giving 'dirty looks' and 'slagging' were among the main causes of conflict between girls and, particularly for those girls who reported acting violently, form the specific criteria used to determine violence. Talking 'behind backs' often takes place in the presence of the 'victim' and involves gestures and posturing, prolonged staring, furtive whispering and sarcastic laughter, which, taken together, constitute a challenging expression of aggression. Such behaviour, particularly when it takes place in the presence of others, is highly provocative, generating anger and the need to strike back. For those girls who routinely use violence and who are also, by and large, those who have excessive experience of violent victimisation, a violent response is considered an entirely appropriate way to react. In some ways, this is reminiscent of findings from research into the violent behaviour of male youths (e.g. Anderson 1998; Fagan and Wilkinson 1998; Polk 1994), where there is a preoccupation with maintaining respect and self-esteem, and violence is used when self-worth or confidence or honour is degraded or under threat. However, while there are gender similarities, there are also gender differences. We take the view – and we share this with other feminist researchers of female violence (e.g. Chesney-Lind 2002; Miller 2001: 11) – that research that over-emphasises gender differences *essentialises* behaviour rather than understands its complexities; and in that which focuses on similarities, inadequate attention is paid to how gender might intersect with various other factors to create different meanings in the lives of women and men. Gender is central to our analyses; it plays a key role in girls' violence. For example, it defines appropriate targets and means, and it affects girls' decisions of whether to use or desist from violence. But these decisions are also structured by other factors and dynamics, such as peer relations, group processes, situational motives and normative responses to violence (Alder and Worrall 2003; Burman 2001; Miller 2001).

We now turn briefly to a different situation, similarly enacted within the context of (ongoing) friendships, to illustrate how the relationships between those involved plays a key role in compelling individuals to act in a certain way, depending on their interpretation of the situation and their views of the others involved. Within the context of friendship groups, (mainly younger) girls often engage in what they call 'play fights' or 'royal rumbles', where they variously hit, poke, pinch, punch, swing round and wrestle one another to the ground; this is accompanied by much laughter and light-hearted shouting. On occasions, it appeared (to us) that play fights escalated into something more intentionally harmful, where certain girls were targeted by others in the group.[10] Yet such actions are held by those participating to be 'not serious', 'just a laugh' and 'not real violence', despite some heavy blows being struck. 'Royal rumbles' involve a particular style of behaving that is conventionally acceptable (and expected) in that situation. Individual girls bring to the 'play fight' situation a set of expectations, formed from previous interactions in the friendship group, that shape their behaviour in that situation. In play fighting, there is no clear perpetrator and seldom a 'winner', or indeed any clear 'contest' in the conventional sense, although more than once, we saw play fights end with one or more girls in tears (although other girls – including those who had dealt the hardest blows – were immediately attentive). Play fights provide a means of relieving tensions, resolving minor (often unarticulated) conflicts or mini power struggles within groups, and for fostering intimacy between girls, as well as providing the opportunity for 'a good laugh'. There are certain rules and conventions to be followed, for example regarding the intensity and siting of blows (no punches in the face), and girls usually adhere to these norms.

Boys, on the other hand, are seen to stretch or flout altogether the rules of 'play fighting' and consequently 'get out of hand'. The following is taken from a discussion between a group of 14-year-old girls living in a northern Scottish city:

MARTINE: Boys like, may hae a caper, like, they'd run up and put you in a heid lock, or elbow you, or punch you or stuff like that [all laugh] … I'm just sittin' and a boy throws me on tae the green or somethin' and I get up and I get really annoyed because its embarrassing.

Martine goes on to relate several incidents of boys going too far and not paying any attention to her protestations of pain. Other girls gave their own examples:

ELAINE: Boys dinna ken, know their ain strength. You say, 'Ah, that's sair [sore]. Will you stop it', and they say 'But I'm only punching you soft', and a'thin'.
CARON: And they'll punch you again.

***

MARTINE: Like I was drying my hair the other day and Garry walks up and punches me right in the back of my neck.
ELAINE: But that's their way of joking with you. Sometimes it's [meant as] a joke and a'thin', but they go too far.
CARON: But you daen't think its a joke, and they dae, so they just punch you, and you just turn around [and whack 'em].

(Group 7)

Boys can also go too far in terms of 'slagging', as in the example that follows, taken from a group discussion between members of a girls' football team who lived on a large housing estate on the outskirts of a major Scottish city:

KELLY: No, if it's like really bad, it really gets to you. Like if people say something about your family.
ANTHEA: Aye, that's what I was going to say. You know what boys are like. Boys will say 'Aye, you're a whore an' all that. And so's your mum.' That's what boys bring up, your mum.

(Group 8)

Like others (Anderson 1998; Artz 1998), we found that common targets of derogatory and critical remarks were family members, particularly mothers. As previously mentioned, verbal abuse impugning family can be a trigger factor for a violent response. Most girls spoke about the desirability of 'standing up' for family and friends. For some girls, particularly those who routinely use violence, slights that degrade or insult their family constitute sure-fire imperatives for justifiable or righteous violence.

Physical violence between siblings provides an example of the ways in which the relationship between those involved plays a key role both in the ascription of meaning to a given situation and in pressuring individuals to act in a certain way. Although fights in the home between siblings are common (59 percent of girls reported fighting regularly with their siblings in and around the home environment), and the stated intention is usually to cause physical harm, the social and spatial context within which this takes place and the relationship of those involved together militate against this behaviour being seen as 'violent', partly because those involved make a consideration of the likely consequences of their actions. Sibling fights are normalised within the context of domestic and family relationships.

As we have remarked elsewhere (Batchelor *et al.* 2001; Burman *et al.* 2001; Burman 2003; Tisdall 2002) there were some resounding 'gaps' and silences in girls' discussion of violence. These silences offer an insight into the contradictory and changeable ways in which violence is conceptualised and remind us once again that young people's views about violence do not always correspond to widely held (adult-led, legal or politicised) definitions. For example, few girls in the study spoke spontaneously of more 'private' forms of violence, such as domestic abuse or violence against women/girls by men/boys who are known to them. Two main reasons can be ventured for this reticence. First, respondents were reluctant to speak about hidden violence (i.e. sexual or domestic) in the public setting of a focus group discussion, due to naivety, embarrassment, privacy, ignorance or a general unwillingness to cooperate. Younger respondents (aged 13–14) in particular voiced confusion about what was encompassed in the term 'domestic violence' (physical, emotional, sexual acts? shouting? arguing?) and who might be involved (men, women, children?), as well as the legitimacy of the behaviour.[11] Second, and importantly, male violence towards women was overwhelmingly associated with the public sphere and (male) stranger danger.

Scary places, dodgy blokes and the public sphere

Girls' concerns about physical and sexual violence cohere around conceptions of dangerous *people*, mostly 'strange men' (but also groups of other young people, who are perceived as hostile or antagonistic) and dangerous *places*. In this study, as in many others (e.g. Day 2001; Pain 1993; Painter 1992; Warr 1985, 1990), fear of sexual attack was expressed as a fundamental safety concern (70 percent reported fear of sexual violence) and considered to be the 'worst thing' that could happen to a woman. Yet this concern was located firmly in the public sphere, not in private spaces as recent policy/practice has acknowledged (Koskela and Pain 2000; Pain 1993; Painter 1992). Girls of all ages and backgrounds held powerful concepts of public space as dangerous generally. The likelihood of encountering *physical* violence was similarly associated with the public sphere (e.g. on the streets, in parks, at the dancing, in school), particularly places of transit (e.g. school buses, corridors, railway stations) and when moving across areas from one (residential, school, leisure) area to another.

'Fear' is a gendered phenomenon, and female perceptions of danger are connected to women's experience and knowledge of what might happen to them (Stanko 1990, 1993). It is this experience, information and local knowledge, embedded in their social relationships, that render some situations, people or places more or less dangerous or threatening. On this basis, women develop personal images of dangerous people and places where they fear violent crime (Valentine 1989, 1992; Stanko 1990; Pain 1993). The association of violence with certain environmental contexts is well established (e.g. Valentine 1992; Pain 1993). The self-report data indicates that almost half (48 percent) of girls reported that there were specific places near where they lived in which they did not feel safe when out alone, and when the threat of violence was tangibly felt. Their apprehensions showed a strong temporal dimension, since specific fears regarding 'dangerous' or 'scary' places were strongly linked with bad lighting, darkness (see also Warr 1990) and restricted surveillance. Accounts of being 'followed', 'stalked' and 'watched' were provided by several girls. In these accounts, the threat of violence was constant, pervasive and demoralising, particularly in those cases where girls were watched in their homes by 'peeping toms'.

Stanko (1990) argues that women know how to negotiate their everyday lives in circumstances that render them more or less safe, and that they do this routinely. Particular 'strategies' adopted by women for negotiating space and 'staying safe' have been noted (Pain 1993) although the predominant strategy is avoidance of dangerous *places* at dangerous *times*. This, in turn, can restrict women's mobility and pressure them into a restricted use of public space. Collective travel, when out and about, is a key precautionary strategy for personal safety for many girls. Other studies have found that travelling with friends is used by young people to manage risks posed by their mobility (Jones *et al.* 2000; Scott 2000). There is an important flipside to this, however, because being in a group of girls can just as easily attract trouble as deter it. Findings from our self-report data indicate that the more time that girls spent in the company of other girls, the more likely they were to have been shouted at, sworn at or called names.

There is a suggestion from this research, and also from other studies (e.g. Rathzel 2000), that girls are spending significant amounts of time in public places. The increased visibility of girls not only has implications for how girls may be perceived (by adults, by the police, by other young people) but also increases their chances of observing and/or participating in violent encounters with other young people. The self-report data indicates that approximately three-quarters of girls spend most of their time 'hanging about' with friends, mostly on streets (in their own areas and/or in city or town centre locations), in parks and play areas, outside shops or in shopping centres, but also congregating in bus shelters and unstaffed railway stations and outside phone boxes.

Girls do not solely experience their everyday lives in relation to the perceived threat of physical or sexual danger. Rather, there is a strong sense that they also engage in risk-seeking behaviour, where the pursuit of excitement, thrills and pleasure takes precedence.[12] There are certain places and contexts that offer the possibility of excitement and, importantly, the opportunity to 'have a laugh'. One such context is that of 'the dancing',[13] a key site of intra-gender, inter-group antagonism and fighting, a place significant in terms of both symbolic and instrumental violence. This offers opportunities to witness and/or participate in fights. It should be emphasised that only a minority of girls actually get involved in fighting however. On a weekly basis, groups of girls (and boys) from different residential areas travel across many major towns and most cities to attend 'the dancing'. There are tangible feelings of trepidation and excitement, not only at the prospect of meeting members of the opposite sex (or potential 'lumbers') but also because 'the dancing' is where an almost ritualistic enactment of antagonisms takes place.[14] Violence between girls (and between girls and boys) occurs here within the context of extensive social interactions. Witnessing outbreaks of physical violence is an anticipated part of the evening's proceedings. Much of this is provoked by the practice of groups of young people (same-sex or mixed gender) assembled together according to sharply defined territorial affiliations and shouting out, above the noise of the music, the name of the area that they come from. There are jostles and verbal confrontations, and fights break out regularly, despite the efforts of the bouncers. At one level, this is violence as spectacle and entertainment, but at another level, it is also a means for young people to declare their pride and allegiance to areas and territories that are otherwise characterised by deprivation and exclusion. It is also an important means of reinforcing social identity, and hence 'sticking up' for friends in the context of the dancing is a social imperative. The risks of encountering violence are well known and, for some girls, like Lauren and Pauline, two 15-year-olds who live in an economically and environmentally marginalised inner-city area that has a longstanding local reputation for violence, provides a good opportunity for a 'proper fight':

PAULINE: Me and Linda went to the dancing about eight weeks ago noo, and I was in for about ten minutes and got papped right out [thrown out]. And I was outside with Linda, and Lauren came outside with a big burst lip, 'cos about twenty lassies jumped her, 'cos she's from a different scheme [housing estate].

***

LAUREN: See when the music goes a bit quiet like everybody will shout wherever they're frae, right. So they started shouting and we were like that 'What are they shouting?' and I was wi' pure hundreds of my pals, right, and ... all these other lassies were growling at me and dancing into me an' all that ... and I just started dancing back into them. And the three of us, like me, Jackie and Ashley, all got into a fight like in a full area of lassies and I had a big burst lip, didn't I? And ma hair was all pulled oot, and it's just growing in.

***

PAULINE: There was a point when I just used to go doon the toon every week – no' to go to the dancing, but I'd go doon there 'cos you get them coming oot. We used to go doon every Saturday, drunk, and wait ootside for them. And fight wi' everybody.

(Group 14)

Such violence is deeply meaningful; it serves to maintain group solidarity, reinforces friendships, affirms allegiances and enhances personal status. But not all girls find violence 'a laugh' and seek it out. Some have deeply ambivalent reactions to physical violence and abusive behaviour, whereas others find physical violence abhorrent. Gendered constructions of femininity shape both definitions of and responses to behaviour that contradict gendered norms (Hey 1997; Lees 1993; Sharpe 1976). When girls do act violently, this is often seen as wholly transgressive by other girls, particularly those who are older and who have been shielded from violent victimisation, and for whom witnessing violence is a rare event.

This research, intended as an exploratory study to establish baseline information on girls' experiences and use of violence and the factors associated with their violent behaviour, has shown how the meaning of violence, for girls, is at once complex, contradictory, contingent and constantly shifting. In order to comprehend the meaning, impact and pervasiveness of violence in girls' lives, we simply cannot ignore the range of behaviour and situations in which girls encounter physical violence or other forms of violation. The meaning(s) of violence for those who use it and experience it are inextricably bound up with lived experiences, subjective identities, and intimate and social relationships. Girls' relationships to violence need to be understood as arising from a complex set of social, material and gendered circumstances and cannot be addressed in isolation from other aspects of their lives.

Notes

1   This research project, 'A View From The Girls: Exploring Violence and Violent Behaviour' (ESRC Award No. L133251018) was conducted by Michele Burman, Jane Brown and Susan Batchelor (Department of Sociology and Anthropology, University of Glasgow) and Kay Tisdall (Children in Scotland and Department of Social Policy, University of Edinburgh). It was one of twenty projects operating under the ESRC's five-year Violence Research Programme.
2   The term 'girls' is used throughout this paper to refer to females under the age of 16. 'Young women' refers to those aged 16–20.
3   Between 1999 and 2000, there was a 19 percent increase (to 336) in the number of custodial sentences for females aged under 21 in Scotland. This was in contrast to

the number of young male offenders similarly sentenced, which, in 2000, was the lowest since 1991. A higher proportion of these young women (22 percent) were imprisoned for crimes of violence (32 out of a total of 148 receptions) than the rest of the female prison population (Scottish Executive 2002).

4 In 2000, females (of all age groups) accounted for 7.5 percent of non-sexual crimes of violence in Scotland. In terms of actual numbers, 315 women had a charge proven against them, and of this group less than one-third (96) were under the age of 21. This compares with 3,808 men who had a charge of non-sexual violence proven against them, 38 of whom (1,445) were under 21 (Scottish Executive 2001).

5 We are relying here on the official statistics relating to *young women* (aged 16–20) processed through the adult courts. It is extremely difficult to obtain reliable information on *girls'* offending due to the distinctive nature of the Scottish system of juvenile justice. In Scotland, in all but the most serious cases, children aged under 16 who commit offences are referred to the Children's Hearing System. Children's Hearings are administrative tribunals where lay members of the public determine whether compulsory measures of supervision are required. The determination of guilt or innocence is considered inappropriate. Figures on the number of children convicted of various offence types are therefore not available, although the Scottish Children's Reporter Association publishes statistics on numbers of offence referrals. However, there are complexities of measurement here regarding the manner in which incidents and referrals are counted: for example, numerous incidents can be involved in one referral; and numerous referrals of the same young person can be made. Also, and crucially, offence referrals are not broken down by offence type but in terms of grounds for referral.

6 The discussion that follows draws on both the quantitative (questionnaire) and the qualitative (focus group and individual interview) data, although percentages refer to the survey data only.

7 Consequently, we are not in a position to claim that our findings are representative of the views of all young women. Only a small number of 'hard to reach' girls with more chaotic and transitory lifestyles took part in the research, for example, and we did not speak to young women in private school settings.

8 For example, 70 percent of girls from the self-report survey described regularly witnessing at first hand some form of physical violence, usually a fight, near or around where they lived, went to school or 'hung out'; nearly two-thirds (65 percent) knew someone personally who had been hurt by physical violence; 42 percent had been frightened by someone threatening, following or chasing them; and 41 percent had been deliberately hit, punched or kicked (usually by another young person).

9 The dichotomisation between 'good' and 'bad' girls also underpins images of young female sexuality; see, for example, Sharpe (1976) and Lees (1993).

10 Elsewhere (Burman *et al.* 2001: 452) we discuss play fighting in the context of the difficulties associated with interpreting and reconciling research participants' words and actions, and balancing these against our interpretations.

11 This mirrors other recent research, which revealed that young people – boys as well as girls – were fairly ambivalent about what 'counts' as domestic violence (Mullender *et al.* 1999).

12 The circumstances in which girls seek out 'danger' and 'risk', and their motivations for doing so, require close investigation, and we are currently developing our analyses in this area.

13 In larger towns, and cities, 'the dancing' usually takes place in nightclubs that have been allocated for the use of 'under 16-year-olds' for certain periods in the early evening (usually 6–9pm on Saturdays).

14 Alcohol is not served on the premises but is consumed beforehand, usually *en route* from home.

References

Alder, C. and Worrall, A. (eds) (2003) *Girls' Violence?* New York: State University of New York Press.

Anderson, E. (1998) 'The social ecology of youth violence', in M. Tonry and M.H. Moore (eds) *Youth Violence.* Chicago: University of Chicago Press.

Artz, S. (1998) *Sex, Power and the Violent School Girl.* Toronto: Trifolium Books.

Baskin, I. and Sommers, D. (1998) *Casualties of Community Disorder: Women's Careers in Violent Crime.* Oxford: Westview Press.

Batchelor, S. (2001a) 'Sensitive subjects: researching "girls" and "violence"', unpublished paper presented to the Social Research Association in Scotland, Edinburgh, May 2001.

Batchelor, S. (2001b) 'Nuts, sluts and the post-feminist criminal: discourses about violent young women', unpublished paper presented at the Workshop for Postgraduate Criminologists, Sheffield, May 2001.

Batchelor, S. (2001c) 'The myth of girl gangs', *Criminal Justice Matters* 43: 26–7 [reprinted in Y. Jewkes and G. Letherby (eds) (2002) *Criminology: A Reader.* London: Sage].

Batchelor, S., Burman, M. and Brown, J. (2001) 'Discussing violence: let's hear it for the girls', *Probation Journal* 48(2): 125–34.

Belknap, J. and Holsinger, K. (1998) 'An overview of delinquent girls: how theory and practice have failed and the need for innovative changes', in R. Zaplin (ed.) *Female Offenders: Critical Perspectives and Effective Interventions.* Aspen, Colo.: Maryland.

Best, J. (1999) *Random Violence: How We Talk about New Crimes and New Victims.* University of California Press.

Bowie, V. (2002) 'Defining violence at work: a new typology', in M. Gill, B. Fisher and V. Bowie (eds) *Violence at Work: Crimes, Patterns and Prevention.* Cullompton: Willan Publishing.

Brinkworth, L. and Burrell, I. (1994) 'Sugar 'n' spice … not at all nice', *The Sunday Times*, 27 November.

Burman, M. (2001) 'Motivations and rewards in girls' violence', unpublished paper presented at American Society of Criminology Conference, Atlanta, Georgia.

Burman, M. (2003) 'Turbulent talk: girls making sense of violence', in C. Adler and A. Worrall (eds) *Girls Violence?* New York: State University of New York Press.

Burman, M., Batchelor, S. and Brown, J. (2001) 'Researching girls and violence: facing the dilemmas of fieldwork', *British Journal of Criminology* 41(3): 443–59.

Campbell, A. (1993) *Out of Control: Men, Women and Aggression.* London: Pandora.

Chesney-Lind, M. (2002) *The Female Offender: Girls, Women and Crime* (2nd edition). Thousand Oaks, Calif.: Sage.

Day, K. (2001) 'Constructing masculinity and women's fear in public space in Irvine', *Gender, Place and Culture* 2: 109–27.

Edgar, K. and Martin, C. (2001) 'The social context of prison violence', *Criminal Justice Matters* 42: 24–5.

Felson, R. (1993) 'Predatory and dispute-related violence: a social interactionist approach', in R.V. Clarke and M. Felson (eds) *Routine Activity and Rational Choice: Advances in Criminological Theory*, Vol. 5. New Brunswick, NJ: Transaction Press.

Fagan, J. and Wilkinson, D.L. (1998) 'Guns, youth violence, and social identity in inner cities', in M. Tonry and M.H. Moore (eds) *Youth Violence.* Chicago: University of Chicago Press.

Gilligan, C. (1982) *In a Different Voice: Psychological Theory and Women's Development*. Cambridge, Mass.: Harvard University Press.

Goffman, E. (1959, reprinted 1972) *The Presentation of Self in Everyday Life*. London: Penguin.

Griffiths, V. (1995) *Adolescent Girls and their Friends: A Feminist Ethnography*. Aldershot: Avebury.

Hardy, A. and Howitt, D. (1998) 'Fighting in adolescent females: a test of gendered representation, gendered trait and gender role conflict/transition theories', paper presented at Psychology Postgraduate Affairs Group Annual Conference, Derby.

Hey, V. (1997) *The Company She Keeps: An Ethnography of Girls' Friendships*. Buckingham: Open University Press.

Hudson, A. (1989) 'Troublesome girls: towards alternative definitions and policies', in M. Cain (ed.) *Growing Up Good: Policing the Behaviour of Girls in Europe*. London: Sage.

Jones, L., Davis, A. and Eyers, T. (2000) 'Young people, transport and risk: comparing access and independent mobility in urban, suburban and rural environments', *Health Education Journal* 59(4): 315–28.

Kennedy, L. and Forde, D. (1999) *When Push Comes To Shove; A Routine Conflict Approach to Violence*. New York: State University of New York Press.

Koskela, H. and Pain, R. (2000) 'Revisiting fear and place; women's fear of attack and the built environment', *Geoforum* 31: 269–80.

Lees, S. (1993) *Sugar and Spice: Sexuality and Adolescent Girls*. London: Penguin.

Leibling, A. and Stanko, S. (2001) 'Allegiance and ambivalence: some dilemmas in researching disorder and violence', *British Journal of Criminology* 41(3): 421–30.

Leschied, A., Cummings, A., Van Brunschot, M., Cunningham, A. and Saunders, A. (2000) *Female Adolescent Aggression: A Review of the Literature and the Correlates of Aggression*, User Report No. 2000–04. Ottawa: Solicitor General Canada.

Littlechild, B. (1997) 'I needed to be told that I hadn't failed: experiences of violence against probation staff and agency support', *British Journal of Social Work* 27: 219–40.

Martin, R. (1997) '"Girls don't talk about garages!": Perceptions of conversation in same- and cross-sex friendships', *Personal Relationships* 4: 115–30.

Messerschmidt, J. (1997) *Crime as Structured Action: Gender, Race, Class and Crime in the Making*. Thousand Oaks, Calif.: Sage.

Miller, J. (2001) *One of the Guys? Girls, Gangs and Gender*. Oxford University Press.

Mitchell, V. (2000) 'What turned this innocent schoolgirl into a murderer?' *Daily Mail*, 10 March.

Motz, A. (2001) *The Psychology of Female Violence: Crimes against the Body*. Hove: Brunner-Routledge.

Mullender, A., Kelly, L., Hague, G., Malos, E. and Imam, U. (1999) *Children's Needs, Coping Strategies and Understandings of Woman Abuse*, Economic and Social Research Council Research Briefing 12, ESRC.

Newburn, T. and Stanko, E.A. (eds) (1994) *Just Boys Doing Business: Men, Masculinities and Crime*. London: Routledge.

Nilan, P. (1992) 'Kazzies, DBTs and tryhards – categorisations of style in adolescent girls' talk', *British Journal of Sociology of Education* 13(2): 201–14.

Norman, R. (1995) *Ethics, Killing and War*. Cambridge: Cambridge University Press.

Pain, R. (1993) 'Women's fear of sexual violence: explaining the spatial paradox', in H. Jones (ed.) *Crime and the Urban Environment*. Aldershot: Avebury.

Painter, K. (1992) 'Different worlds; the spatial, temporal, and social dimensions of female victimisation', in D. Evans, N. Fyfe and D. Herbert (eds) *Crime, Policing and Place: Essays in Environmental Criminology*. London: Routledge.

Polk, K. (1994) 'Masculinity, honour and confrontational homicide', in T. Newburn and E. Stanko (eds) *Just Boys Doing Business? Men, Masculinity and Crime*. London: Routledge.

Rathzel, N. (2000) 'Living differences: ethnicity and fearless girls in public places', *Social Identities* 6(2): 119–42.

Sasson, T. (1995) *Crime Talk: How Citizens Construct a Social Problem*. New York: Aldine de Gruyter.

Scott, C.A. (2000) 'Going home with the chaps: concerning the degradation of young urbanites and their social space and time', *Youth and Policy* 69: 17–41.

Scottish Executive (2001) *Criminal Proceedings in Scottish Courts, 2000*. Edinburgh: Scottish Executive.

Scottish Executive (2002) *A Better Way: The Report of the Ministerial Group on Women's Offending*. Edinburgh: HMSO.

Sharpe, S. (1976) *Just Like a Girl: How Girls Learn to Be Women*. London: Penguin.

Sommers, I. and Baskin, D. (1993) 'The situational context of violent female offending', *Journal of Research in Crime and Delinquency* 30(2): 136–62.

Sparks, R. (1992) *Television and the Drama of Crime*. Milton Keynes: Open University Press.

Stanko, E. (1990) *Everyday Violence*. London: Virago.

Stanko, E.A. (1993) 'Ordinary fear: women, violence and personal safety', in P. Bart and E. Moran (eds) *Violence against Women: The Bloody Footprints*. London: Sage.

Stanko, E. (2001) 'Murder and moral outrage: understanding violence', *Criminal Justice Matters* 42: Winter 2001/2002.

Stewart, H. and Tattersall, A. (2000) *Invisible Young Women: Hearing the Stories of Young Women who Present with Violent, Challenging and/or Offending Behaviour*. Victoria: Young Women's Project.

Tisdall, K. (2002) 'The rising tide of female violence? Researching girls' own understandings, attitudes and experiences of violent behaviour', in R. Lee and E. Stanko (eds) *Researching Violence: Essays on Methodology and Measurement*. London: Routledge.

Tonry, M. and Moore, M.H. (eds) (1998) *Youth Violence*. Chicago: University of Chicago Press.

Valentine, G.M. (1989) 'The geography of women's fear', *Area* 21: 385–90.

Valentine, G.M. (1992) 'Images of danger: women's sources of information about the spatial distribution of male violence', *Area* 24.

Warr, M. (1985) 'Fear of rape among urban women', *Social Problems* 32: 238–50.

Warr, M. (1990) 'Dangerous situations: social context and fear of victimisation', *Social Forces* 68(3): 891–907.

5 'Hi, I'm Ramon and I run this place'

Challenging the normalisation of violence in children's homes from young people's perspectives

Emma Renold and Christine Barter

Introduction

Concern over violence in residential care for children during the last 30 years has surfaced as the subject of media attention mainly in relation to individual and/or institutional physical and sexual abuse of residents by their adult supposed 'carers'. Examples include the Staffordshire 'pindown' regime, in which children were routinely humiliated by staff (Levy and Kahan 1991), and more recently the North Wales judicial inquiry, which investigated over 250 reports against staff in residential children's homes from as far back as the 1970s, confirming widespread physical and sexual abuse (Waterhouse 2000). However, while accounts of (institutional) adult–child abuse often reach the headlines and shape our perception of violence as something that adults do to children, recent research into children in residential care indicates that young people may be significantly more at risk of physical and sexual violence from other residents than from staff. This is possibly due to the fact that UK children's homes now frequently accommodate children of varying ages with very challenging behaviour and diverse and conflicting needs (*ibid.*) – a finding that resonates with recent research, which argues that abuse outside the home most commonly involves boyfriends and fellow pupils rather than adults (Cawson *et al.* 2000). However, given the possible effect that this may have upon the climate of violence between children, and a number of reminders within wider studies of children in residential care, which state that bullying and peer violence are a common feature of residential life (Sinclair and Gibbs 1998[1]), children's experience of peer violence has received little attention and even less understanding (Barter 1997) – an absence and imbalance that our research has aimed to redress.

When violence between children, be it physical, sexual or emotional, has been uncovered, the language of description often shifts from acts of 'violence' to that of 'bullying'. This is true of both the limited research into residential children's homes and (perhaps inherited from) the growing field of children's school experiences. For example, while the Utting Report (1997: 99) estimated that 'possibly half the total abuse reported in institutions is peer abuse', only one of the twelve sections on 'abusers' referred to children. And while the main recommendations mentioned peer violence, it was not expanded upon and was omitted from the list of principal recommendations. However, the report did include a separate discussion on 'bullying', implying a clear conceptual distinction between the two types of behaviour that is difficult to justify. Indeed, while the wider bullying literature embraces a much broader and varied understanding of peer violence, such as physical, verbal and emotional bullying, and 'indirect' (using others, rather than oneself, as a means of attack) and 'relational' bullying (harming others by social exclusion or spreading rumours), it could be argued that the term itself may be used to play down the significance and impact of aggressive behaviour among and upon children, perceiving and treating it as less serious than an identical act carried out by an adult (Cawson *et al.* 2000). Indeed, the normalisation of peer violence as an inevitable and incontrovertible part of children's culture or *growing up* (discursively constructed through the language of 'bullying') often means, as this chapter illustrates, that much of the behaviour perceived by young people as harmful and abusive is overlooked. Our study into peer violence in residential children's homes goes some way towards deconstructing and challenging normalised and often adult-centred conceptualisations of violence and violent behaviour by prioritising children's own subjective experiences and tapping into young people's definitions, perceptions and evaluations of both incidence (i.e. type of violence) and impact (subjective experience).

The study

The central aim of the study was to map and investigate young people's experiences of peer violence within the residential setting by exploring their own definitions and perceptions of the meanings and effects of violence, including the impact it had on their lives and the coping and protective strategies they employed. The research also set out to examine staff and residential managers' evaluations, responses and working practices concerning peer violence, which enabled the research team to explore the extent to which young people and staff shared a common reference system for understanding and dealing with violence. Combining staff and young people's perspectives was crucial to unpacking the intergenerational relationship between largely adult-defined institutions and the activities and social relationships that children construct for and between themselves, particularly, as this chapter goes on to illustrate, the ways in which young people and staff differ in their evaluations and experiences of different forms of violence. Indeed, one of the main aims of the study was to enable children's own definitions and interpretations of violence to inform the development of policy and practice surrounding peer violence in residential settings, rather than simply reflecting adult realities and solutions. To this end, the research reflects and draws upon more recent developments within what has come to be known as the 'new sociology of childhood', in which children are seen to be knowledgeable and actively involved in the construction and shaping of their own social lives and whose perspectives are viewed as being important in their own right and not just in relation to their social construction by adults (Brannen and O'Brien 1996; James and Prout 1998). Before we outline the development of our methodological framework, a brief overview of the sample is provided.

The sample

The research was conducted in fourteen residential children's homes run by local authorities (nine), and by the voluntary (two) and private sectors (three). Ten homes were mixed-sex, and four were all-male. Twelve of the fourteen units were for adolescents, and two were for young children. While ages ranged from 6 to 17, the majority were teenagers between 13 and 16 years old. Seventy-one young people participated in the study, forty-four boys/young men and twenty-seven girls/young women. Of the seventy-one young people, 21 percent were from minority ethnic groups, representing the national balance of 'looked after' children more generally. Seventy-five residential staff also participated, representing a range of different ages, genders, ethnicities, grades (from residential workers to managers), experience and length of service.

Conceptualising violence: a question of methods

Theorisation of the term 'violence' remains under-developed and problematic (Richardson and May 1999). As Curtin and Litke state in their preface to *Institutional Violence*, 'it is never entirely clear what violence is' (1994: xi), particularly when it can be both condoned in one context/culture and condemned in another. However, traditional *common sense* understandings of violence often emphasise visible, physical and quantifiable (and consequently a preoccupation with male) violence over less visible manifestations such as emotional, verbal or psychological harm (Gabe *et al.* 2001) – an outcome that feminist scholars suggest may omit behaviour that many people understand and experience as violence (Hanmer and Saunders 1984; Kelly 1988; Maynard 1993; McNeill 1987; Stanko 1990, 1995; Wise and Stanley 1987). In response, these commentators, among others, have developed a broader and more inclusive social definition of violence that encompasses a wider spectrum of behaviour that is rooted in and can cope with the complexity of experience from the standpoint of the individual concerned. Such a definition is fundamental to our project, a central aim of which is the representation of children's and young people's experiences of violence, whose voices (and thus experiences) have historically remained silent and marginalised.

We drew upon Kelly's (1987) inclusive framework for violence as a continuum of harm in which physical, sexual, emotional and psychological abuse of power at individual and group levels allows for a much more fluid theorisation of violence where a whole range of interactions and actions can be positioned according to participants' own evaluations and interpretations.

Indeed, we were increasingly aware during the fieldwork how violence needs to be situated within a continuum that recognises its multifaceted and often contested status if young people's accounts are to be incorporated and taken seriously. For example, a continuum can include a diverse range of violent behaviour from isolated flashes of physical violence to systematic longitudinal verbal attacks. It was also imperative to map the intersections of both incidence and impact if we were to tease out the meanings and roles that different forms of violence play in young people's lives. Consequently, in addition to our theoretical framework, we needed to develop a methodology in which young people (and staff) could define and contextualise their own personal experiences of violence. Semi-structured interviews were used in this first instance. However, given the loaded nature of the term 'violence' a decision was taken early on not to describe our research interest using this term but rather to call it an investigation into 'the positive and negative aspects of residential life' more widely. Indeed, we were very keen to use the research process as a platform to enable children to articulate their experiences as they are significant and meaningful to them and, furthermore, to allow them to wield some control over the focus and direction of the research (see Alldred 1998).

We also needed a methodology that could engage young people to participate in what is a potentially sensitive research topic and enable a discussion of types of violence that they may not have encountered directly. A complementary technique to the qualitative interviews was the use of vignettes depicting different forms of violence along the continuum described above, and which young people could respond to and locate themselves within. Thus, where the semi-structured interviews offered a platform for participants to draw upon their own experiences of violence, the vignettes provided the opportunity for young people to comment on types of violence they had not encountered, or maybe felt too uncomfortable to disclose through direct discussion (see Barter and Renold 2000). Alongside these more formalised data collection strategies, the research also used ethnographic techniques as a considerable amount of time was spent in each field setting informally observing and interacting with participants. Accessing young people's social networks and cultures was a vital component of the research process in terms of understanding the process of the normalisation of violence and violent behaviour.

'We have our own rules': children's cultures and the normalisation of violence

INTERVIEWER: If a young person was coming into the home for the first time, what do you think they should be aware of?

YOUNG PERSON: I dunno … about the way other kids are and about the rules … what to do and what not to do, 'cos kids have their own rules. We have our own rules.

(female, age 15)

Children's cultures have been relatively neglected and under-theorised in the literature on residential children's homes. This is often due to a narrow definition of 'culture', with its presumption that there needs to be a stable and static peer group for the development of shared cultural norms, thus excluding children in children's homes because of the fluidity and movement of children between children's homes and different types of care (e.g. foster care). However, a small number of studies have commented that one of the reasons stated by young people for going missing from children's homes was the powerful peer group culture (Wade *et al.* 1998). Others have evidence that the culture of violence is a persistent feature of residential life (Morris and Wheatley 1994). Following Geertz's (1973) general approach to culture and more recent accounts of children's cultures within the 'new sociology of childhood' (see James *et al.* 1998), the concept of children's cultures is no longer viewed solely as a distinct or separate children's world with its own 'lore'. Rather, it is seen to be produced by the contexts in which children live out their everyday lives. James *et al.* thus characterise children's culture as 'a form of social action contextualised by the many different ways in which children choose to engage with the social institutions and structures that shape the form and process of their everyday lives' (*ibid.*: 88). Thus, in relation to the current study, 'violence' was the particular form of social action under investigation, and the children's home, with its own formal and informal regulations and structures, was the institution in which children's actions, behaviour and cultural norms were contextualised.

We found that tapping into and understanding children's (peer group) cultures is central to the way in which violence is mediated and experienced by young people – as the quote for this section illustrates, 'kids have their own rules'. Indeed, many young people in the study were aware of specific micro- and macro-cultural codes and practices in relation to their behaviour and conduct within the peer group, most of which pivoted around modes of acceptable and unacceptable behaviour, or in the words of one boy, 'what to do, what not to do'. We refer to *micro-cultural codes* as a way of theorising the situatedness of 'violence' within local peer group cultures in each individual home and *macro-cultural codes* as a way of theorising wider peer group cultures and dynamics that cut across all children's homes and children's lives, such as their perceptions and constructions of ethnicity, gender (masculinities and femininities) and age (young/old child or child/adult). However, we are aware that the division is conceptual and that the macro and the micro intersect and shape each other.

The following sections illustrate the ways in which the micro- and the macro-cultural codes within and between peer groups led, with constant exposure over time, to the normalisation and desensitisation of different forms of violence and violent behaviour. We also explore how the process of normalisation and subsequent desensitisation varied between and within children's homes. Some young people's normalisation of violence was highly personalised and specific to their past experiences of violence, rather than being embedded in a wider culture within the peer group or children's home. Others were related to their acculturation into a shared yet hierarchical peer group culture on first entering a home. The following section expands upon the former.

'It's got a reputation, this home has': violence as situated and localised

While there seemed to be a shared or common culture of low-level verbal abuse in the form of 'swearing' in all but two of the children's homes, the meaning and subsequent impact of violence could not be divorced from the local context in which it was produced and understood by young people. This was particularly the case in terms of the existence or severity of violence within each home, which in turn led to the normalisation of violent behaviour. For example, a culture of violence within each home was often apparent from our first visits, during which we negotiated access. In one home, the authors were immediately confronted with verbal and non-verbal forms of intimidation, such as spitting and swearing, and were eventually locked in a vacant bedroom for approximately half an hour while a group of residents ran screaming and shouting around the different floors of the children's home (see Barter and Renold 2002). In another home, we encountered residents sitting quietly and calmly in the TV room, and when 'dinner' was called they each walked to their place at the dinner table, showed us to our seats and chatted about their day at school and future social/leisure activities that night. The contrast was stark indeed. Young people themselves were also acutely aware of the culture of violence within each home, to the extent that the culture of some homes was transmitted, not on direct exposure to the peer group, but solely via the circulation of gossip and rumour. One young person, for example, learned of the culture of what he termed as 'bullying' in the home he was shortly to be admitted to via his social worker's 'guilty knowledge':

INTERVIEWER: So what was it like when you first came here then?
YOUNG PERSON: ... my social worker said I'd get bullied.
INTERVIEWER: Your social worker told you you'd get bullied?
YOUNG PERSON: He said children will take advantage of you when I come in here.

(male, age 14)

Our study attempted to position homes along a continuum of different forms of violence based upon impact, from low-level violence to high-level violence. This provided us with an overall exploratory framework to identify in which homes the culture of violence was stronger than others and the institutional factors that may influence such cultures (such as control over admissions, high staff turnover, single sex). However, although such variables were possible associates of high- or low-level violence, the meaning that young people attached to living in a home with high or low levels of violence often differed. For example, where the 'violent' reputations of some homes instilled fear in young people, they could also be revered precisely because of their history of housing young people with challenging and violent behaviour, as the following extract illustrates:

YOUNG PERSON: It's a pretty good home this, 'cos when you come in this home, you have to be pretty mature to come in this home 'cos it's an [sic] hard home to be in, you know 'cos it's got a reputation this home has for like ... you know if like people are annoying, they'll threaten to send them to [name of home].

(female, age 14)

However, a culture of violence in a home did seem to impact directly upon young people's definition and experience of harm to the extent that particular forms of violence could vary in qualitatively different ways depending upon the level of violence within the home. In a home categorised as exhibiting 'low-level violence', for example, pushing someone was considered to have a similar impact to being threatened with a knife in a home categorised as exhibiting 'high-level' violence. Indeed, exposure over time to violence led some young people to become desensitised to its impact:

INTERVIEWER: Would you like it to be less violent?
YOUNG PERSON: I don't mind.
INTERVIEWER: It doesn't bother you now?
YOUNG PERSON: No, it doesn't bother me ... if I had first come in [to the home] then I would probably like it changed like, asked for the bully to be stopped. But, but now I just get used to it. Seven months living here, you get used to it.

(male, age 15)

Similarly, the term 'bullying' was used by young people in a variety of ways, including to denote persistent systematic physical acts of violence as well as isolated incidents of being wronged by another child. One boy, when asked what he meant by the term 'bullying', commented:

YOUNG PERSON: Um ... punching, hitting people, swearing, not swearing I mean verbal abuse ... there's hundreds of kinds of bullying, you've got physical abuse, verbal abuse, too many kinds ... it's, there's many kinds of bullying.

(male, age 14)

The difficulty for some young people in conceptualising various forms of violence that could take impact and harm into account led one young man to construct his own definition. He described how the harm caused by a prolonged verbal attack was more significant than isolated forms of name calling and subsequently chose to call the former 'name bullying'.

What became evident in the early stages of the project was that conceptual-ising violence as contextually contingent and, to some extent, temporal was vital if we were to assess the meaning and impact that different forms of violence had for young people. Indeed, understanding violence as local and situated in children's cultures was crucial in our investigation into the processes that lead to the normalisation of violence. And as the next section illustrates, it became increasingly evident that young people's perceptions of violence were highly contingent upon their place and role within the peer group, and there was an emerging relationship between perception of harm, severity of violence and stability of peer group culture.

Violence as social and interpersonal: peer group hierarchies and pecking orders

A consistent (and re-emerging) theme was the centrality of the peer group dynamic in young people's and staff's accounts of how the cultures of violence were mediated and normalised. Given that the 'peer group culture partly emerges out of the temporal demands laid on children and young people by the institutional structures through which their growing up is regulated and controlled' (James *et al.* 1998: 77), it could be argued that the residential component of the children's home placed an extra pressure upon the peer group in so far as they would often have no choice but to be in close physical proximity with someone they may or may not know, over long periods of time. It thus came as little surprise that the peer group was often fraught with tension and that embedded in young people's accounts of residential peer group cultures was a constant reference to hierarchical peer group dynamics. In all but one of the residential homes, both young people and staff described this phenomenon as being present in their home at the time of the fieldwork. While the precise language used to denote the hierarchical structures differed (with staff uniformly referring to it as the 'pecking order'), both described a peer culture in terms of there being a dominant member of the peer group who, via various forms of oppression and control, could impose their will upon other members of the peer group. Staff generally referred to this person or persons as 'top dog'. One residential worker, discussing problem behaviour, revealed:

STAFF: I think, I don't know, I think it's, with the boys I find it's top dog, you know top dog's gone so there's a big battle for top dog position, and it's not a question of how good you can be, it's how bad you can be.

(male, residential worker)

Another continued:

STAFF: There are a lot of issues that come up, I mean at the moment, well, we had five boys in before Tara came and there's a lot of, um, peer group pressure between them and there's a lot of arguing about who wants to be top dog.

(female, senior residential worker)

Young people had a larger repertoire, including, 'the boss', 'the ruler', 'top kid' or 'the leader', as one girl described it:

YOUNG PERSON: You have to have a leader, init ... and like everybody knows who it is but doesn't say you know, doesn't let on, and like all the other kids get pushed around.

(female, age 14)

Both staff and young people framed their descriptions in terms of domination and subordination, and many could not only identify who was situated at the top of the hierarchy, and other relative subordinate positions within the hierarchy, but also who would inherit the 'top' position once it became vacant:

YOUNG PERSON: I'm sort of second you could say now. I don't have to do anything. I've just come second – I'll take over the place the same. Then, when Ben moves out ... I would, I would be totally top.

(male, age 12)

However, there was no clear or consistent profile of those who were likely to be positioned at the top of the hierarchy. And while age, maturity, status (being, in their words, 'hard' or 'cool'), height, physical stature/strength, intelligence, manipulative powers, criminal record/experience and length of stay in the home were all characteristics of those positioned as 'top dog', none was a prerequisite. In one home (catering for boys between the ages of 11 and 16), for example, the next young person to ascend to the top of the hierarchy was a 12-year-old boy (see earlier interview extract). In another home, two relatively slight 15-year-old girls were controlling the peer group, which included a 16-year-old male and an older and bigger 16-year-old female. Rather, it was the ability to manipulate and control the rest of the peer group, whether through individual physical force or by more subtle means (threats, intimidation), which marked the 'leaders' from the 'pack', as one girl described it. Thus it was not simply a matter of bruising your way to the top but a complex process that often combined the deployment or threat of physical force with a range of manipulative negotiating skills.

Young people and staff alike identified that flashpoints for physical and non-contact violence within the peer group hierarchy occurred upon a new admission, or when a young person at the top of the hierarchy left, thus leaving a vacancy for one of the other members to occupy. Workers identified that at these times the internal stability of the group collapsed due to the transitions in power and fractures in social relations, which often resulted in shifting alliances within the peer group. A consequence of such disruption included feelings of broken loyalties and sometimes jealousy, which often led young people to feel threatened and insecure. Such transitions usually took the form of a struggle of wills, described by workers as 'acting out', which often resulted in physical conflict and intimidation. At these moments, young people talked about the need to 'stand my ground' or 'stand up for myself'. Some workers' comments also reflected the young people's accounts in so far as they too felt the anxiety a new admission created for young people, possibly due to an invasion of space, which they felt led many young people to 'protect their patch'. However, workers identified that following a period of flux (in which power struggles erupted) the peer group would 'settle down' and young people would 'find their place'. Consequently, a 'new social order' could be established (which they identified as lasting a couple of days to a few weeks), and the *status quo* would be regained. However, young people's accounts regarding the positioning process and the means of attaining a stable peer group culture were markedly different to staff interpretations. They described how the peer group structure needed constant maintenance and how their relative position within the peer group hierarchy involved continuous covert practices (although to varying degrees) of domination and subordination, thus giving the appearance of a settled peer group dynamic. Indeed, young people's and staff's accounts of the practices of subordination/domination and the function of the peer group became further demarcated, as the following section highlights.

'He rules the place and bullies everyone': bullying as a 'natural' and inevitable peer group dynamic?

The majority of workers stated that the 'pecking order' was a constant and common feature of residential life. Previous research has also described the existence of 'top dog' networks, where children exercise considerable power and influence over others by actual or perceived physical strength and manipulation (Brannen *et al.* 1993; Parkin and Green 1997; Sinclair and Gibbs 1998). Overwhelmingly, however, the process and maintenance of the peer group hierarchy were perceived as 'natural' and 'normal', or at least inevitable, as the following quote illustrates:

STAFF: There's always, there's always a pecking order ... any group in my opinion, even, even adult groups because there's some sort of pecking order, you know, as subtle as it can be sometimes but definitely with children. They need, you know, they need to have that pecking order ... I've always, I've always felt that it's fairly natural, it's fairly normal and it needs to, sometimes they need to sort it out themselves. Do you know what I mean? Especially when you have this very settled place, unit, and a new child arrives in it, you know, you can plan for the next four or five weeks, shifts, that there's gonna be ... there's gonna be realignment, there's gonna be, I

don't know, a lot of disruptive behaviour because the pecking order needs
to be sorted out again.

(female, residential worker)

Thus, for many workers, 'pecking orders' were an enduring aspect of peer relations. And although many felt that the residential dynamic exacerbated the
importance of the pecking order in the lives of young people, they still regarded
the hierarchical structuring of peer relations as a common aspect of children's
social relationships. However, such functional interpretations have alarming
consequences in so far as workers' normalisations of the peer group hierarchies
desensitised, diluted and sometimes denied the role that intimidation and coercion played in the maintenance of such structures. Some workers even viewed
the process as beneficial to children's life experiences. Moreover, while workers
did not overtly conceptualise peer group hierarchies as necessarily detrimental,
they were usually associated with intimidation and misuse of power. The fact
that such awareness regarding intimidation and coercion was presented as
synonymous with, and thus an accepted aspect of, children's cultures' meant
that much of what went on was overlooked and unchallenged.

As the title for this section illustrates and the quote below further demonstrates, young people's accounts of their experiences of the 'pecking order' and
peer group dynamics was quite different:

INTERVIEWER: So you when you first came here he was?
YOUNG PERSON: He reckoned he was big and hard and owned the place.
INTERVIEWER: Did the other kids think he was top dog as well?
YOUNG PERSON: Yeah, 'cos he kept bullying him and stuff.

(male, age 16)

There was only one home in which young people reported a stable and relatively equal distribution of power relations. Indeed, talk of safety and 'feeling
safe' was closely linked with stable and non-hierarchical peer group dynamics.
Over half of those who discussed their experiences of hierarchical peer group
dynamics framed their accounts within discourses of 'bullying'. And despite the
wide-ranging definitions of 'bullying' (outlined briefly in the opening section),
'bullying' was often referred to in this context as an abuse of power, as the
following quotes go some way to illustrate:

YOUNG PERSON: Gavin, he's the eldest, 'cos he's not here everything seems to
go so easy, but when Gavin's here, because he's the eldest he thinks he rules
the place and he bullies everyone. He's always hitting me.

(male, age 13)

INTERVIEWER: I know that one of the boys was causing grief … could you tell
me about that?

YOUNG PERSON: He was just bullying everyone ... the younger ones as well ... the little ones you know like Neil and that ... all the little ones he was bullying and shit ... beating them up, taking their money, scaring them ... stuff like that ....

INTERVIEWER: What sort of things did he do to scare them?

YOUNG PERSON: Real weird stuff ... like mind stuff you know telling them they couldn't do this or that or he'd beat the shit out of them that night ... like not to eat or say he's going to get one of them so they'd be scared all day not knowing when he would do it ... he just liked making people scared of him, made him feel big I suppose doing that sort of shit.

INTERVIEWER: Do you know how long he was doing this?

YOUNG PERSON: About three months, quite a long time he did it for, 'cos they daren't do anything 'cos ... I think a lad before him had done the same to this kid and then he was chucked out and he started on the others thinking he was the boss.

(male, age 15)

Only one young person (female) perceived hierarchical peer group dynamics and the bullying tactics used to maintain their structure as a natural phenomenon. Overall, young people's reports of hierarchical peer group dynamics was perceived as something that had to be endured on entry into the home. While inevitable, they were viewed as a wholly negative part of residential experience, with nearly all young people perceiving such dynamics as fundamentally harmful and abusive. Indeed, their accounts were a long way off interpreting it as a 'beneficial' experience or perceiving it as a 'natural' part of peer relations or 'growing up'. However, there were differences in terms of the ways in which peer group hierarchies were maintained, particularly in relation to the levels of bullying and types of violence deployed. For example, in one home, one young man manipulated and tyrannised the whole peer group (younger boys and girls) with physical, psychological, verbal and sexual violence over a period of three months (unbeknown to staff). In another home, two girls ruthlessly and in an intimidatory manner placed all but one girl into subservient positions via threats and psychological coercion. A third home saw a group of girls subordinating a new resident by vandalising her belongings and threatening similar action if she resisted conforming to their rules. All three examples reveal, either through a single dominant individual or through combining dominant forces, how the peer group is manipulated and controlled via oppression and subordination, whether it is through physical force or intimidation.

It was only when staff were aware of the physical forms of violence that they routinely intervened, often stating that the 'dynamics' had 'got out of hand'. However, this conceptualisation seemed to allow the perceived normality of the peer group hierarchy to remain unchallenged while enabling workers to identify that individual young people only occasionally used unacceptable means to either challenge or reinforce their superior positions within the peer culture.

More worryingly, several residential workers were complicit in reinforcing some young people's position as 'top dog', and thus the hierarchical structure, by informally employing some young people to act as mediators for the views and actions of other residents, thus providing a valuable resource for controlling the peer group. One manager even went so far as to delegate supervisory responsibilities if a staff member was absent at particular moments in the day!

YOUNG PERSON: I help the staff out a lot … sometimes if like someone's kicking off and like if I think I can like calm them down I do, and like staff are giving it like the, 'Well done' and that.

(male, age 15)

Furthermore, the almost instinctive reflex to respond only to physical violence, which was routinely and almost exclusively used by boys and young men, allowed more covert forms of violence (such as intimidation, threats and verbal attacks), used by both male and female residents (although in different ways), to go undetected, as the next section on the masculinisation of violence illustrates.

The masculinisation of violence

YOUNG PERSON: People just fight … because they want to try and look big, and impress everyone.

(male, age 15)

Between a rock and a hard place: projecting hardened masculinities

Violence has long been recognised as a 'reference point for the production of boys and men' (Hearn 1998: 7) and been associated with 'normalised' forms of masculinity. Yet while such behaviour is universally condemned, it is simultaneously legitimised through essentialistic discourses of 'boys will be boys' (Miedzian 1992). The residential setting was no exception, and the gender regimes operating inside the homes echoed much of the literature on other institutions, such as school and prisons (see Mills 2001). It also reflected the masculinisation of violence within wider society (Connell 1995) and studies that suggest that the majority of violent behaviour and incidents are perpetrated by boys and young men (Home Office 2000). Indeed, some boys talked about the need to project a tough and inflated masculinity, which in many cases had the effect of instilling fear in other boys:

INTERVIEWER: What was it like when you first came here, what was your first day like?
YOUNG PERSON: It was scary, not like I was scared because like there's so many big boys and they're just big, puffed up, all hard and I was very worried.

(male, age 14)

Indeed, the majority of violence engaged in by boys, both as 'receivers' and 'doers', was physical violence, and much of the physical violence was normalised and naturalised by both boys and staff as just 'what boys do', as one young person commented:

YOUNG PERSON: People will fight, always, no matter what ... fighting is just a normal thing for me.

(male, age 13)

For staff, the most commonly presented scenario of male-on-male violence often centred upon a specific argument, which resulted in a 'fight' and which was quickly forgotten by both parties. In this context, boys' violence was presented as an unsophisticated although 'honest' method of conflict resolution. Thus, in these cases, 'low-impact' physical violence was validated by workers within the construction of certain forms of masculinity and, as such, viewed as a developmental practice employed by young men in their progression to adulthood:

STAFF: That's what normal kids do. They get into little arguments. I think so anyway and I think they need their space to do that sort of thing. That's part of growing up in a way, isn't it? They have to learn by their mistakes. If they're going to call somebody bigger than them a name then the chances are they're going to get hit .... If they stand in a club when they're 18 and they're having a drink and they call somebody a stupid **** you're going to get a whack across the face. So they have to learn by their mistakes.

(male, deputy manager)

Often, boys' deployment of physical violence was framed in terms of their expression and projection of a particular hegemonic (i.e. culturally exalted) masculinity, or as one staff member put it, 'flexing their proverbial muscles'. To this end, many incidents were conducted in full view and knowledge of staff. Awareness that workers would intervene to prevent any serious physical harm provided a context, for male residents, in which there could be a 'safe' instigation of violence. In these situations, boys could position themselves as 'aggressors', thereby confirming their masculinity to others:

YOUNG PERSON: Most kids want the staff to be there because when they kick off they are going to get restrained and it makes them look like they've just beaten him up. So I could walk to a really big kid, go and hit him and as soon as they've restrained me he can't touch me, so it will make me look like I've just, can you see what I mean?

(male, age 14)

Although workers did consistently intervene in all (known) cases of severe physical violence, such incidents were still framed within discourses of what we have termed *uncontrollable masculinities*, with physical violence as the sole (and accepted) property of hegemonic masculinity. Such essentialist notions, as Mills states, serve to 'take the responsibility for violence away from the perpetrator. They imply that illegitimate male violence in a "civilised" society cannot be helped' (2001: 57). However, a minority of workers provided a more complex analysis, equating hegemonic masculinities with the 'deprived' environments from which most of the young men came. These workers argued that, due to the limited opportunities available to these boys, the only way they could reinforce their own reputations and feelings of self-worth was through the use of violence and intimidation. Gilmore, for example, suggests that 'the harsher the environment and the scarcer the resources, the more manhood is stressed as inspiration and goal' (1990: 224). This echoes other studies, which stress that physical toughness and violence became major vehicles for the assertion of masculinity in the absence of any other available avenues (Newburn and Stanko 1994). However, such views continue to suggest that male violence is somehow inevitable and thus unchangeable. To this end, the justification narratives framed within a language of male rights ('my right to fight') continued to supersede all notions of personal responsibility and were, by and large, left unchallenged.

An additional and often unforeseen (by staff) relationship in the pressure to project a tough masculinity involved an uneasy alliance between *being hard*, which denied many boys the option of seeking emotional support from their peers and staff, and *doing hard*, which involved the justification of physical retaliation to anything that they perceived as threatening their masculinity. The most severe example of the former involved physical retaliation to verbal attacks that were aimed at their mothers or sisters, commonly termed 'mother cussing'. Many boys felt that they had to take it upon themselves to deal with their experiences of violence, often described through a language of planned revenge and protection from further attacks:

YOUNG PERSON: Revenge is best served cold. What it means, is that you got to plan it before you do it, because it's like, if you just go into it wobbly and you don't know what you're doing and you just crack him one and hurt him really badly, you'll be happy but then you could get nicked – but what I'm trying to say is right, if you plan it easily enough like, to just run up to him and crack him in the face and run off and go out or something, so staff think oh no he's just messing around again.

(male, age 14)

INTERVIEWER: Have you ever thought about not getting back at him?
YOUNG PERSON: If you don't get back at him, he does it again and he does it again and what someone needs to do is box him across the head ... I'd like to break his nose so he feels it, so every time he looks in the mirror he remembers me and his face all cut up and he will remember who did this to him.

(male, age 15)

Implicit in these narratives was the notion that boys would do anything to avoid being positioned as the *victim*, which suggested weakness or vulnerability:

YOUNG PERSON: Say like some, like new kid came here and like one of the kids asked him to do something and he said no for some reason then he'd get bullied they'd [other residents] say he's quite weak or something. Then he doesn't stand a chance.

(male, age 14)

YOUNG PERSON: There are some kids that do get targeted ... but they will try and snap back just to look as though they won't take any crap.

(male, age 16)

Thus, where girls sought *emotional support* (disclosing and sharing experiences with their peers), the majority of boys sought what could be described as *functional support*, often in the form of physical violence. For them, it seemed to be the only acceptable response, possibly because of the perceived association of emotion with effeminacy and emotional release with emasculation (Frydenberg 1997). A consequence of boys' non-disclosure was that many serious incidents of physical violence and intimidation went undetected. To this end, many boys' experiences of violence, normalised and embedded within wider hegemonic notions of masculinity, continually positioned them 'between a rock and hard place'. Moreover, staff's preoccupation with the visible, physical or masculinist notion of violence led to an ignorance around the impact of more covert forms of violence. For example, as the following quote illustrates, both male and female residents perceived systematic verbal attacks and intimidation as having a longer-lasting and more damaging effect on their social lives and future welfare than isolated physical forms of violence:

YOUNG PERSON: Verbal hurts more then hitting ... with hitting it's like, oh, a punch, the pain is over in a few seconds, but when you get verbal it stays in you for quite a few days.

(male, age 15)

Violence legitimized as social justice

Most young people, when subjected to any form of violence, advocated retaliation. In fact, when young people discussed their involvement in violent activity they almost always framed their accounts within discourses of justification (e.g. 'I never hit him before he hits me'). Indeed, with the majority of young people providing detailed rationales for their actions, it made more complex the usual binary identification of recipient and perpetrator, with over half of young people, when recounting their involvement in 'violent' scenarios, positioning themselves as both perpetrator and recipient. Only a tiny minority framed their involvement in different forms of violence in terms of internal causes, such as 'loss of temper', thus often absolving themselves from the consequences of their actions. Only a few were able to avoid situations of conflict by walking away, ignoring taunts or jibes or getting staff to intervene. For the majority of young residents, 'fighting back' was perceived as a form of social justice. Justification narratives were less about defence and more about retaliation, framed within discourses of revenge, prevention, protection of honour/status within the home or peer group, and other narratives that positioned recipients as deserving retaliation. In the words of one young person: 'you can't just sit there and take it'. Many young people emphasised the importance of gaining 'respect' through their willingness to employ violence in conflict situations (Batchelor *et al.* 2001) and thus maintain a 'credible threat of violence', to borrow a phrase from Daly and Wilson (1988: 128), in their day-to-day lives. This was particularly the case for homes in which there were high levels of violence. However, and not unexpectedly, there were significant gender differences with each justification narrative. For boys, retaliation was not simply about revenge or protecting oneself; it also seemed to be one of the predominant routes to constructing, if not 'proving' (and improving), their 'hard' macho exteriors:

YOUNG PERSON: He tried picking on everyone.

INTERVIEWER: And why do you think he was doing that?

YOUNG PERSON: Because he thought he was like trying to test us all out ... like a hard man, he wanted to be the boss so he had to fight us all, but I'm not going to put up with all that so I kicked the shit out of him and he didn't come near me after that.

(male, age 15)

Girls, on the other hand, more often explained the use of violence more pragmatically, justifying their behaviour in terms of survival, particularly in relation to preventing the onset or continuance of bullying, as the following quotes highlight:

INTERVIEWER: So when you say you were like picked on and stuff, did you ever do that yourself, to other young people?

YOUNG PERSON: When I first moved I did, because I wanted to get out of the, I didn't want it to be me, so I thought well if I do it then they won't bully me, so I did it, but not for long and not bad things either .... I wouldn't be the one putting stuff in the hair and that, it'd be the rest of the group, but I would be there, if you know what I mean.

(female, age 13)

INTERVIEWER: Why do you think some young people get bullied more than others?

YOUNG PERSON: 'Cos when you live in a kids' home you've got to stick up for yourself, the ones who don't are the ones that get picked on, because they think oh 'huh, what are they gonna do', so you've got to learn to stick up for yourself or you're not going to live are you.

(female, age 14)

The consensus that violence begets violence seemed to be embedded within the social codes of these young people's worlds. Those who viewed retaliatory violence as a legitimate response invested strongly in their own sense of what we have termed *reciprocal justice*. Indeed, for many young people (particularly those living in homes in which there was a higher degree of violence) to retaliate rarely produced moral discord (provided that there was a fairly equal distribution of power relations between perpetrator and recipient). However, while such views were, in the main, rarely shared or condoned by residential workers, there were occasions when violence, as a form of reciprocal justice, was supported both covertly and overtly by staff.

Close analysis of the cases in which staff chose not to intervene or delayed intervention in recognisable acts of violence, categorised in our study as *professional non-intervention*, revealed an emerging and consistent theme in relation to the recipient or 'victim' of the attack. Delaying or choosing not to intervene was generally framed within young people's accounts of *deserving victims*. The majority of these violent attacks occurred in the context of retorts to deliberate and repeated provocation by the 'victim', often over a prolonged period of time. In a number of instances, young people stated that individual staff had forewarned the *provocateur* that if they persisted in their aggravating behaviour they would cease to intervene in any subsequent reprisals. In the majority of these cases, the sanctions that would have routinely accompanied the use of physical violence were reduced, as the following account reveals:

YOUNG PERSON: There was about three or four of us that did [physically hurt her]. But staff couldn't do anything, 'cos they had warned her that if we did hit her they're going to turn their backs, 'cos she drove us to that. And it took us like three weeks before we lost our patience completely and staff just couldn't say anything to us and they told her mum as well, that if we were to hit her there is nothing they can do, the police won't be called.

(female, age 16)

In these specific contexts, the non/delayed intervention was generally viewed by the majority of the young people concerned as reasonable so long as the violence in *their* estimation was acceptable. Obviously, this may reflect the fact that many of these accounts were from the perpetrators of the physical retort, although a third of accounts came from witnesses who shared this view. Overall, the young people felt that the actions of these staff reflected their ability to view the situation from their perspective and to recognise the unreasonable demands that such antagonistic behaviour placed on their self-control mechanisms. Indeed, it appeared that non-interventionist practices most commonly occurred when a clear consensus emerged that identified a young person as a persistent *provocateur*. Consequently, this fostered a climate of victim culpability within the home and was indeed another route through which violence became not only normalised but also tolerated and condoned.

Conclusion

This study is rooted in a critical field of research where, as Christensen and James (2000: 2) reveal, 'researchers are increasingly having to address the theoretical and policy implications of treating children as social actors in their own right in contexts, where, traditionally, they have been denied those rights of participation and their voices have remained unheard'. Indeed, it could be argued that the voices of young people in this field are doubly marginalised, both in their relatively powerless position as children *per se* and as children 'looked after' by the state, in which there is a long history of silence in the suppression of children's voices and experiences. Consequently, grounding our understanding of the nature of violence from young people's *own* experiences and perspectives is paramount: first, in terms of reflecting and assessing the diversity and impact of different forms of violence (enabled by our appropriation of Kelly's 'continuum of harm' framework); and, second, by prioritising the 'children's standpoint' (Alanen 1994) and intersecting children's and staff's accounts, the processes of the normalisation of peer violence can be unpacked and adult-centred conceptualisations of what counts as 'violence' can be challenged. This approach enabled us to explore which forms of behaviour are discursively constructed as 'normal' or 'natural' (rather than harmful or abusive), and which get overlooked, tolerated or at worst accepted.

While by no means exhausting the ways in which different forms of peer violence are normalised, this chapter has attempted to identify the process and consequences of key normalisation practices present within the residential setting. First, we argued that paying close attention to, and situating our understandings of peer violence within, children's cultures was a fundamental step in the process of deconstructing the processes of normalisation. Central to this was the need to recognise the localised culture of violence and conceptualise violence as contextually contingent. Second, the impact of violence was embedded within, and was almost always positioned by young people in terms of, the wider power dynamics within their peer group cultures. The maintenance of the hierarchical peer group structure, via subordination and oppression, was one of the key ways in which violence in the residential setting was mediated. However, such intimidation and coercion were presented as synonymous with, and as an inevitable feature of, children's cultures and the progression towards adulthood. Such accounts were in stark contrast to young people's portrayal of 'pecking orders' and 'top dog' networks as 'bullying' and an abuse of power. Third, much of the physical violence, bullying and intimidation between boys was normalised and justified as just 'boys being boys', where the pressure to project hardened masculinities denied many boys the option of seeking emotional support. Indeed, although not explored in this chapter, staff's preoccupation with the masculinisation of violence led them to underestimate girls' involvement in physical violence and lessened its significance by referring to 'cat fights' and 'bitching matches'. Moreover, the final section expanded the consequence of justification narratives and the legitimation of violence as a form of social justice via a discourse of retaliation, reciprocal rights and deserving victim status, which generated a climate, shared by both young people and staff, of victim culpability.

In summary, this chapter extends other research findings, arguing that adult perceptions of violence between young people are inadequate. Not only does the concept of violence need to be more inclusive, but our study also strongly suggests that there can be no one single definition of violence. Rather, it needs to be situated within a continuum that recognises its multifaceted and contested status if we are to take seriously the views and experiences of children and young people. Debates surrounding how violence is defined and theorised are not simply stimulating intellectual exercises; they hold wide-ranging and far-reaching practical implications. Unravelling the ways in which particular forms of violence are normalised, and thus what counts as violence, affects whether that behaviour is brought to the attention of someone authorised to intervene and/or assist the 'victim' or assailant (Kelly 1988). Our research stresses the need to move beyond traditional, adult-centred thinking, which undermines much of what children and young people experience as harmful and abusive. Such understandings need to be situated within children's evaluations of impact and a more critical and connected relationship with their peer group cultures and social (particularly gender) identities more widely. If children's experiences and relative positions within society are taken into account, then established adult wisdom surrounding violence needs to be reconsidered. Only then can policy formulations and professional responses and interventions be appropriate and effective.

Note

1 Sinclair and Gibbs' study reported that 44 percent of the 223 residents interviewed had been bullied during their stay, and children's (81 percent) main anxiety regarding residential living related to 'getting on with their peers'.

References

Alanen, L. (1994) 'Gender and generation: feminism and the child in question', in J. Qvortrup *et al.* (eds) *Childhood Matters: Social Theory, Practice and Politics*. Aldershot: Avebury.

Alldred, P. (1998) 'Ethnography and discourse analysis: dilemmas in representing the voices of children', in J. Ribbens and R. Edwards (eds) *Public Knowledge and Private Lives*. London: Sage.

Barter, C. (1997) 'Who's to blame: conceptualising institutional abuse by children', *Early Child Development and Care* 133: 101–4.

Barter, C. and Renold, E. (2000) '"I wanna tell you a story": exploring the application of vignettes in qualitative research with children and young people', *International Journal of Social Research Methodology* 3(4): 307–23.

Barter, C. and Renold, E. (2002) 'Dilemmas in control: methodological implications and reflections of foregrounding children's perspectives on violence', in R. Lee and E. Stanko (eds) *Researching Violence: Essays on Methodology and Measurement*. London: Routledge.

Batchelor, S.A., Burman, M.J. and Brown, J.A. (2001) 'Researching girls and violence. Facing the dilemmas of fieldwork', *British Journal of Criminology* 41(3): 443–59.

Brannen, J. and O'Brien, M. (1996) *Children in Families: Research and Policy*. London: Falmer Press.

Cawson, P., Wattam, C., Brooker, S. and Kelly G. (2000) *Child Maltreatment in the United Kingdom: A Study of the Prevalence of Child Abuse and Neglect*. London: NSPCC.

Christensen, P. and James, A. (2000) *Research with Children*. London: Falmer Press.

Connell, R.W. (1995) *Masculinities*. Cambridge: Polity Press.

Curtin, D. and Litke, R. (eds) (1994) *Institutional Violence*. Amsterdam, Atlanta: Rodopi.

Daly, M. and Wilson, M. (1988) *Homicide*. New York: Aldine de Gruyter.

Frydenberg, E. (1997) *Adolescent Coping: Theoretical and Research Perspectives*. London: Routledge.

Gabe, J., Denney, D., Lee, R.M., Elston, M.A. and O'Beirne, M. (2001) 'Researching professional discourses on violence', *British Journal of Criminology* 41(3): 460–71.

Geertz, C. (1973) *The Interpretation of Cultures*. New York: Basic Books.

Gilmore, D. (1990) *Manhood in the Making: Cultural Concepts of Masculinity*. London: Yale University Press.

Hanmer, J. and Saunders, S. (1984) *Well-founded Fear: A Community Study of Violence to Women*. London: Hutchinson, in association with the Explorations in Feminism Collective, affiliated to the Women's Research and Resources Centre.

Hearn, J. (1998) *The Violences of Men*. London: Sage.

Home Office (2000) *Criminal Statistics England and Wales 1999*. London: Home Office.

James, A., Jenks, C. and Prout, A. (1998) *Theorising Childhood*. Cambridge: Polity Press.

James, A. and Prout, A. (eds) (1998) *Constructing and Reconstructing Childhood* (2nd edition). London: Falmer Press.

Kelly, L. (1987) 'The continuum of sexual violence', in J. Hammer and M. Maynard (eds) *Women, Violence and Social Control*. London: Macmillan.

Kelly, L. (1988) *Surviving Sexual Violence*. Cambridge: Polity Press.

Levy, A. and Kahan, B. (1991) *The Pindown Experience and the Protection of Children*. Stafford: Staffordshire County Council.

Maynard, M. (1993) 'Violence towards women', in D. Richardson and V. Robinson (eds) *Introducing Women's Studies: Feminist Theory and Practice*. London: Macmillan.

McNeil, S. (1987) 'Flashing: its effects on women', in J. Hammer and M. Maynard (eds) *Women, Violence and Social Control*. London: Macmillan.

Miedzian, M. (1992) *Boys Will Be Boys: Breaking the Link between Masculinity and Violence*. London: Virago.

Mills, M. (2001) *Challenging Violence in Schools: An Issue of Masculinities*. Buckingham: Open University Press.

Morris, S. and Wheatley, H. (1994) *Time to Listen: The Experience of Young People in Foster and Residential Care*. London: ChildLine.

Newburn, T. and Stanko, E.A. (1994) *Just Boys Doing Business? Men, Masculinities and Crime*. London: Routledge.

Parkin, W. and Green, L. (1997) 'Cultures of abuse within residential child care', *Early Child Development and Care* 133: 73–86.

Richardson, D. and May, H. (1999) 'Deserving victims? Sexual status and the social construction of violence', *Sociological Review* 47(2): 308–31.

Sinclair, I. and Gibbs, I. (1998) *Children's Homes: A Study of Diversity.* Chichester: John Wiley & Sons.

Stanko, B. (1990) *Intimate Intrusions: Women's Experience of Male Violence.* London, Boston: Unwin Hyman.

Stanko, E. (1995) 'Women, crime and fear', *The Annals* 53: 46–58.

Utting, W. (1997) *People Like Us. The Report of the Review of the Safeguards for Children Living Away from Home.* London: HMSO.

Wade, J. and Biehal, N., with Stein, M. and Clayden, J. (1998) *Going Missing.* Chichester: John Wiley & Sons.

Waterhouse, R. (2000) *Lost in Care: Report of the Tribunal of Inquiry into the Abuse of Children in Care in the former County Council areas of Gwynedd and Clwyd since 1994.* London: HMSO.

Wise, S. and Stanley, L. (1987) *Georgie Porgie: Sexual Harassment in Everyday Life.* London: Pandora.

6 Understanding racist violence

Larry Ray, David Smith and Liz Wastell

In this chapter, we discuss the findings of research into the perpetrators of racist violence in the Greater Manchester conurbation.[1] Our main focus is on the offenders' own accounts of themselves and their offences as obtained through interviews, and our interpretation of what they said. These accounts are situated in the context of the local cultures of violence, grievance and racism that characterise the neighbourhoods where offenders tend to live. We will suggest that much racist violence can be understood as a product of the shame, resentment and hostility experienced by young white men who are disadvantaged and marginalised economically and culturally, and thus deprived of the material basis for enacting a traditional conception of working-class masculinity. Such emotions readily lead to violence only in the case of young men (and occasionally young women) for whom resorting to violence is a common approach to settling arguments and conflicts. Tendencies to this behaviour are widely shared among white residents of disadvantaged neighbourhoods on the fringes of metropolitan Manchester. First, however, we want to set the research findings in two contexts: that of racist violence as a public issue in England and Wales and in Greater Manchester, and that of the Manchester conurbation's economic and cultural development.

Racist violence as a public issue

Bowling cites a range of sources to show that 'violent racism' has a long history in Britain and that therefore 'violent racism has always been on the political agenda' for ethnic minorities in Britain (1998: 57). But it was not until 1978 that the Metropolitan Police began to record crimes and other events as 'racial incidents', and not until 1982 that such incidents were defined in a way that stressed the racial motivation of the perpetrator, as alleged by anyone involved or as interpreted by the investigating officer. The redefinition followed the publication of the first government report on racist violence (Home Office 1981), which signalled the appearance of the problem on a formal policy agenda, and the first recognition by government that the rate of racially motivated victimisation was much higher among ethnic minorities than among the white population. The first Islington Crime Survey (Jones *et al.* 1986) specifically sought to remedy the omission of racist attacks and harassment from the first British Crime Survey (BCS), and the 1988 BCS included for the first time a 'booster' sample in an attempt to measure victimisation risks among ethnic minorities, including risks of racially motivated crime (Mayhew *et al.* 1989). Subsequent reports using BCS data concentrated on racially motivated crime (Aye Maung and Mirrlees-Black 1994) and ethnic minorities' experiences of victimisation and racial harassment (Fitzgerald and Hale 1996). The most recent report, based on data from 2000, found, like previous surveys, that members of ethnic minorities were more at risk of all crimes than the overall white population (explained largely as a result of their concentration in the poorer parts of large cities, where victimisation risks tend to be highest for all groups) and more likely to report victimisation they believed to be racially motivated: the estimated rates were 0.3 percent for whites, 2.2 percent for black groups, 3.6 percent for Indians and 4.2 percent for Bangladeshis and Pakistanis (Aust *et al.* 2001).

The 2000 BCS reports lower estimated rates of racially motivated offences (about half of them actual attacks) than in the 1995 survey (280,000 against 390,000), in line with its findings of reduced rates of all forms of victimisation. This picture of a falling rate of racially motivated crime is dramatically at odds with the data on racially motivated incidents recorded by the police during the same period. The police figures (Home Office 2000) show a rise of 75 percent nationally between 1998 and 1999, and a further doubling to about 48,000 in 2000, half of those in the Metropolitan Police area. In Greater Manchester, the figures followed a similar pattern, rising from 624 in 1997–98 to 1,224 in 1998–99 and 2,341 in 1999–2000 (Greater Manchester Police 2000). Aust *et al.* (2001) and the Section 95 Home Office report for 2000[2] concur that the discrepancy between the BCS and police figures can be explained by greater willingness on the part of victims to report incidents to the police and better recording by the police of incidents reported to them.

Two particular developments provide an immediate explanation of the increase in recording of racial incidents. One is the publication in early 1999 of the Macpherson Report on the killing of Stephen Lawrence in 1993, the police reaction to it, and the subsequent investigation of the case. Macpherson (1999) indicted the Metropolitan Police for 'institutional racism' and proposed a new definition of racially motivated incidents as 'any incident which is perceived to be racist by the victim or any other person' (Macpherson Report, Chapter 47, para. 1). The second is the introduction of the category of 'racially aggravated' offences in the Crime and Disorder Act of 1998. The Home Office (2000) reports that in the first full year of recording for this new type of offence, 21,750 offences were recorded, half of which were offences of harassment, including threatening and disorderly behaviour; 3,815 defendants were prosecuted, 1,073 convicted at magistrates' courts, and 990 committed for trial at Crown Courts. In comparing these figures with the 47,810 recorded racial incidents, it is clear that the attrition rate between recording, prosecution and conviction is high (and the BCS suggests that under 20 percent of incidents are even recorded).

Neither the Macpherson Report nor the provisions of the 1998 Act appeared out of a vacuum. The family of Stephen Lawrence had campaigned long and effectively for an inquiry, against the background of efforts by groups repre-senting the interests of ethnic minorities and by some local authorities, especially in London, to bring the issue of racist violence and the police response to it onto the policy agenda (Bowling 1998). The establishment of the Macpherson Inquiry can thus be regarded as one outcome of a successful social movement for the recognition of the reality of racist victimisation and of the claims of victims to adequate protection. The category of racially aggravated offences can also be seen as an achievement for social movement politics, organised around the themes of identity and oppression, in making what was previously a private problem into a public issue. The provisions of the Crime and Disorder Act represent the clearest recognition in British law of the concept of 'hate crime', which originated in the USA in the early 1980s. Conviction for a racially aggravated offence is meant to lead to a more severe sentence than for the same offence without a racial motive, on the grounds that to be assaulted or otherwise offended against because of one's identity as a member of a particular social or ethnic group is more frightening and emotion-ally disturbing than to be selected as a victim for other reasons. The BCS provides some empirical support for this argument (Aust *et al.* 2001). 'Hate crimes', especially racist violence, thus tend to be conceived as the acts of consciously motivated 'haters' who are strangers to their victims (as in the Stephen Lawrence case) and who target the victim as a member of the hated social group. As we will see, this image of racist violence is problematic in the light of our research.

We noted that the number of racist incidents recorded by the police in Greater Manchester increased by a similar proportion to the national figures between 1998 and 2000. However, there is a peculiarity in the Greater Manchester figures, which shows how the definition of 'hate crime' can be shaped by local influences – the media, the presence of political interest groups, and the construction of the problem by authoritative figures – in this case the local police divisional commander. The police division covering Oldham has, since 1994, had a pattern of recorded racist incidents different from any other division in Greater Manchester (Greater Manchester Police 2000); not only is the number of incidents disproportionately high for Oldham's population, but the number of incidents with white victims consistently far exceeds that of any other division. The problem of racist violence in Oldham has been defined as essentially a problem of 'hate crimes' by young South Asian men against vulner-able whites. We have discussed the processes involved in constructing this definition, and its effects, elsewhere (Ray and Smith 2001); here, we want only to note that racist violence as a public issue can be constituted by particular local pressures that have developed over time, and in which police perceptions and practices, media interpretations and political interventions are arguably more important than the material facts of demography, economy and social interaction.

Culture, economy and community in the post-industrial city

Haslam (1999: 254), discussing the 'pop cult' status of Manchester in the context of its development as the first major city of the Industrial Revolution ('Cottonopolis'), notes that it 'is becoming a must-see city' for young people, with a global identity and status associated with iconic music and its possession of Europe's richest football club. He also notes, as had Engels in his account of the condition of the English working class in 1844, that in modern Manchester there are 'two nations, still grim areas of real, deep poverty a world away from glittering sites of civic splendour' (*ibid.*: 270). Taylor *et al.* (1996), in their comparison of Manchester with Sheffield as 'post-Fordist' cities, recognise Manchester's cultural capital and its aspirations as a headquarters city, with, for example, its own stock exchange, while being sceptical about the likelihood of their achievement. They cite an observer who wrote in 1840 that there was 'no town in the world' where the gap between rich and poor was as wide as in Manchester, and they suggest that in the mid-1990s the same claim could reasonably have been made (*ibid.*: 171). In 1993, just under 300,000 people were employed in manufacturing in the Manchester conurbation, compared with almost 740,000 in a broadly defined service sector, 38 percent of whom were in finance, insurance and real estate occupations (*ibid.*: 303). According to Taylor *et al.* (*ibid.*: 61), the best estimate is that at least 207,000 manufacturing jobs disappeared in Greater Manchester between 1972 and 1984, most of the loss taking place in the recession after 1978.

Racist violence should be understood in the context of the profound economic and social changes that Manchester, in common with other cities and towns that grew with the Industrial Revolution, has undergone with the decline of Fordist systems of production and consumption. Modes of working-class life, which had come to be seen as natural and permanent, became mere memories and dreams within less than a generation. The new labour market provides opportunities for skilled professionals and entrepreneurs in the financial, commercial and cultural spheres, but it denies opportunities to the unskilled and disadvantaged: it creates a local economy that sharply divides insiders from outsiders, the skilled and competent from the largely unskilled, who lack the resources to adapt to a post-industrial labour market. Communities once defined by the shared experience of manufacturing industry lose coherence and stability along with affluence; long-cherished cultural expectations of working-class masculinity become unrealisable with the erosion of their material basis (a process powerfully described in relation to the original skinheads of East London by Cohen (1972)), and the inherited meanings of territory and neighbourhood become fractured and uncertain.

Both the social fragmentation consequent upon economic restructuring and the relative success of Manchester in establishing a global cultural identity are important here. For those with the economic means and the cultural capital, Manchester is a city of rich possibilities, with an active music scene, a legendary sporting heritage and an expanding leisure and hospitality industry. For those without such means, it is a city of exclusion and deprivation, and among the excluded new forms of defence are mobilised to maintain threatened individual and collective identities. Symbolic boundaries, defining access to housing, jobs, transport and cultural goods, are imposed on mental maps of the city drawn on the basis of territories and communities of belonging that have ceased to have a real demographic or social basis. Those excluded from Manchester's global, cosmopolitan culture come consciously to reject and despise it, retreating instead into 'fundamentalisms' (Giddens 1994) of territory, class, gender and ethnicity. The mental maps become racialised, as ownership and belonging are reasserted against the threat of change and difference, and a sense of resentment and grievance acquires a specifically racist content. This, in summary, is our interpretation of the economic, social and cultural processes underlying the acts of racist violence that formed the core of our research; we hope that the findings that follow and our discussion of them will make the interpretation plausible.

Identifying the perpetrators of racist violence

It was inherent in our conception of this research project that we should contact perpetrators of relatively serious acts of racially motivated violence. Previous work, such as that of Hewitt (1996) and Sibbitt (1997), had tended to concentrate on acts of harassment, name calling and bullying – acts that can undoubtedly erode the quality of life of their victims to the point of producing routine misery but in many cases do not amount to crime and thus do not attract the attention of the police. We were encouraged by the work of Bowling (1998),[3] who in his conclusion called for a shift of focus in research from the victims to the perpetrators of violent racism. He wrote that 'The perpetrator is unknown', so that it was impossible to understand or interpret his or her behaviour: 'we have no idea about perpetrators' backgrounds, their relationship to politically organized or disorganized racism or the relationship between instrumental and expressive elements of their motives' (*ibid.*: 304–5). The work of Hewitt and Sibbitt is interesting and suggestive about the processes of transmission of racist ideas and assumptions through peer groups and family generations, respectively, but it says little about the issues that interested Bowling and us.[4] In Sibbitt's case, this was not for want of trying: she reported her frustrations in trying to contact racist offenders through one probation service where, she suggested, 'the very culture ... appeared to militate against offenders ever admitting this aspect of their offending' (1997: 93–4). The culture was one of 'political correctness', in which offenders were repeatedly reminded of the unacceptability of racist language and attitudes; Sibbitt also suggested that probation officers often had a stereotypical image of violent racists, which made them nervous about working with them.

Our rationale for approaching the probation service in Greater Manchester was that the service ought to have some contact, even if fleeting (as in the preparation of a pre-sentence report for court), with all adult perpetrators of racist violence serious enough to have led to prosecution and to a guilty plea or a conviction, and thus be able to facilitate access to the subjects who were the focus of our research. However, Sibbitt's experience was a reminder that – even with the full support of the service's senior management, which we had – the process of gaining access to research subjects might be less than straightforward (see Ray *et al.* 2002). Quite apart from organisational and professional obstacles to access, there are inherent problems of defining racist violence and interpreting the racist content of criminal acts. Our research began before the implementation of the 1998 Crime and Disorder Act, which introduced the concept, new in criminal law, of the racial aggravation of offences. If a substantial number of offences had been recorded as racially aggravated, the initial identification of prospective research subjects would have been easier. But the prosecution of racially aggravated offences is itself the product of a complex process of definition and assessment of the evidence on the part of the police and the Crown Prosecution Service. As we will see, the presence of racist motivation is rarely clear-cut. Rather, it is inherently disputable and contestable, and the definitions of criminal justice practitioners, social researchers and offenders themselves often conflict.

We identified and collected data on sixty-four offenders who had committed acts of violence in the recent past in which some racist motive was judged to have been present. The basis for this judgement was the use of racist language in the context of the offence, or indications in the prosecution case that racial difference was relevant to understanding the offence. This number was lower than we had originally envisaged, the shortfall reflecting definitional difficulties, inconsistent recording practices and, possibly, a smaller volume of known racist violence than we had expected. In their demographic characteristics, the sample resembled other samples of people in contact with probation services (e.g. Mair and May 1997; Stewart and Stewart 1993). This was most clear in the age and gender composition of the sample: the majority consisted of young men (only five of the sixty-four were female), and their average age was 24, forty-eight being under the age of 25 when identified as research subjects. We estimated that half were currently unemployed (reliable information on employment status was not available for all the sample), and those who were in work tended to have jobs that were poorly paid, casual or insecure, and low-skilled. Forty-one (64 percent) had, according to their probation records, left school with no qualifications, and none had passed more than basic school examinations. Over half had in the past committed offences that were similar to those that triggered our interest, often involving victimisation of the same premises and people. However, they were non-specialist offenders: 64 percent reported having or were known to have convictions for other offences, mainly involving theft, assault and drugs, and this figure is almost certainly an underestimate. Very few – perhaps three – gave any political articulation or justification of their violence, and only slightly more showed any knowledge (beyond awareness of their existence) of, or interest in, far Right and racist organisations.

We believe that if we had gone to probation service sources in search of a sample of offenders convicted of violent offences without any discernible racist motive, we would have found a very similar demographic pattern. That is, contrary to some of our speculations before beginning the research, there was virtually no evidence of specialisation in racist violence. If racist violence is driven by overt political motives, or even by an intent to intimidate ethnic minority people with a view, for example, to forcing them to move house, one would expect to find people convicted of offences of racist violence and of nothing else. In fact, we found very little evidence of any violence that was, in Bowling's (1998) terms, instrumental rather than expressive. Here 'instrumental' is taken to entail the presence of some 'rational' calculation that violence is a means of achieving ends other than those that arise from the immediate situation of conflict. Even one of the few interviewees who was able to articulate a politicised racist ideology, and who claimed to be well connected in the leading circles of a fascist organisation, was plainly involved in dealing illegal drugs. So the racist violence of offenders in the sample was in virtually all cases part of a wider pattern of criminality, which for many included the routine use of violence as a means of resolving disputes. We should not be surprised, therefore, by the further finding that the victims of their violence were rarely complete strangers to their attackers: the parties were usually known to each other, although not well. The image of racist violence constructed by the media after the publication of the Macpherson Report, that it is generally the work of politically motivated offenders who select strangers as their victims purely on the basis of their perceived membership of some social group, accords with the classic account of racist attacks as a form of 'hate crime'. The image that emerges from our research is very different.

Life on the margins of the global city

One of our research interests was to explore how far racist sentiments and ideas were shared by white residents, other than known offenders, of the neighbourhoods where identified offenders lived. To do this it was first necessary to locate neighbourhoods that seemed to house a disproportionately high number of racist offenders. We identified two estates as standing out markedly in this respect, and another two that could be placed less certainly in the same category. All these estates were on the outskirts, to the north and west, of the Greater Manchester conurbation; all were environmentally run down, economically impoverished and socially and culturally deprived. They were also virtually all-white. On a visit by the research team to one of these estates (built in the mid-1950s to house the families of workers at nearby petrochemical plants, many of which had closed), we found that all three pubs were closed and boarded up, licences having been withdrawn as a result of persistent violence; a visit to another estate coincided with a local news story that the (South Asian-owned) fish and chip shop had caught fire on the evening before, and that arson was suspected. From such evidence, and still more from the accounts of offenders resident in these estates, we concluded that high levels of violence were an element of everyday life on the estates.

These findings are largely in line with the conclusions of previous UK researchers interested in the demographic and environmental characteristics of areas where there is most support for racist ideas and racist violence. Taylor (1982) suggested that electoral support for the National Front was highest in areas of predominantly white residence close to areas with larger ethnic minority populations, who symbolised threatening change and competition over resources. Similarly, Hewitt (1996) found the highest rates of racist attitudes in areas where white residents felt territorially threatened, within a 'white hinterland' vulnerable to encroachment. Sibbitt (1997) argued that the areas with the highest rates of racist violence and harassment were socially and economically deprived and contained a high proportion of dysfunctional families, people with mental health problems and men with criminal records; people who experienced difficulties in managing their own lives were liable to scapegoat ethnic minorities rather than take responsibility for their own failures. One can infer that in such neighbourhoods violence might be part of everyday life. Even without Sibbitt's stress on social pathology, we would expect residential segregation on ethnic lines to be positively associated with racist violence. Census data (Rees and Phillips 1996) show that ethnic groups are more spatially differentiated in outlying parts of Greater Manchester than in the city itself. And within local authority areas like Bury, Oldham, Rochdale and Trafford there are estates, sometimes quite small (*cf.* Back 1996), which appear as all-white enclaves that are economically and socially distinct from adjacent areas, and that are characterised by a sense of exclusion, dispossession and resentment among their residents.

This sense of grievance emerged in the course of discussion groups conducted in the later stages of the research with residents of the two areas identified as particular sources of perpetrators of racist violence. Members of the groups included older people, young mothers, and young people attending a youth club. While generally disavowing actively racist beliefs and expressing disapproval of violence, racist or otherwise, the adult residents especially expressed a sense of being overlooked: their estates were seen as ignored by those in charge of regeneration projects and the resources associated with them; recognition of problems and ameliorative action were seen as concentrated nearer the centre of the conurbation, in areas (like Moss Side) that had acquired national notoriety. The poverty, decline and increasing criminality (according to older residents) of small, outlying estates went unregarded. It was not difficult for residents to construe this exclusion from the benefits of economic and environmental regeneration in racialised terms: the areas that gained were those with substantial ethnic minority populations, those that lost were white. A sense of collective isolation, of being disregarded and devalued, compounded the material realities of marginality. There were few local jobs or cultural resources, and public transport to the city centre was virtually non-existent after 8pm. Together, these produced a collective resentment among residents of these areas that readily acquired a racist dimension and was shared by known perpetrators of racist violence.

Not all the perpetrators of racist violence identified in our research came from the outskirts of Manchester, or at least not all were currently living there. There are ways of being marginalised from the cosmopolitan city even while living close to its centre. This was the case with a sub-group of the sample, perhaps ten in number, who typically lived in poor-quality temporary accommodation or in hostels, arranged for them by their probation officers. These young men often had a history of family breakdown, were estranged from their families or had been rejected by them. While they lived in or near areas of lively cosmopolitan culture, they were effectively excluded from participation in it both by poverty and by their internal rejection of it in favour of a nostalgic hankering for some vanished 'imagined community' (Anderson 1983) – white, stable, and homogeneously working-class. Interviewees in this group included the most overt and extreme cases of failure in basic social functioning of the kind described by Sibbitt (1997). Materially and emotionally incapable of enjoying the visible goods of Manchester's global identity and culture, they were no less excluded than those who lived on the fraying, impoverished estates of the periphery.

Racist violence in context

Very few interviewees talked of themselves, their lives or their neighbourhoods with any sense of achievement or pride. Few, for instance, were in jobs or personal relationships that seemed to bring satisfaction or fulfilment, and interviewees were far more likely to complain about their areas of residence than to declare themselves content with them. Typically, they saw their neighbourhoods as having declined during their lifetimes, not from a fantasised community of peace and harmony but from conditions that were habitable to those that were barely so. They explained the decline in terms familiar to criminologists – of a downward spiral starting with real or symbolic 'broken windows' (Wilson and Kelling 1982) and culminating in a loss of public order and safety, associated with public drug dealing and the violence it brought in its wake (Skogan 1990). The drug dealers and perpetrators of violence were, from offenders' own accounts, generally young men like themselves, and the fact that they deplored the impact of drugs and violence on the neighbourhood suggests an ambivalence and unhappiness, an unacknowledged sense of shame (Retzinger 1991; Scheff 1994, 1997) about their own way of life, since in many cases they were clearly part of the problem as they themselves defined it.

Many interviewees also revealed a disjunction between their self-identity and the material conditions that could have sustained it. These young men often presented themselves in terms derived from the traditions of the industrial working class. They claimed to see themselves as 'hard grafters' in traditional manual labouring occupations, notably on building sites, even though very few had in fact any substantial employment history. Their capacity for hard manual work was an important part of the common ground they claimed to share with men of African or Caribbean origin: 'blacks' were 'more like us', in terms of the shared cultural interests in music and football and in a common experience of the economy and labour market. Blacks were to be found working on building sites, for example, while South Asians – universally described as 'Pakis', a term that some claimed had been stripped of all offensive racist meaning – allegedly were not. Not surprisingly, the victims of the racist violence of this sample of offenders were almost exclusively South Asian, not African or Caribbean, in origin.[5] But the sources of aggression and hatred towards South Asians tended to be expressed in the language not of race hatred but of class hatred and resentment. Like the violent racists described by Webster (1999), many interviewees presented themselves as being the 'real' victims – of the processes of exclusion and neglect explored above, and sometimes of persecution by the police, who allegedly sought to aggravate some offences by stressing evidence of racial motivation (racist abuse and obscenities, for example). Violence can be a recourse for those who experience themselves as powerless as well as for the powerful.

South Asians were often presented by interviewees as having become economically successful without deserving to be so. In traditional working-class imagery, they were unlike both whites and blacks (who were 'more macho, more like us, really') because their work was in 'corner shops and businesses', not on building sites, and this meant that they were 'money grabbers' who, given a chance, would 'rip you off'. This construction enabled offenders to deploy one classic technique of neutralisation, denial of the victim by invalidating his or her moral status (Sykes and Matza 1957). All five of Sykes and Matza's neutralisations appeared in interviewees' accounts of their offences: denial of injury; denial of responsibility (as a result of drunkenness or being otherwise 'out of it'); an appeal to higher loyalties (standing by your mates); and condemnation of the condemners (the claim that everyone, including the police, is secretly racist). But the fifth neutralisation, denial of the victim, seems to be the crucial element in a process that appeared in many accounts: offenders did not deny their violence; indeed, in many cases they were apparently content to acknowledge that they often used violence to achieve their ends, in settings where supposedly one could not otherwise survive. What they repeatedly denied, minimised and neutralised was racist motivation. Denial of the victim is crucial in allowing racist motivation to be recast as motivation based on class hatred, the justified – or at least intelligible – resentment of the illegitimately rich and successful on the part of the poor and powerless.

Part of the traditional language of class hatred is a contrast between the strength and masculinity of the oppressed and the weakness and effeminacy of the oppressor. South Asians were 'effeminised' by stressing their supposed lack of aptitude for stereotypically masculine work. They were constructed as passive, lacking the physical attributes required for successful violence. Several violent offences seem to have been triggered by the refusal of victims to accept this passive, subordinate status. For example, two young white men, after drinking heavily, entered a South Asian-run corner shop, picked up a tray of cans of lager and made for the door, calling vaguely to the shopkeeper that they would pay for the drink later. The shopkeeper tried to prevent them taking the beer from the shop, which, according to the interviewee, came as a surprise, because he had allowed them to take beer and pay for it later on previous occasions. This was the trigger for a serious assault. Another incident arose from a dispute over a taxi fare. Interviewees were dependent on taxis for transport home at night because of the lack of public transport, and there were several references in interviews to the fact that taxis were usually owned and driven by South Asians, who, it was claimed, cheated on the fares or at least overcharged. The two young white men involved in this incident offered to pay less than the fare asked for, an offer the driver not surprisingly refused. In the ensuing argument, the taxi driver allegedly took action to defend himself, and his resistance was interpreted as a provocation.

It is important to note that we found few incidents of violence in which the victim and the offender were complete strangers. More often there was some existing relationship between them; they knew each other, but not well. Often, as in these examples, the relationship was a purely commercial one: in fact, offenders who lived in outlying estates often had no contacts with South Asians except in commercial transactions; the shops on the estates were mainly owned and staffed by South Asians, but understandably they did not live above the shop. Offenders were thus confronted in all their interactions with South Asians with the apparent fact that they were dealing with people more economically successful than themselves. In the absence of traditional 'hard graft', that success was seen as undeserved. But this perspective – again, a common theme in the imagery of class hatred – was complicated by envy. Interviewees frequently spoke of how South Asians had cultural and social advantages denied to them. These included strong extended kinship networks ('They look after each other'), close immediate family bonds, and access to vivid, lively religious and cultural traditions. Several interviewees also claimed to believe that ethnic minorities were deliberately favoured in the allocation of public resources such as housing and further education; one even spoke authoritatively of the wing in a local prison whose regime had been designed for the exclusive benefit of 'Pakis'.

As we saw, very few of the offenders in our sample could be regarded as remotely successful in economic terms, and many came from fragmented or rejecting family backgrounds, making for sharp and painful contrasts with the situation of their victims, of which they were well aware. And in contrast with the visible, colourful cultures associated with the religions of the Indian subcontinent, to be white and English ('just normal') was effectively to be invisible, part of the ground against which difference stood out as figure. A few interviewees tried to differentiate themselves from this background normality, for example by claiming Irish roots. But for most their inability to define their own cultural identity was a further source of damage to self-esteem and even of 'ontological insecurity', the term Giddens (1991) borrowed from R.D. Laing to describe the unique ontological stresses of modernity. Interviewees were asked about their knowledge of ethnic minorities and their cultural practices, and in this context several of the younger offenders remembered anti-racist or multicultural classes at school, in which the religions of South Asians had been, as they saw it, celebrated; but the effect of this had only been to deepen their resentment at the lack of attention paid to their own white English culture. It seems likely that anti-racist education can be experienced as a further form of condemnation and devaluation when its recipients already feel devalued by and alienated from school, as these interviewees had been. But this education had also presumably been among the influences that led all but a handful of interviewees to deny racist motivation even as they acknowledged acts of violence: 'I didn't mean it and he knew that' was a typical response to interview questions about racially abusive remarks in the context of violent offences. Such denials and minimisations testify both to offenders' sense of the social unacceptability of racist language and to the complexity and ambiguity inherent in the concept of 'racist motivation' in relation to acts of violence such as those we have described. They can also be interpreted as indications of an underlying, unacknowledged sense of shame, an emotion that, as we show below, need not be accompanied by remorse.

The emotions of racist violence

Research into violence has stressed the importance of the emotion of shame as a trigger for acts of violence as a means of restoring lost or threatened pride or honour. Writing from a clinical psychiatric perspective, for example, James Gilligan (2000) has claimed that a sense of having been shamed, that one's masculine honour has been challenged or damaged, is the most frequent immediate cause of male homicidal violence. The claim is in line with Cooney's (1998) observation that 70 percent of homicides (and, for Cooney, assaults that stop or are stopped short of killing) are 'moralistic' rather than predatory, in the sense that they are conceived by their perpetrators as acts of 'righteous slaughter' or revenge, through which the moral order is restored and damaged honour and status are reasserted. The most elaborate account from a sociological perspective of the relationship between shame and violence – mediated by 'humiliated fury' – is that developed by Thomas Scheff (1994, 1997), who claims that unacknowledged shame is the central emotion behind the urge for violent revenge, not only at the interpersonal level but also between ethnic and cultural groups and nation states. For example, he argues (1994) that the two world wars of the twentieth century can be understood as resulting from France's national shame following defeat in the Franco-Prussian War in 1871, and from Germany's shame following national humiliation by the Treaty of Versailles in 1919, respectively.[6] While Scheff has arguably not succeeded in showing the value of his approach at all these levels, we have found his position productive in understanding the immediate interactions between perpetrators of racist violence and their victims.

For insights into interpersonal violence and conflict Scheff draws on the work of Retzinger (1991), who analysed marital disputes in terms of the partners' experiences of the universal emotions of shame and pride in their interactions. According to Retzinger and Scheff, shame arises when one's social bond with others is threatened, weakened or broken, for example when one feels that one has been treated with disrespect. When social bonds are strong and intact, we experience not shame but pride, the emotion that makes possible cooperation and connectedness with others. If shame is openly acknowledged, the parties to an interaction can renegotiate their relationship on a basis of renewed mutual respect. If, as is more common, given what Scheff (1997) sees as the destructive tendency of modern societies to deny and repress the emotion, the shame remains unacknowledged, the result will be an anger that, unless respect is restored, can build into fury and rage. In a state of shame, according to Retzinger, we feel reduced and belittled, the object of scorn and ridicule, helpless and passive; we feel psychological and sometimes somatic pain and unease; we feel childish, devalued and unable to cope; our very identity is threatened and insecure. In contrast, the perceived source of the shame, the other who scorns and ridicules us, is seen as powerful, active, secure and in control, a confident adult who ignores our distress and abandons us when we are at our most vulnerable. The rage that makes violence possible is a defensive response to this distress and is directed vengefully against those who are seen as having caused it.

We think that the frequent use of what Scheff calls 'shame cues' by our interviewees justifies the inference that many were in a state of unacknowledged shame. Such cues can be detected in their self-definition as victims (as found by Webster (1999)) and in their complaints that the 'Pakis' 'have all the power'. Far from being the parties with power in their relationships with South Asians, offenders insisted that, properly understood, they were in the weaker position, overlooked, disregarded and abandoned to their fate. Like other residents of poor white estates, they saw their home areas as systematically disadvantaged in the allocation of resources. Near their estates, there were signs of South Asian encroachment: an adventure playground where white kids used to play had been replaced by a mosque; 'they are just going to take over and we are just going to be pushed aside'. They complained that racism was always seen in terms of white prejudice and aggression towards ethnic minorities, but that South Asians could be racist too. It was whites, not Asians, who were justified in feeling fearful on the streets: Asians were protected by their sheer numbers as well as by their solidarity. Even in the incidents that had led to their recent convictions, whites were often the real victims, more sinned against than sinning. South Asians, in contrast, were privileged, successful and in control of their lives, sustained by strong bonds of mutual support, by a rich and meaningful cultural tradition, and by special treatment by public authorities: 'the Asians are getting mosques and special schools ... but the English aren't getting nothing'. The English were just being told 'what to do ... to stop being racist'. But the success of South Asians was undeserved and illegitimate: 'they just come in England and a week later they've got a shop .... It's funny'. A language of hostility regularly accompanied a language of shame and failure, as one would expect, given the link between shame and fury.[7]

Not all interviewees were as open about their hostile fantasies or revealed the connections between shame and the emotions associated with violence as clearly as the one cited in the preceding paragraph. But the themes articulated there recurred often enough for us to conclude that these offenders were typically in a state of shame rather than pride. If, as Retzinger and Scheff have argued, shame results from weakened or broken social bonds, from a lack of connectedness to others, it could have many complex sources in the lives of these offenders, who, as we have said, tended to come from fragmented families, and many of whom lacked stable and affectionate relationships with partners. Feeling powerless, insecure and neglected, they sought a scapegoat, someone or something to blame for their distress. Against a background of the routine, taken-for-granted racism that characterised their neighbourhoods, and in the context of a shared sense of being invisible and ignored, young men and more rarely young women for whom violence is an accessible and habitual cultural resource will readily identify those who are visibly different and visibly (or apparently) more successful as the causes of their shame and humiliation. Acts of racist violence can then be understood as situationally specific expressions of the convergence of these cultures of racism, grievance and violence. Such acts are, in Bowling's (1998) term, 'instrumental' only in the narrowest of senses, that they relieve fury and frustration and replace, however fleetingly, shame with pride. They are better understood as 'expressive', and what they express is unacknowledged shame and the anger and rage that this breeds.

Conclusions

Racist violence as it emerges from our research is a more complex and contradictory phenomenon than is suggested by the imagery and language of 'hate crime'. At the same time, our findings do not contradict those of previous researchers such as Hewitt (1996), Sibbitt (1997) and Webster (1999). Like them, we see racist violence as intimately connected with wider cultures of racism, of exclusion and, crucially, of violence, and as capable of being understood only in this context. Individuals with some pathological propensity to violence undoubtedly exist, and were represented in our sample, although in small numbers; ideologically driven perpetrators of instrumental racist violence also exist, but they barely appeared in the sample. More typically, racist violence is the work of young men with no commitment to racist politics, who are indeed more inclined at the conscious, cognitive level to disavow racist ideas than to embrace them. Nevertheless they are deeply marked by racist assumptions, which they share with many residents of poor white estates on the outskirts of the city. It is because racist language is routine and endemic that it was plausible for offenders to deny in interviews that it had any special significance in the violent incidents they recounted, and to claim that the use of this language did not amount to evidence of racism. Cognitively, most interviewees agreed that racism was morally wrong and socially divisive; although a few said that their parents actively disapproved of racism, they were more likely to attribute racism to their parents' generation than to their own. We see no reason to question the sincerity of their disavowal of racist ideas: this is what they *thought*. What they *felt* is another matter, and we have suggested that the racist sentiments that were voiced in the course of violent incidents were released at moments of strong emotional engagement, in which the threatening otherness of South Asians released fundamental emotions of shame and rage.

Simmel (1955) remarked that instead of thinking of separation as the result of conflict we should see it as its cause: conflict comes not from closeness but from alienation, or, in Scheff's terms, from weakened social bonds. The riots in the spring of 2001, fuelled by racial antagonisms and anxieties, broke out not in mixed cosmopolitan areas of inner cities but in towns and cities in England with a high level of residential segregation on ethnic lines – Burnley, Oldham, Bradford. For many of the offenders in our sample, their only routine contacts with South Asians were in commercial transactions; they came from all-white neighbourhoods in some of the most segregated parts of Greater Manchester.

One of our conclusions about possible routes towards reducing racist violence is therefore (perhaps uncontroversially) that means should be found of reducing the physical and social separation and distance between ethnic groups. This could have implications for housing policy, for education, and for training and employment. Another conclusion arises from our stress on the emotional, 'irrational' elements in racist violence: purely educational approaches to combating racism are unlikely to be successful. Nor is an approach based on denunciation and condemnation; perpetrators of racist violence have been denounced and condemned for much of their lives. Programmes for offenders that aim to reduce the likelihood of repeat racist violence will therefore need to make clear the unacceptability of such violence (and of racism), but to do so in ways that do not simply compound offenders' shame and further undermine their self-esteem. In other words, they must convey respect for the person while firmly labelling his or her actions as unacceptable (Braithwaite 1989). The cognitive-behavioural emphasis of the programmes that have developed recently in the work of the probation service rests on a considerable volume of empirical research that suggests, at the very least, that it is more effective than other approaches in changing attitudes and reducing reconvictions (e.g. Chapman and Hough 1998). But, at least in the case of racist violence, changing cognitions – and the behaviour that is thought to stem from them, in more or less predictable ways – may not be enough. The roots of racist violence are less in faulty thinking processes than in emotions produced by the complex and interacting effects of family relationships, institutional experiences, peer groups, life in particular neighbourhoods, access to cultural capital, and economic activity. Effective programmes are therefore likely to have to attend to emotion as well as to cognition, and to face the seemingly paradoxical challenge of enabling racist offenders to move from shame to pride, from alienation to connectedness.

Notes

1 Fieldwork for the research was conducted from June 1998 to May 2000, funded for 18 months by the ESRC (Award No. L133251019) and for six months by the Greater Manchester Probation Service. We are grateful to the service both for its financial support for the work and for allowing us to use probation resources to gain access to the relevant research subjects. These research findings are based on one area of England, and we recognise that the patterns may be different elsewhere, especially in countries with different histories and configurations of ethnic relations.

2 Section 95 of the 1991 Criminal Justice Act requires the Home Office to publish annual statistics on race and the criminal justice system, primarily for the benefit of criminal justice professionals.

3 This was kindly made available to us before its publication.

4 These include an interest in identifying the responsibilities of the police for dealing with violent racism and protecting ethnic minorities from it. Bowling is critical of the use of multi-agency approaches to blur lines of responsibility and accountability.

5 The predominance of South Asians as victims of racist abuse in part reflects the distribution of ethnic minorities in the UK. In 1991, in an ethnic minority population of 3 million (about 5.5 percent of the total) South Asians represented 50 percent, Afro-Caribbeans 16.6 percent and Chinese 5.2 percent. In addition to Manchester, ethnic minorities are highly concentrated in a few urban areas: London, the West and East Midlands, and West Yorkshire. However, a similar study undertaken elsewhere in the UK might have found a different pattern of victimisation.

6 Karl Marx anticipated this analysis when he suggested that 'Shame is a revolution in itself .... Shame is a kind of anger turned in on itself. And if a whole nation were to feel ashamed it would be like a lion recoiling in order to spring' (Marx 1843).

7 This analysis draws on projection theories of racism, which cannot be discussed in detail here. One might further note Kristeva's claim that animosity towards the Other projects fear of 'the foreigner within us' (1991: 191).

References

Anderson, B. (1983) *Imagined Communities: Reflections on the Origins and Spread of Nationalism*. London: Verso.

Aust, R., Clancy, A., Hough, M. and Kershaw, C. (2001) *Crime, Policing and Justice: The Experience of Ethnic Minorities. Findings from the 2000 British Crime Survey*. London: Home Office.

Aye Maung, N. and Mirrlees-Black, C. (1994) *Racially Motivated Crime: A British Crime Survey Analysis*. London: Home Office.

Back, L. (1996) *New Ethnicities and Urban Culture: Racisms and Multiculture in Young Lives*. London: UCL Press.

Bowling, B. (1998) *Violent Racism: Victimisation, Policing and Social Context*. Oxford: Clarendon Press.

Braithwaite, J. (1989) *Crime, Shame and Reintegration*. Cambridge: Cambridge University Press.

Chapman, T. and Hough, M. (1998) *Evidence-based Practice*. London: HM Inspectorate of Probation.

Cohen, P. (1972) 'Subcultural conflict and working class community', *Working Papers in Cultural Studies* 2 (Spring): 5–51.

Cooney, M. (1998) *Warriors and Peacemakers: How Third Parties Shape Violence*. New York: New York University Press.

Fitzgerald, M. and Hale, C. (1996) *Ethnic Minorities: Victimisation and Racial Harassment. Findings from the 1988 and 1992 British Crime Surveys* (Home Office Research Study 154). London: Home Office.

Giddens, A. (1991) *Modernity and Self-Identity: Self and Society in the Late Modern Age.* Cambridge: Polity Press.

Giddens, A. (1994) *Beyond Left and Right: The Future of Radical Politics.* Cambridge: Polity Press.

Gilligan, J. (2000) *Violence: Reflections on our Deadliest Epidemic.* London: Jessica Kingsley.

Greater Manchester Police (2000) *Racist Incident Report 1998–99.* Manchester: Greater Manchester Police.

Haslam, D. (1999) *Manchester, England: The Story of the Pop Cult City.* London: Fourth Estate.

Hewitt, R. (1996) *Routes of Racism.* Stoke-on-Trent: Trentham Books.

Home Office (1981) *Racial Attacks: Report of a Home Office Study.* London: Home Office.

Home Office (2000) *Statistics on Race and the Criminal Justice System: A Home Office Publication under Section 95 of the Criminal Justice Act 1991.* London: Home Office.

Jones, T., Maclean, B.D. and Young, J. (1986) *The Islington Crime Survey.* Aldershot: Gower.

Kristeva, J. (1991) *Strangers to Ourselves.* New York: Columbia University Press.

Macpherson, W. (1999) *The Stephen Lawrence Inquiry. Report of an Inquiry by Sir William Macpherson of Cluny* (Cm 4262). London: HMSO.

Mair, G. and May, C. (1997) *Offenders on Probation* (Home Office Research Study 167). London: Home Office.

Marx, K. (1843) 'Letter to Arnold Ruge, March 18th 1843', Marx/Engels Internet Archive *[http://marxists.org/archive/marx/works/1843/letters/43_03.htm].*

Mayhew, P., Elliott, D. and Dowds, L. (1989) *The 1988 British Crime Survey* (Home Office Research Study 111). London: HMSO.

Ray, L. and Smith, D. (2001) 'Racist offenders and the politics of "hate crime"', *Law and Critique* (November) 12(3): 203–21

Ray, L., Smith, D. and Wastell, L. (2002) 'Racist violence from a probation service perspective: now you see it, now you don't', in R.M. Lee and E. Stanko (ed.) *Researching Violence.*

Rees, P. and Phillips, D. (1996) 'Geographical patterns in a cluster of Pennine towns', in P. Ratcliffe (ed.) *Ethnicity in the 1991 Census, Volume 3: Social Geography and Ethnicity in Britain: Geographical Spread, Spatial Concentration and Internal Migration.* London: Office of National Statistics, 271–93.

Retzinger, S.M. (1991) *Violent Emotions: Shame and Rage in Marital Quarrels.* London: Sage.

Scheff, T.J. (1994) *Bloody Revenge: Emotions, Nationalism and War.* Boulder, Colo.: Westview Press.

Scheff, T.J. (1997) *Emotions, the Social Bond and Human Reality: Part/Whole Analysis.* Cambridge: Cambridge University Press.

Sibbitt, R. (1997) *The Perpetrators of Racial Harassment and Racial Violence* (Home Office Research Study 176). London: Home Office.

Simmel, G. (1955) *Conflict and the Web of Group-Affiliations.* Glencoe, NY: Free Press.

Skogan, W.G. (1990) *Disorder and Decline: Crime and the Spread of Decay in American Neighbourhoods.* New York: Free Press.

Stewart, G. and Stewart, J. (1993) *Social Circumstances of Younger Offenders under Probation Supervision*. Wakefield: ACOP.

Sykes, G.M. and Matza, D. (1957) 'Techniques of neutralization: a theory of delinquency', *American Sociological Review* 22: 664–70.

Taylor, I., Evans, K. and Fraser, P. (1996) *A Tale of Two Cities: Global Change, Local Feeling and Everyday Life in the North of England. A Study in Manchester and Sheffield*. London: Routledge.

Taylor, S. (1982) *The National Front in English Politics*. London: Macmillan.

Webster, C. (1999) 'Inverting racism', paper to the 1999 British Criminology Conference, Liverpool.

Wilson, J.Q. and Kelling, G. (1982) 'Broken windows: the police and neighbourhood safety', *Atlantic Monthly* (March): 29–38.

7 The constitution of fear in gay space

*Leslie J. Moran, Beverley Skeggs,
Paul Tyrer and Karen Corteen*

Introduction

In studies on fear of crime to date, little attention has been paid to the impact of sexuality. More specifically, while lesbians and gay men have long been produced and examined as objects of fear (Duggan 2000; Hart 1994; Moran 1996), their appearance as subjects of fear is something of a new departure. The importance of fear in lesbian and gay experiences of danger and safety associated with violence still remains largely unexamined.[1] It is now perhaps a trite point, but one worth repeating within the frame of a lesbian and gay politics of violence, that fear of crime is for many more important than direct experiences of criminal acts in the generation of experiences of danger and safety. In this chapter, we begin an exploration of the geography and politics of fear that informs lesbian and gay perceptions of danger and safety.

Our specific objective is to explore lesbian and gay experiences of fear of crime through an analysis of data generated as part of a major research project, 'Violence, Sexuality and Space'.[2] In general, the research concentrates on how three specific groups (gay men, lesbians and heterosexual women, all identified as 'high-risk' groups by various crime surveys) produce and make use of space in two contrasting geographical areas, a large city and a much smaller city, both in the northwest of England. Manchester is a major city at the heart of a large conurbation. It has an identifiable and well-established gay space known as 'the village'. The village is the location that gives concrete form to what has been described as 'the strongest and most vibrant lesbian and gay community in the country'. This 'gay Mecca' (Healthy Gay Manchester 1998) offers gay men in particular high visibility and spatial concentration. It is a 'Mecca' characterised specifically by way of various forms of cultural capital: 'pleasure', consumption, 'style', fashion, cuisine and more specific events such as a Queer Arts Festival. Lancaster offers a sharp contrast. It is a much smaller provincial city 50 miles to the north of Manchester. It has no clearly identifiable and durable gay space.[3]

The project data were generated using a reflexive, multi-method approach. In each location we conducted a space census survey, semi-structured interviews with key informants, and focus groups for lesbians, gay men and straight women.[4] In this chapter, after situating our work on lesbian and gay fear within the wider contemporary debates on fear of crime, we begin our analysis from the findings generated by the survey, to date the UK's largest survey of lesbian and gay experiences of safety and danger.[5] The survey generated some surprises relating to the importance of fear of violence in lesbian and gay definitions of safety and danger in our two locations. Having set out a summary of these findings, we then explore their meaning through an examination of the project's wider research data on safety and danger, generated through the focus group discussions and semi-structured interviews. We develop an analysis of the complexity of definitions of fear of violence and safety. We then turn to considering the spatial themes that inform fear and safety talk in the data. Our data not only draw attention to the importance of taking the location of fear seriously but also point to the importance of fear in the production of location. We examine the challenges that these spatial themes raise for those who seek to understand fear and safety and for those who generate policy in response to it.

Lesbian and gay politics of violence and fear of crime

Victim surveys have played a key role in drawing attention to violence against lesbians and gay men. Debate continues as to whether these surveys document previously unrecorded levels of violence or constitute a new 'epidemic' of violence (Jacobs and Potter 1998; Moran 2000). However, they consistently show that the wide spectrum of homophobic violence, from physical assault to harassment and verbal abuse, is an everyday experience for lesbians and gay men. This documentation of violence has been used to demand changes to policing practice and crime control provisions more generally, including new reporting procedures, enhanced punishment provisions and new offences. The use of victim surveys by lesbians and gay men appears to follow a standard pattern of political activism (Jenness and Broad 1997; Jenness and Grattet 2001; Mason and Tomsen 1997). In sharp contrast to this, lesbian and gay activism has paid less attention to a second dimension of victim surveys; their use to document fear of crime.

In many ways this silence is surprising. Fear of crime has been a major growth area in criminological and criminal justice work at the level of practical intervention and policy debates, and in academic circles (Hale 1996). Ditton and Farrall (2000) reported an explosion of interest in this area. In a four-year period, conference papers, monographs and books on the subject increased from just over 200 to more than 800. Reviews of the literature on the fear of crime draw attention to the highly problematic and contested nature of the domain. Most recently, Bannister and Fyfe (2001) have suggested that a recent explosion in the literature indicates that interest has outstripped the conceptual development of fear of crime.

The themes of fear of crime literature resonate with many individual and collective ills highlighted by a lesbian and gay politics of violence (Jenness and Broad 1997; Jenness and Grattet 2001). For example, scholars suggest that fear of crime is closely connected to the processes of victimisation as a consequence of a breakdown in social control or as being mediated by the urban environment

(Bennett 1990; Hale 1996). Others have noted that fear of crime has an important role in the production of social division and social exclusion by way of its psychological, physical and economic impact on individuals (Stanko 2000). This has strong spatial significance. In response to fear there is a withdrawal into the private realm. In turn, this withdrawal generates the decline and deterioration of the community and the public realm, which in turn gives rise to more crime in public places (Hale 1996).

The characterisation of fear in this literature is also of interest. It is dominated by a particular set of associations. This fear is endlessly portrayed as a threat or danger associated with the unknowable and characterised as the unruly, that which is beyond control (van der Wurff *et al.* 1988; Bannister and Fyfe 2001: 808). More specifically, the fear of crime literature foregrounds the body. It is the primary location of fear experiences. Fear is emotion, pain, uneasiness and anxiety caused by a sense of impending danger (Bannister and Fyfe 2001). Fear is personalised and individualised in and through the body. In its association with the body, fear is understood predominantly in this literature as unreason and irrationality.

Engagement with the fear of crime literature does pose some problems. On occasions, 'fear' has been replaced by other terms, such as 'terror', 'anxiety', 'worry', 'anger' and 'loss of trust' (Jefferson and Hollway 2000; Stanko 2000; Walklate 2000, 2001). These distinctions, their individual significance, their interrelations and their connection to fear have been used to challenge much quantitative research into fear of crime (Hale 1996: 84–94), and to generate calls for new approaches to fear of crime research (Ditton *et al.* 1999). Another site of controversy has been over the meaning of 'crime' in this context. Work that documents fear associated with aspects of well-being, quality of life and lifestyle (Hindelong *et al.*1978: 244) has been challenged. 'Fear of crime', it is suggested, is a phrase that should only be used in the context of a fear of a particular range of legally proscribed acts, usually limited to serious physical violence and property crime (Hale 1996). Others have challenged resort to this narrow, pedantic definition of crime.

Stanko's critique (2000) of the resort to narrow definitions of 'crime' in the context of fear is of particular importance here. She suggests that it has had both particular and more general effects. It has been an important factor in reducing fear of crime to a debate about victims, more specifically a debate about good victims and bad victims and the needs of the former and the culpability of the latter. More generally, she suggests, it has had the effect of erasing the structural and political issues of social hierarchies and inequalities, which have been not only a key factor in the generation of victim surveys but also a central feature of the data. For us, 'crime' (and our interest here focuses on violence as crime) must be widely construed. In part, this draws upon feminist and lesbian and gay scholarship that draws attention to the urgent need to recognise the multiple forms of violence and its different effects.

There is also support for this position in the fear of crime literature. Sally Merry's work (1981) has particular significance, challenging resort to narrow definitions of crime. She argues that broad definitions are necessary. A whole range of experiences generates fear of crime (fear of violence), from physical injury to experiences of minor impropriety that threaten ontological security and belonging. The adoption of broad definitions enables a full account of the 'multi-dimensional nature of fear of crime' to be generated (Hale 1996: 84). Fear, we argue, is linked to security, the sense of being safe, of having some control over one's life, of being able to make sense of being.

An increasing amount of work has highlighted the spatial dimension of fear (Gold and Revill 2000), which in general is concerned with how people experience and interpret (urban) space. We are interested in an examination of the physical and social characteristics of place and the familiarity of that space, which are implicated in the formation of fear. In effect, people read the environment as a barometer of risk and protective factors. In order to make these readings, they draw on the discourses to which they have access to make sense of their own and others' occupation of space. This always involves visual evaluation of the built environment as well as visual evaluation of others (Skeggs 2000). Space is always discursive space; for the individual, it cannot be known beyond the information that is used to make sense of it, or even feel it. This information is not evenly available and is dependent upon the prior social positioning of the reader, or what Bourdieu (1986) would refer to as predispositions.

There is also another side to the spatial aspects of fear. Some scholars have noted that as we read spaces for fear in order to know what to avoid, we may also seek out places of fear. Neill (2001) argues[6] that we need to understand how urban fear can attract as well as repel. He suggests that fear can be a better release from boredom and consumerism, which now threatens to make our experiences homogeneous. Fear, Neill suggests, has a close relationship to desire. Furthermore, conquering fear allows us to be heroic. It holds out the illusory possibility of conquest and thereby an experience of escape from anxiety. With these introductory remarks in mind, we want to turn to our survey data and to highlight some of the findings that surprised us.

The survey data

The first surprise is that gay men in the village sample (37 percent – the largest group of survey respondents in the village) were the group most likely to find Manchester's gay village unsafe.[7] Another unexpected result is the stark difference between gay and lesbian respondents using the space. Gay men are twice as likely to perceive the village as unsafe as lesbians. When we examine the gay men's responses in more detail, we find that those who have closest contact with the village, living in or near the city centre and/or making regular visits to the village, report the lowest safety ratings. In sharp contrast, gay men from out of town report the highest.[8]

These findings are perhaps even more startling when we compare the Manchester 'gay Mecca' data with the survey data from Lancaster, which has none of the resources and characteristics associated with visible and vibrant spatial concentrations of lesbians and gay men. In Lancaster, lesbians and gay men are the groups most likely to find Lancaster safe. There is also little reported difference between the two: 84.1 percent of gay men and 85.9 percent of lesbians reported Lancaster to be safe.[9] In the first instance, these findings appear to offer a challenge to a baseline hypothesis of the research: that the 'gay Mecca' offers and is experienced as safer space.

But the challenges do not stop there. The data also suggest that the composition of experiences of safety and danger may vary from location to location. When we asked our Manchester survey participants to tell us their reasons for avoiding parts of the village (its streets or bars), we were surprised by the responses. Manchester's gay men and lesbians rarely mention experience of violence. In fact, they reported the lowest levels of experience of violence. The most important reason given for avoiding bars and areas is 'perceptions of danger'.[10] Lancaster differed in this respect. Experiences of violence play a much more prominent role in the rationalisation of avoidance behaviour by both gay men and lesbians. Gay men reported the highest level of experiences of violence as the basis for avoidance (41.7 percent). In Manchester, gay men reported the lowest level of experiences of violence (9.8 percent) of any sexual category. Violence also played a more important role for lesbians in Lancaster (30.6 percent), in stark contrast to low reports of violence by lesbians in Manchester (8.9 percent).[11]

One dramatic difference between the two locations is the presence of 'straights' as a distinct category of danger in Manchester. It is a category that has little significance for the Lancaster respondents.

The data also draw attention to the fact that these different factors may have particular spatial significance within each research location. For example, in Manchester 'perception of danger' is a reason for avoidance particularly associated with two locations: 'cruising areas' and 'secondary streets'. 'Experiences of violence' is particularly associated with the avoidance of the main thoroughfares ('central drags') and 'the bus station'. 'Straights' is a category of danger associated, perhaps unsurprisingly, with 'straight bars and areas' and the main thoroughfares. In Lancaster, council estates appear as a specific location of danger. Both experiences of violence (50 percent) and perceptions of danger (44.4 percent) inform this finding.

The picture becomes even more complex when gender is added to the data. Reading across our data provides some information about the relationship between identity and the spatial significance of reasons for avoidance. For example, in Manchester fear of straights associated with particular locations ('straight bars' and 'central drags') is a located rationalisation of unsafety, particularly in lesbian experiences of safety. For gay men, the location most likely to be avoided is 'gay bars and areas'. Here 'perceptions of danger' rather than 'experiences of violence' seems to be a dominant factor.

The survey data not only challenge one of our research presuppositions, that the 'gay village' would be experienced as safer space, but also complicate our understanding of the impact of public gay space. More specifically, the experience of Manchester's gay village as a space of danger is an experience associated with those who use it most frequently. Perceptions of danger rather than experiences of violence seem to play a key role. Finally, one of the effects of established gay space may be a change in the way danger is perceived. 'Straights' become a category of danger associated with the village.

How are we to make sense of these surprising Manchester findings?[12] We want to examine these findings in more detail. First, we want to examine 'straights' as a distinct category of danger. Second, we want to explore the spatial context and significance of this danger. In pursuing an analysis of these two dimensions, we turn to our qualitative data from Manchester; the structured interviews with key informants and our focus group transcripts.

Categorising 'straights'

Our qualitative data from Manchester suggest that the category 'straight' needs to be treated with some caution. While 'straight' is always sexualised, it is important to take account of the difference that the distinction between lesbian and gay may have on the formation of 'straight'. As one lesbian explained:

> there are different issues for men and different issues for women. Straight women can't stand lesbians. Although they like to be around gay men they are really threatened about being around lesbians ... people have had arguments with straight women in gay bars.

In contrast, one of the gay men from our focus group explained: 'it's about fear, it's about being frightened ... I certainly don't feel frightened by straight women, but I do feel frightened, threatened by straight men'. When read together, these two extracts draw attention to the fact that while 'straight' as danger may be sex/gender neutral, it may also be informed by gender. In different contexts this danger may be 'straight men', in others 'straight women'. Furthermore, 'straight' may also connote safety. Through sex/gender and sexuality, 'straight' is formed as both safe and dangerous.

Our data also suggest that class is important, although rarely directly spoken. Working class as danger is usually referenced through geography (housing estates or named areas), or appearance (hair = big, clothing = sportswear, opal fruit, i.e. checked shirts, mini-skirts, fluffy bras, platform shoes), or the terms 'lad' and 'scally'. For example, Norman, a gay man who has been involved in several gay businesses, including a gay bar, in the village explained:

> you only need a couple of straight lads to come down here and have a good time and they start fetching their friends; it's when you get gangs of twelve or fifteen leaving pubs in Salford and it's like let's go down the gay village and kick a fucking queer's head in, and it happens, believe me.

Terms such as 'lads' (and in other examples, 'yobs'), and the reference to 'Salford' (a city that adjoins the northern borders of Manchester and is always historically represented as working-class), give the gendered danger of 'straight' a strong working-class inflection (Moran 2000). We have explored elsewhere how feminine-appearing women are usually read as straight, hence making the femme invisible. This reading is nearly always informed by class[13] (Skeggs 2000, 2001). Thus there is a need to proceed with some caution when considering 'straight' as a sign of danger. It may be just another way of reproducing class through sexuality. As one of the gay men from the Manchester focus group noted, there is a tendency to assume that:

> all heterosexual people are gay men haters or that there is some element of homophobia going on with straight people … I think that's wrong … some heterosexual people are being really violent to some gay men – you know its not generic.

This draws attention to the way that our research participants use 'straight' as both a general category of sexualised danger and as a category of sexualised danger that is formed by gender and class. This is particularly pertinent in the way that straight women stand out, not as a traditional sign of violence but as a division drawn between groups on the basis of taste. One of our key informants, Steph, a bar manager, explained:

> I see some terrible sights over the weekend, like hen parties dragging like 'L-signs' and blow-up men, dolls, sort of things like that. But again I don't know. I don't think it's the right space for them. That's what I think personally. But there are bars further up the street that do cater for straight women.

When asked whether the bar she managed was the right place for straight women, she explained:

> Trendy women, yeah, trendy, but the normal everyday Sharon and Tracey I would say 'No. I don't think that you would enjoy yourself in Manto. You're best going somewhere like Bar 38', where it's the complete opposite, where it'd be 70 percent straight and 30 percent gay.

Danger is here figured through taste respectability. It is those who threaten the production of taste for consumption who produce a disruption of the space. Their difference is institutionalized in bar policies. They are less a sign of fear in comparison with working-class men, but they still serve to name straights as disruption, matter out of place.

Straight danger

We now want to turn to the particular dangers associated with 'straight'. Our Manchester focus group data provide examples of the many different forms of danger associated with 'straights'. This ranges from physical attacks and violence ('who commits the violence … its definitely heterosexual people') to verbal abuse, to more abstract characterisations of danger, such as 'hostility' ('most of the hostility which people tend to recognise comes from straight men'). Another manifestation of danger is found in the following extract from one of the men in the gay group. He explained:

> a small but very obnoxious group of straight people, unreasonably pissed, [were] affecting the whole character of the bar … they were dancing, there's a dance floor downstairs but you don't do it in the middle of a busy bar … and it was done in a particular way that I don't expect in a gay bar … they seem to be more controlled in gay bars … but the aggression that goes with heterosexual people … was self-evident.

Here danger takes the form of the place and mode of dancing. These straight acts were out of place. As such, they might be characterised as disorderly behaviour or acts that violate particular expectations of civility. One of the lesbian focus group participants characterised the problem as 'sheer lack of respect'. One of the incivilities most commonly referred to in our focus group data is 'looking'. As a member of the lesbian focus group explained:

> there has been a lot of straight people in there and I've been in there with my partner and we don't even hold hands … because we feel as though we are being looked at and stared at … we were surrounded by heterosexual people who were snogging.

The danger associated with this disorderly practice is marked in the change ('self-policing') of behaviour. In general, the focus group participants characterised this as an illegitimate restraint on behaviour in lesbian and gay space. It is expressed in various ways but most commonly in terms of 'feeling uncomfortable' and an inability to be 'relaxed', in becoming 'more self-conscious'. When one of the gay men in the focus group was asked to explain why he felt safe in a particular gay club, he explained: '0.2 percent straight people are there. You know it is just fully gay … you just go there to lose your inhibitions … to be who you want to be'. Here the virtual absence of 'straights' is an experience of ontological security and belonging. The disturbance that is marked by the policing of behaviour, loss of comfort and the inability to relax represents the experience of 'straights' as a threat to identity.

This talk of danger, safety and ontology also has another dimension. It is always a talk about place (*cf.* Girling *et al.* 2000). It is to these geographies of 'straight' as danger that we now want to turn.

Place talk takes various forms. Our Manchester survey data suggest that experiences of danger and their composition are place-specific. For example, straights as danger was particularly associated with straight bars. As one of our gay focus group participants explained:

> when I go into a straight bar then my direct experience is there's an expec-
> tation of violence ... [gay men] have a sensitivity that they will pick up
> more quickly that there is something going on ... In the straight scene
> [violence] seems to be the first option.

Here the experience of 'straight bars' as places of violence seems to bring
together direct experience of straight violence in straight bars and expectations
of danger. The bus station is another location of danger highlighted in our
survey data. One of the gay focus group participants describes his experience of
that location in the following terms:

> the bus stop is a bit of a black spot ... if you start going in that direction
> basically then there's a lot more drunkenness, but straight drunkenness or
> people pissing in corners and that kind of romantic behaviour, then you
> start feeling a bit more kind of self-conscious basically as opposed to just
> letting your mind drift or be happy or whatever.

In this instance, the danger/safety of the place is explained not in terms of
direct violence but by reference to a reading of the urban landscape and particular practices as signs of a certain incivility and thereby as signs of danger.

Reading bars and clubs through the relation between straight and danger not
only produces those places as 'straight bars' in contrast to 'gay places' but also
maps those places as dangerous and safe, respectively. As one of the men in the
gay group explained: 'when I go into a straight pub then my direct experience is
there was an expectation of violence whereas if I go into a gay bar or a gay pub I
don't expect it'. In turn, the characterisation of the village as the 'gay village'
connotes straights as elsewhere, in another place. The village is thereby a place
of safety over against danger, which is always elsewhere.[14]

This brings us to another spatial theme, which is variously characterised as
straight 'colonisation', 'takeover' and most commonly as 'invasion' of the gay
village. The invasion narrative appeared early in our research as a pervasive
theme in the Manchester key informant interviews. It was also an important
theme in the lesbian and gay focus group discussions. Key informants explained:

> Well I think that most gay people feel it's their space. ... It's their only
> place and it's being invaded. Invade sounds a bit dramatic but it is being
> invaded somewhat by straight people. So there is a bit of animosity there.
>
> (Ben)

> You see it doesn't bother me, the fact that there's a lot of straight people in
> at the weekend because I'm not there. But for the [gay] men who tradition-
> ally go out, it obviously seems to affect them because their own private
> space is being invaded in their eyes.
>
> (Sue)

These extracts illustrate common features of the 'straight invasion' theme. First, invasion not only constitutes bars as gay in contrast to straight but is also important in the constitution of 'the village' as gay space against straight space, which always lies elsewhere. They also illustrate another important dimension of the experience of the village as a place of danger and safety. As 'our' space and as 'private' space, the village is a gay place that is understood by way of a very particular relation to space. Here being and belonging is constituted through repertoires and metaphors of investments of 'property', 'propriety' and 'entitlement'; of ownership (Moran and Skeggs 2001).[15] Through these investments, an identification is made with the place. Territorialisation becomes a matter of identity. As one gay focus group member explained, 'it is the invasion of straights ... you lose the identity of the place so you have to ... look further, make a bigger effort to find the identity again, which otherwise got diluted'. A final dimension of the spatial theme of invasion is how boundaries are figured. As one of our lesbian focus group members explained: 'the village has always been the boundaries that have been defined'. Boundaries define not only the wider entity of the village but also the particular bars and clubs that make up the village. Invasion generates boundaries through the threat of their violation.

Invasion narratives also invest these boundaries with a temporal dimension. One aspect of this might be characterised as nostalgia. They constitute an imagined time, before the invasion, when the gay village was a pure gay space, a village without straights, without danger. A second temporal dimension is illustrated by a gay focus group participant, 'Friday and Saturday it can be straights-ville'. Here the invasion takes place at particular times of the week. Others pinpoint particular times of the day:

> come twelve o'clock all the gay people piss off to Cruz and Paradise and Poptastic, and then all the straight people who don't want to come into any clubs or anything know these places are still open till two ... Friday and Saturday is primarily straight, it is very, very straight.

Before we leave the topic of the boundaries of gay space, we want briefly to explore two further issues. The first is the relationship between fear of straights and power. The second is boundaries as the locus of a politics of estrangement.[16] First, let us turn to the question of power.

Gay and lesbian space is about power over and against the power of straights. Being in the majority, for a change, puts you in the position of 'the one in power'. As such, one of our gay male focus group members explained: 'I can do what I want in front of them and they've got to like it or they've got to get out the door'. One of the lesbians in the focus group explained that in the gay village:

> you are in the majority and for the very first time in your life you are in the majority and it's a fantastic feeling to know that you are with other people who are exactly like you and all the others fade into insignificance.

Fear of straights, explained one gay man, is about power over straights and in particular about power over straight men.

The experience of power takes an ontological form (*cf.* Stanko 1997). It informs the fabrication of expressions of 'confidence' and 'self-assurance'. Another ontological dimension was mentioned by a gay group participant. He explained:

> we are less tolerant of violence as gay men than heterosexuals are ... they go out for a good night out on a Saturday night and ... they're expecting [violence] so our tolerance of violence is lower than that ... in the heterosexual environment.

These differences may be given form and are institutionalised not only by a different civility but also by new sensitivities and different expectations:

> we will pick up more quickly that there is something going on and our expectations of a civilised response to a challenge is higher ... that we don't immediately go to fisticuffs if there was a problem.

This, as one of the gay male participants noted, may make lesbians and gay men 'more conscious of straight people being on the scene'. It may also result in the number of straights being overestimated, producing particular amplification effects within the context of the 'invasion' story. The same participant, playing devil's advocate, suggested:

> we don't necessarily like straight people accessing the scene quite as much and in order to justify that to ourselves we say it compromises our safety, whereas it might not necessarily but it makes us feel better, it sits better on our shoulders if we believe that that's the reason we do not like it.

The power to exclude associated with boundaries is part of a strategy of building a safe identity and community. Articulating and locating threat and fear become a necessary part of identity and community formation, of making a boundary.

It is at this point that it is useful to turn to the politics of estrangement and to consider the uses of estrangement in the reading of straights in the village as danger. Of central importance here is the fact that straights as danger are not remote from the gay village but close to it. As Simmel (1964) and others (Bauman 1991; Bhabha 1996; Ahmed 2000) have noted, it is the proximity of strangers that forces, figures and enables the production of difference, in this instance the difference between gay and straight. The straight as danger is not the remote enemy that threatens but the one who is close, presenting anxieties generated by reading, interpretation and judgement. It is their proximity that generates the need to separate straight from gay, and safer straight from dangerous straight.

Ahmed (2000) argues that it is stranger fetishism that figures difference in contemporary society. She argues that stranger fetishism can be read not only as a displacement of social relations on to an object (in the traditional Marxist take on fetishism) but also as a transformation of objects into figures. She argues: 'stranger fetishism is a fetishism of figures; it invests the figure of the stranger with a life of its own insofar as it cuts "the stranger" off from histories of its own determination' (*ibid.*: 5). She shows how narratives that construct 'the strange culture' as their object (distance) are also contaminated by that very object (by proximity). They involve, simultaneously, social and spatial relations of distance *and* proximity:

> Others become strangers (the ones who are distant), and 'other cultures' become 'strange cultures' (the ones who are distant), only through coming *too close to home*, that is, through the proximity of the encounter or 'facing itself'.
>
> (*ibid.*: 12; emphasis added)

Estrangement requires that persons (and things) have to be located out of place primarily because they inhabit the same space. The gay village of our research is a place where people of many differences are made proximate, but only some are metaphorically located outside. This politics of estrangement appears to be at work in the figuring of straight as stranger and therefore danger.

But the boundaries constituted and invested in and through a politics of estrangement appear to be fragile. This is illustrated in the following observation by one of the gay male focus group members. He explained: 'a couple of straights ... enhance it a bit'; but another responded: 'it's when it starts going over the line ... when it starts to shift that percentage too much'. Here the fragility of power takes the form of the difficulty of deciding the undecidable: how many straights does it take? That fragility is also recognised in the context of the wider landscape and experience of inequality between gays and straights. For example, it is spoken of in the following extract, which contrasts the straight invasion of gay bars with gay invasion of straight bars: 'there aren't many bars ... that have been straight but invaded by gay people ... it doesn't happen'. The power imbalance between gay and straight is in the one-way traffic described here. 'Gay' has a particular fragility. Fragility is also connoted by way of references to the speed of change and the temporal shift in the nature of the space. At best, there seems to be an awareness here that the politics of estrangement has at best a tactical and spatially limited significance.

Conclusions

The novelty of work that explores lesbians and gay men as subjects of fear makes us hesitate to draw firm conclusions from the research data. Our analysis draws attention to the complex relationship between fear of crime, sexuality, gender, class and its impact upon individuals and communities in different locations.

Our particular concern in this study has been to examine the unexpected finding that the gay village, far from being experienced by its most frequent gay users as a safe space, was experienced as a space of danger and a location that was unsafe. Furthermore, we wanted to explore the meanings associated with the emergence of 'straights' as a distinct category of danger found in that location. Within the parameters of that study, we also want to emphasise the importance of the contexts in which the geographies and politics of fear discussed above have emerged and need to be understood.

First, the research data we have used come from participants who predominantly were users of the village. For example, those who contributed to the Manchester survey were in the village on a Friday, lunchtime and evening, which the key informant interviewees suggested was the time associated with high levels of 'straight invasion'. More specifically, those who expressed the highest concerns about danger in the village in that survey were the people who had the highest frequency of use. This is important. Those who expressed most concern about fear of crime had not withdrawn from the public sphere. But there is a need for caution here. This does not suggest that their mode of occupation was not affected by fear. Nor does it suggest that fear of crime does not have dramatic damaging consequences for lesbian and gay individuals and communities. More research over longer periods of time is needed to study these issues.

Second, during the period when we were gathering our data, discourses of danger and safety of lesbians and gay men had a high profile in the village (*cf.* Stanko 1997). This culture of safety and danger was produced by campaigns about hate crime and local crime-reporting initiatives. It influenced tourist and publicity material about the village produced to promote the local, national and international profile of the village by the local authority. Within a longer time frame and the wider politics of HIV/AIDS, which has had a high profile in the village, danger and safety have been key themes within contemporary sexual politics to which lesbians and gay men have been alerted for some time.

Third, Manchester's gay village is predominantly a commercial space, which may produce this culture of safety and danger in very particular forms. While these spaces of entertainment were initially generated from political campaigning, they are now resolutely commercial. The demand for profit generates a very specific social and cultural instability. The form and impact of fear on these particular spaces may differ from its impact upon 'neighbourhoods', characterised predominantly as locations of privacy and domesticity (Valentine and Johnston 1995). However, at the same time, for lesbians and gay men, commercial and entertainment spaces may have a different significance from that associated with the hetero-normative. These 'public' spaces are an important location for experiences of privacy, intimacy and domesticity, of home (Moran 2002).

Fourth, in the research data most references to straights as danger, violence and the threat of violence are both an effect of invasion and its cause. Straight use of the space is explained in terms of access to late-night drinking. Other explanations given by lesbians and gay men include straight desire to access the high subcultural capital associated with gay male culture – it is 'trendy', 'fashionable', 'cool'.[17] Another is to be found in the following extract:

> when you get to like ten o'clock and half past ten you are getting groups of lads coming in here you see. Plus there are groups of girls coming in and so groups of lads are following them you know, to cop off. It is the old mentality.

Here male heterosexual desire is the rationale for invasion, and straight women act as the medium through which straight men enter the space. Common to all these explanations of invasion is the absence of any direct references to violence.

One of the challenges of the gay and lesbian spaces and politics of fear is to understand how people who have for so long been the objects of a politics of fear turn to a politics of fear to produce themselves as subjects. The data collected in our research suggest that far from eradicating myths of the dangerous other, lesbian and gay identity politics reinvents those myths for a different politics. Morley (2000) notes that there is a long history, from the Greeks and the Romans onwards, of imaginary geographies, in which the members of certain social groups locate themselves at the centre of the universe, at the spatial periphery of which they picture a world of threatening monsters and grotesques. They produce these pictures to both centre themselves and enable them to identify and exclude others. In a space where many different groups come together, where Bhabha (1996) would argue it is important to know the differences, stranger proximity requires an ability to read and identify the potential threat in order to produce the self as safe.

Thus our reference to myth in this context is not in order to connote the need to move from the falsehood of myth to the truth of post-myth condition (Gilloch 1996) but to point to the urgent need to examine the nature and effects of our very limited repertoire of ways of making sense of being, belonging and social order. Fear is therefore constitutive of many different ways of existing.

Notes

1 A rare exception to this is Valentine (2000).
2 The 30-month project was funded by the Economic and Social Research Council (ESRC). Data were generated between May 1998 and March 2000. Lewis Turner and Carole Truman also participated in some parts of the research. Full details of the project can be found at *http://les1.man.ac.uk/sociology/vssrp*.
3 At the time of the research only one bar in Lancaster appeared in gay listings as gay-friendly. In the summer, the bar was predominantly a family tourist space. City centre redevelopment threatens the continued existence of this bar. After the research was completed, a gay bar opened in Lancaster.
4 Fifty-eight structured interviews (twenty-one in Lancaster, thirty-seven in Manchester) were undertaken, with key informants chosen because of their commercial, institutional (both public and private) and community links and interests.

Questions dealt with three main themes: the historical and contemporary development and use of space, safety issues, and policy and safety initiatives. Six focus
groups were held with each group of lesbians, gay men and straight women in each
location. We also collected archival data, tourist information, information from local
TV and newspapers, council documents and minutes of relevant meetings (see
website for full information).

5 The survey was conducted in our two research locations. The Lancaster survey,
undertaken over two nights in May 1999 in venues identified as lesbian- and gay-
friendly, generated 219 responses from 230 distributed questionnaires. The survey of
Manchester's gay village focused upon thirteen of the village venues (selected so as
to provide a sample of the different types of venue). It was undertaken on a Friday
(lunchtime and evening) in early February 1999. 703 questionnaires were completed
(a response rate of 79 percent). Of those that responded (682) to the question of
their sexual and gender identity, 19.8 percent (135) were lesbians, 35.9 percent
(245) were gay men, 19.5 percent (133) were straight women, 13.6 percent (93)
were straight men, 1 percent were transgender, 2.9 percent (20) were bisexual
women and 3.8 percent (26) were bisexual men.

6 Neill draws upon Gilloch's analysis of the work of Walter Benjamin. See Gilloch
(1996) for an analysis of this theme in the work of Walter Benjamin.

7 Our statistical analysis (using logistic regression) confirms that being a gay man is
significant.

8 Gay men were the group that used the village the most: 86.5 percent of the gay men
surveyed visited the village once a week or more. Logistical regression added another
dimension to this: address was significant. Individuals living outside Manchester
perceived the village to be safer than individuals from Manchester. Those who were
most remote from the village (i.e. from outside Manchester) scored the highest
rating for perceptions of the village as 'safe' (80 percent), in contrast to those living
in the city centre, who had the lowest rating for perceptions of 'safety' (48.6
percent). The design of the questionnaire also enabled us to examine the impact of
other factors upon experiences and perceptions of safety and danger: age, means of
transport to/from venues, arriving alone or with friends. However, analysis of the
data suggested that none was significant in terms of perceptions of danger. This was
true for both locations.

9 In Lancaster, straight men were the group with the lowest perceptions of safety.
Straight men were almost twice as likely to find Lancaster unsafe than our lesbian
and gay respondents. There is a need for some caution here, as the sample of straight
men surveyed was small.

10 Perceptions of danger was the most popular reason given by all groups.

11 It is important to note here that we were not able to ask the same spatial questions
in each location. So in Manchester we asked about safety and danger in the village.
As no equivalent space exists in Lancaster we posed the question in terms of
Lancaster more generally, with a follow-on question relating to safety and danger
associated with particular streets and bars in Lancaster. In Manchester, the follow-on
question focused on the village.

12 The Lancaster findings have been explored in some detail in Corteen (2002).

13 There has been a long and detailed historical debate in lesbian literature on how
femme is taken as straight (Butler 1998; Martin 1996).

14 At the same time, this absolute division is problematic. Straight bars and 'mixed'
bars (dominated by straights, according to our census survey) exist in the village.

15 Comfort, and its associations with home, are other modes of investment; see Moran
(2001).

16 We have explored other problematic aspects of boundaries in Moran and Skeggs
(2001).

17 In contrast, the straight women's group had stopped using the space because it was no longer seen to be cool. A historical time lag is occurring here.

References

Ahmed, S. (2000) *Strange Encounters: Embodied Others in Postcoloniality*. London: Routledge.

Bannister, J. and Fyfe, N. (2001) 'Fear of crime', *Urban Studies* 38(5–6): 807–13.

Bauman, Z. (1991) *Modernity and Ambivalence*. Cambridge: Polity Press.

Bennett, T. (1990) 'Tackling fear of crime', *Home Office Research Bulletin*. London: Home Office.

Bhabha, H. (1996) 'Rethinking authority: interview with Homi Bhabha', *Angelaki* 2(2): 59–65.

Bourdieu, P. (1986) *Distinction: A Social Critique of the Judgement of Taste*. London: Routledge.

Butler, J. (1998) 'Afterword', in S. Munt (ed.) *Butch/Femme: Inside Lesbian Gender*. London: Cassell.

Corteen, K. (2002) 'Lesbian safety talk: problematizing definitions and experiences of violence, sexuality and space', *Sexualities* 5(3): 259–80.

Ditton, J., Bannister, J., Gilchrist, E., and Farrall, S. (1999) 'Afraid or angry? Recalibrating the "fear" of crime', *International Review of Victimology* 6: 83–99.

Ditton, J. and Farrall, S. (eds) (2000) *The Fear of Crime*. Aldershot: Ashgate Dartmouth.

Duggan, L. (2000) *Sapphic Slashers: Sex Violence and American Modernity*. Durham, NC: Duke University Press.

Gilloch, G. (1996) *Myth and Metropolis: Walter Benjamin and the City*. Cambridge: Polity Press.

Girling, E., Loader, I. and Sparks, R. (2000) *Crime and Social Change in Middle England: Questions of Order in an English Town*. London: Routledge.

Gold, J.R. and Revill, G. (2000) *Landscapes of Defence*. Harlow: Prentice Hall.

Hale, C. (1996) 'Fear of crime: a review of the literature', *International Review of Victimology* 4: 79–150.

Hart, L. (1994) *Fatal Women*. Princeton, NJ: Princeton University Press.

Healthy Gay Manchester (1998) *Healthy Gay Manchester's Lesbian and Gay Guide to Greater Manchester*.

Hindelong, M., Gottfredson, M. and Garofalo, J. (1978) *Victims of Personal Crime*. Boston: Bollinger.

Jacobs, J.B. and Potter, K. (1998) *Hate Crimes: Criminal Law and Identity Politics*. New York: Oxford University Press.

Jefferson, T. and Hollway, W. (2000) 'The role of anxiety in fear of crime', in T. Hope and R. Sparks (eds) *Crime, Risk and Insecurity*. London: Routledge.

Jenness, V. and Broad, K. (1997) *Hate Crimes: New Social Movements and the Politics of Violence*. Hawthorn: Aldine De Gruyter.

Jenness, V. and Grattet, R. (2001) *Building the Hate Crime Policy Domain: From Social Movement Concept to Law Enforcement Practice*. New York: Russell Sage Foundation.

Martin, B. (1996) *Femininity Played Straight: The Significance of Being Lesbian*. New York: Routledge.

Mason, G. and Tomsen, S. (eds) (1997) *Homophobic Violence*. Sydney: Hawkins Press.

Merry, S. (1981) *Urban Danger: Life in a Neighbourhood of Strangers*. Philadelphia: Temple University Press.

Moran, L.J. (1996) *The Homosexual(ity) of Law*. London: Routledge.

Moran, L.J. (2000) 'Homophobic violence: the hidden injuries of class', in S. Munt (ed.) *Cultural Studies and the Working Class*. London: Cassell.

Moran, L.J. (2002) 'The poetics of safety: lesbians, gay men and home', in A. Crawford (ed.) *Crime, Insecurity, Safety in the New Governance*. Cullompton: Willans Publishing.

Moran, L.J. and Skeggs, B. (2001) 'The property of safety', *Journal of Social Welfare and Family Law* 23(4): 1–15.

Morley, D. (2000) *Home Territories: Media, Mobility and Identity*. London: Routledge.

Neill, W.J.V. (2001) 'Marketing the urban experience: reflections on the place of fear in the promotional strategies of Belfast, Detroit and Berlin', *Urban Studies* 38(5–6): 815–28.

Simmel, G. (1964) 'The stranger', in *The Sociology of Georg Simmel*, trans. K.H. Wolff. New York: Free Press.

Skeggs, B. (2000) 'The appearance of class: challenges in gay space', in S. Munt (ed.) *Cultural Studies and the Working Class: Subject to Change*. London: Cassell.

Skeggs, B. (2001) 'The toilet paper: femininity, class and mis-recognition', *Women's Studies International Forum* 24(3–4): 295–307.

Stanko, E.A. (1997) 'Safety talk: conceptualising women's risk assessment as a "technology of the self"', *Theoretical Criminology* 1(4): 479–99.

Stanko, E.A. (2000) 'Victims R Us: the life history of "fear of crime" and the politicisation of violence', in T. Hope and R. Sparks (eds) *Crime, Risk and Insecurity*. London: Routledge.

Valentine, G. (2000) '"Sticks and stones may break my bones": a personal geography of harassment', in G. Valentine (ed.) *From Nowhere to Everywhere: Lesbian Geographies*. Harrington Park: Howarth Press.

Valentine, G. and Johnston, L. (1995) 'Wherever I lay my girlfriend, that's my home: the performance and surveillance of lesbian identities in domestic environments', in D. Bell and G. Valentine (eds) *Mapping Desire: Geographies of Sexualities*. London: Routledge.

van der Wurff, A., Stringer, P. and Timmer, F. (1988) 'Feelings of unsafety in residential surroundings', in D. Canter, C. Jeusiono, L. Soccka and G. Stephenson (eds) *Environmental Social Psychology*. The Hague: Kluwer.

Walklate, S.L. (2000) 'Trust and the problem of community in the inner city', in T. Hope and R. Sparks (eds) *Crime, Risk and Insecurity*. London: Routledge.

Walklate, S.L. (2001) 'Fearful communities?' *Urban Studies* 38(5–6): 929–31.

Part III
Violence, meaning and social contexts

8 Defined by men's abuse
The 'spoiled identity' of domestic violence survivors

Rosemary Aris, Gill Hague
and Audrey Mullender

Previous research in the UK and elsewhere has shown that, despite recent improvements, there is widespread misunderstanding of the nature of domestic violence, not just among the general public but also among workers in the statutory agencies to whom the majority of women experiencing abuse and seeking help turn for assistance and support (Smith 1989). This lack of understanding has had, and continues to have, serious consequences for survivors of such violence and their children in relation to access to services; indeed, it has cost some women their lives (Home Office Homicide Statistics, annual). It is clear from repeated and well-publicised tragedies that the safety of women and children depends on how well service providers understand the scope and scale of domestic violence and the complexities of women's attempts to escape. Male partners may escalate violence, abuse and threats to prevent their partners from leaving; women may feel tied by bonds of love, marriage, children and financial security; and the interaction between the emotional impact of the abuse and the difficulty that survivors have in negotiating the maze of ill-coordinated legal and welfare services is well known (e.g. Mullender 1996). Above all, service providers need to understand how advocacy, self-help and support services can empower women through this process on their own terms.

If, as some commentators have emphasised (Mullender and Hague 2001), this understanding can best be acquired by listening to, and learning from, the survivors of domestic violence themselves, then user involvement is crucial in improving agency responses to domestic violence. This view is supported by Home Office and other investigations in the UK into the adequacy of services in relation to domestic violence (Humphreys *et al.* 2000; Smith 1989) and has prompted a small number of new initiatives designed to place survivors at the heart of service provision and policy making. These include survivor advisory groups to domestic violence forums, and systematic consultation through Women's Aid, the key national agency providing refuge and support services for abused women and their children. The Home Office is also currently funding a series of projects designed to assist in developing good practice in domestic violence work, and some of these specifically take account of the views and voices of abused women themselves. However, our recent study of user consultation and participation (on which this chapter is based) found that such an emphasis remains rare. More often, these views and voices are overlooked (Hague *et al.* 2001).

Against this general background, such research findings – that survivor involvement does not appear to have improved (except in a few cases), or has diminished, as provision has increased – are depressing. The women's refuge movement, which began in the 1970s, has always had principles of collective and individual empowerment. Through its efforts, the perspectives and views of abused women did inform earlier work on domestic violence and have, in large part, contributed to the spread of information and support for survivors and their children (Hague *et al.* 1996). However, it seems that empowering, participative policies of this type have not kept pace with more recent developments across the service sectors involved.

It could be argued that, while depressing, this finding is not surprising when problems with the theory and practice of empowerment through user involvement are so well documented. These problems revolve around issues that include professionalisation, power and budget-driven managerialism (Anderson 1996; Croft and Beresford 1992; Ramcharan 1997). Similar issues have emerged in our research and have contributed to the under-involvement of survivors and to the difficulties encountered by users in initiatives aimed at responding to domestic violence (Hague *et al.* 2001). However, the literature that attempts to explain the frequent dilution of user involvement schemes has tended to focus on strategies employed by professionals, in male-dominated organisations, to avoid the transfer of power (Croft and Beresford 1992). The findings of this study indicate a more complex picture and suggest that there is an unacknowledged tendency, employed by professionals in the field of domestic violence (who are frequently women), to engage in a practice that aims to protect survivors but, paradoxically, acts to silence them. This silencing tendency, we will argue, leads survivors to minimise the extent and nature of the abuse they endure and may discourage their participation in initiatives designed to assist them. By labelling/ constructing survivors as 'being in the experience', workers in the domestic violence field sometimes unwittingly constrain and disempower those who are ostensibly being helped.

It has long been recognised in psychology, sociology and social policy that identity is multi-layered and fractured, and that 'professionals' and institutions play a key role in reformulating identity (Garfinkel 1974; Goffman 1963; Smith 1978; Weider 1974). Berger and Luckman (1967), for instance, in their classic study of the social construction of reality, claim that identity is a phenomenon that emerges between the individual and society. Identities exist in part by virtue of social definition and are internalised as realities in the course of socialisation (Berger and Luckman 1967: 195). It will be argued later in this chapter, with reference to Goffman's notions of 'spoiled identity' and 'stigma', that, in the field of domestic violence, professionals often do not realise the key role they play in identity formation (Goffman 1963). As we will outline in this chapter, our research has shown that survivors of domestic violence will frequently avoid contact with professionals as a way of preventing their identity being tainted by men's abuse. The crystal-clear awareness, demonstrated by many abused women, of the negative processes commonly set in motion by disclosure of abuse (which can mean that they become defined by the condition in a way that detrimentally affects all other social interaction as well as their self-image) leads many to keep silent or, where that is not possible, to edit the information they communicate to professionals. This has two principal consequences. First, it limits the help that survivors receive, as professionals become frustrated by what they may see as lack of cooperation. Second, it exacerbates the problem of gauging the extent of domestic violence. In conclusion, we will claim that professionals need to recognise this failure of communication, since it has serious implications for the safety of survivors and is a major impediment to the service improvements to which professionals and activists in the domestic violence field, and local and central government, are committed (Women's Unit of the Cabinet Office 1999).

The organisation of the research

In this research, we aimed first to find out how far and in what ways survivors of domestic violence are involved in the development and delivery of services for women and children who have experienced domestic violence. Second, we were particularly interested in examining the participation of survivors in multi-agency forums, where different agencies work together to improve services and safety, and in looking at examples of good practice. Third, we wanted to hear what women say about the effectiveness of services and about the extent and nature of their participation. Last, we were interested in the extent to which initiatives to involve abused women are adding to knowledge and understanding of domestic violence and are empowering women by increasing their control over the services they need.[1]

The research took place in the UK, but it does have relevance for service provision in other countries. It was carried out in two stages. Stage 1 consisted of a questionnaire-based mapping study of all inter-agency forums and refuges and of selected other specialist domestic violence projects throughout England and Wales. This section of the project aimed to establish what was available across the country in terms of projects involving service users in their services or having consultation mechanisms in place. Stage 2 aimed to chart the involvement of survivors in this support system in more detail and consisted of in-depth fieldwork in three main research sites in London, the southwest and the West Midlands, supplemented by work in two policy profile areas in South Wales and in the north of England, together with two small case studies in London boroughs and one in the north.

This second phase of the research was based on semi-structured interviews with a sample of eighty-five declared domestic violence survivors. The sample (a purposive one as far as could be achieved) was drawn from a variety of sources, including refuges, temporary accommodation, women's self-help groups, multi-agency forums and the general public. This was supplemented by interviews with groups of women, bringing the overall interview total to 112. Semi-structured interviews were carried out with eighty-two officers of statutory, voluntary and community organisations and multi-agency forums, including social services, police domestic violence units, local authority housing departments, Victim Support and refuges. This data set was further supplemented by interviews with key personnel in national agencies. Data were also collected by attendance and observation at forum and agency meetings and strategy groups, and at women's self-help support groups, and through the collection and analysis of documentation, practice guidance and policies.

The project was supported by an advisory group of professionals and activists, many of whom were declared survivors of abuse, and by a group of domestic violence service users. The Women's Aid Federation of England, the key national specialist agency for abused women and their children, acted as consultant to the study.

User involvement and the identity of survivors

Almost all participants in the research welcomed the idea of user involvement in policy making and in the provision of services in relation to domestic violence, as Box 8.1 indicates.

However, at the time of the study, few survivors who had used services were directly involved in domestic violence forums, in decision making in statutory agencies and domestic violence projects or in service provision (although some abused women were active in other ways, and individual workers in the research sites were working hard to try to ensure that service users were heard). Across the country, few inter-agency forums and projects had concrete procedures and mechanisms in place for carrying out meaningful consultation, and the majority had little concept of how to go about it. While refuges emerged specifically as somewhat better at user involvement than other agencies (as would be expected from their activist history), even here the picture was not always encouraging. The majority of survivors interviewed had never heard of their local domestic violence forums, felt distanced from decision-making processes in refuge organisations and statutory agencies, and believed that there was no arena in which they could be heard.

Box 8.1

- 81 percent of survivors thought that survivors should actively participate in domestic violence forums and service provision;
- 91 percent of agency and project workers thought that survivors should be actively involved in domestic violence forums and service provision;
- 90 percent of refuges consulted with service users, but only 40 percent of forums did so.

Attempts had been made to improve this situation. In one of the study areas, there was a theatre group, and survivors had been closely involved in the running of a public awareness-raising campaign. In several of the research sites, there were survivor support groups that were sometimes consulted (although, in one, this group had been suspended and has not restarted since). Often, if survivors were represented on their local domestic violence forums, it was by refuge workers or other women's projects, and they also attended as professionals, either disclosed or undisclosed as survivors. One study site had had an active survivors' forum advising on policy and represented on the local domestic violence forum itself, although the latter arrangement had been problematic without the provision of sufficient support and resources to overcome the difficulties involved.

Despite these examples of tentative user consultation and involvement, in most cases throughout the study survivors were represented in local forums and agencies by no one at all. Overall, in spite of the best efforts of some workers in the localities concerned, the majority of the women we interviewed felt that their views were overlooked to a considerable extent by service providers and that their needs were not adequately met. They felt silenced, regarded as not important, and unable to achieve the type of service and policy responses they sought. Many interviewees also believed (often at the same time) that agency practice had improved in various ways over recent years. Even so, most felt that they were powerless to influence the direction of policy or service development and gave accounts of inadequate or potentially dangerous responses by agencies.

Analysis of the research revealed five main barriers to user involvement. These were distributed throughout the layers of organisation that make up multi-agency approaches to domestic violence and also service responses. They compounded one another to lessen the impact of survivors on policy making and service provision. These barriers include problems encountered in domestic violence forums (including members' lack of commitment to user participation and to diversity and equalities issues); difficulties in accessing survivors; hierarchical organisation in domestic violence work; the construction of the identity of survivors as 'being in the experience'; and the understandable unwillingness of professionals to disclose that they may also be survivors. Each of the barriers is explored further in various ways in the following sections, and the extent to which 'being in the experience' links each of them is developed at the end of the chapter in relation to theorising about stigma and identity more broadly.

Problems with domestic violence forums

A number of weaknesses were identified in the organisation of domestic violence forums that reduced their effectiveness and made the participation of survivors more difficult. In one of the research sites, for example, the domestic violence coordinator, the members of the police domestic violence unit and other members of the forum who represented statutory agencies said that they had no idea how to involve survivors or keep them involved. They hoped that the research reported here might provide inspiration. Previous attempts had been made at different times to involve individual survivors from local refuges in forum meetings, but these had been short-lived. According to the coordinator, one of the two survivors who had participated had used the experience to 'make a career' in domestic violence work, and the other had encountered family difficulties and could no longer attend. The coordinator had subsequently convened discussions/workshops to look at ways of involving survivors in the forum as this was 'something we need to be working towards', but she had encountered resistance to user involvement and, in her words, 'there are still members of the forum and representatives of agencies who attend discussions and workshops who are very traditional in their outlook and hold on to their professional high ground'. In one group discussion about user participation in service provision, this view was strongly advanced by a representative of a statutory agency and supported by representatives of other statutory agencies. He appeared to think that being a survivor was an insufficient qualification to enable abused women to offer advice to domestic violence forums, and he emphasised that 'while we appreciate survivors' views it's really a job for professionals'.

For their part, almost all refuge, agency and project workers, who were themselves members of multi-agency forums, welcomed the idea that survivors should be involved in multi-agency forums and other initiatives aimed at combating domestic violence. Many voluntary agency representatives and refuge workers saw the setting up of such forums as a significant step forward for survivors. Of the refuge and agency workers interviewed, 36 percent thought that domestic violence forums promoted understanding of domestic violence, and 27 percent thought they provided an opportunity for survivors' voices to be heard through refuge workers, but only 9 percent thought they ensured more appropriate services. Domestic violence workers who were interviewed identified many specific weaknesses as well as strengths in domestic violence forums, including, in this context, that forums were exclusive, for professionals only, and that there was no access for service users.

Difficulties in accesing survivors in domestic violence work

A wide range of respondents in the study thought that the absence of domestic violence service users and ex-users from decision-making structures and policy-making consultations was a major barrier to the development of a more effective response to domestic violence. They agreed that the participation of survivors would have improved understanding of domestic violence and that it might perhaps have led to a more serious approach to attendance at meetings by decision makers in statutory agencies. However, although there was widespread interest in this issue, rarely was much effort expended to put participation into practice or to provide the required resources. Clearly, the first problem identified was how to obtain the practical commitment of agencies, including that of senior managers, to user consultation in the domestic violence field.

Where this battle had been won in principle, at least partially, carrying it through still presented very real practical difficulties. There was often a problem in accessing survivors who wished to be directly involved. Domestic violence service users facing extreme personal crises may not be in a life position to contribute to service provision, and serious issues of safety and confidentiality are at stake. In addition, survivors may move on – either in their lives or geographically – and may be available for only a short period for consultation and participation activities. In one research site, the numbers of survivors who had been initially involved in a domestic violence survivors' forum dropped off rapidly as time went by and personal situations changed. In another area, the domestic violence coordinator had encountered practical difficulties in contacting survivors directly. In her experience, survivors could mainly be contacted through the local refuges, where there were often problems because of security needs, with refuge workers acting protectively towards their residents, and it had been difficult to contact survivors who had left refuges or had never been in one. In all cases, confidentiality was a difficult issue to confront to ensure safety. Another complexity was representation. Domestic abuse affects women from all social and ethnic backgrounds. Taking on issues of diversity and equality in building consultative processes, and reaching out to women in all local communities, are important issues in accessing survivors willing to partici-pate, but we found few examples where they had been taken on effectively.

Hierarchical organisation as a barrier

Some forum members interviewed believed that the lack of attention to survivor voices owed less to confidentiality and access issues and more to hierar-chical organisation, in refuges as well as in statutory agencies. In their experience, key staff in some refuge organisations sometimes gave the impres-sion of 'owning' survivors – they acted as 'gatekeepers', and forums could gain access to survivors only through them. Forums also performed their own gate-keeping in that some project workers who provide support/refuge/advice in relation to domestic violence (in addition to the main organisations that provide refuge accommodation for survivors) complained that they were, or had been, excluded from the forum and that survivors were not referred to them by statutory agencies. The manager of one black women's organisation complained that a particular statutory agency had never referred survivors to that organisa-tion. They were referred only to the main refuge providers, because these were seen to be the 'experts' in domestic violence. This meant that other, often small, women's support organisations were unable either to participate them-selves or to contribute to service user participation initiatives.

For their part, while some refuge workers were keen to facilitate service user involvement in domestic violence work outside their own project, some also expressed a variety of concerns about the dangers of participation in forums for survivors. They emphasised the vulnerability of survivors to exploitation or to being treated like exhibits. Several respondents argued that, in their experience, many women did not want to be involved and would rather put the experience behind them and move on. Others, like the statutory representative cited earlier, believed that survivors were out of their depth in the forum or meeting environment. They believed that the experience of domestic violence was not enough to equip them for this role (in which they would be representing other survivors) and that women would not understand what was going on or what was being discussed, as this often required training, insider knowledge and familiarity with jargon.

Certainly, women ex-users who were interviewed in the study, and who had represented other survivors on domestic violence forums, talked of how the experiences had often been distressing and inappropriate (although the involvement of service users in this way had also been successful on various occasions). Our informants reported feeling silenced and patronised or even, on occasion, subjected to potentially racist or discriminatory responses from agency workers, even where the agencies or forums concerned said they were trying hard to avoid these outcomes. Other service users who were interviewed reported amazement at the 'talking shop' nature of many official meetings and the apparent waste of time involved.

Where domestic violence survivors were well known to the forum members concerned and were personally strong and confident or, most importantly, where they represented a support group or agency (in common with participating professionals), participation at meetings worked more effectively. In general, however, the study found that involvement of this type remains problematic in regard to issues of intimate personal abuse, although not impossible to achieve (and it should be remembered that there has been a move in policy and legislation, for example Best Value, to require this sort of community involvement and user consultation). Where it is attempted, various support, compensation and training issues for the women doing the work are likely to be raised. These include the provision of child care, transport, expenses, interpreting and the possibility of payment; the use of safe venues; support to attend meetings; and training in the procedures used.

Due to the difficulties of direct involvement of domestic violence service users in inter-agency forums and agency meetings, including as a result of thehierarchical and potentially exclusive nature of these events, various other methods of consultation are currently being tried out to a small extent around the country. These include domestic violence survivors' forums and advisory/monitoring groups, which usually also become support groups for the women involved. A group of this type has successfully operated for six or seven years in Liverpool, for example. Other mechanisms include women's focus groups, structured representations through Women's Aid and women's projects, community arts and theatre, consultative processes required by new legislation (e.g. Crime and Disorder Audits and Best Value reviews), surveys and questionnaires, and research projects to seek user views. There are resource implications in all of these, and the provision of support and possibly training for women who participate is of key importance. On the whole though, they do work better.

Some domestic violence workers interviewed for our study expressed a degree of scepticism or cynicism about who was expected to do the work necessary to make user involvement a success and whether survivors were really going to benefit from such initiatives. There was a perception that policy makers expected schemes to involve women who have experienced domestic violence to be implemented and run by women, usually existing domestic violence workers. However, refuge groups and women's projects rarely have the spare capacity to engage in this work unless structures and resources are agreed by all the agencies involved to enable them to do so. User consultation is not a cheap option and needs to be resourced properly if it is to work. In most localities investigated, however, few – or no – resources or staff were available, and workers in both the statutory and voluntary sectors were already being pushed to their limits.

'Being in the experience': agency and refuge workers and the remaking of survivors' identity

In a study of Women's Aid refuges in the early 1980s, Pahl (1985) concluded that women who had participated in decision making while they were in a refuge and who had shared in the running of the house were more likely to live independently after leaving the refuge. As a result of their participation they had gained in strength, confidence and control over their lives.

The vast majority of refuge and project workers interviewed for this study appeared to subscribe to this view. They thought that user participation was a good thing, both in refuges and in domestic violence forums, although, at the time of the research, the majority (81 percent) of residents interviewed in refuges were not directly involved in making decisions about running refuges, for example on management committees. Some refuge workers interviewed were very protective of their residents. When asked to talk about why they thought this was and about how survivors could be involved in policy making and provision of services in relation to domestic violence, the same qualification (echoed by voluntary and statutory agency representatives alike) was often applied, although sometimes expressed slightly differently. This was that survivors should be involved, but not while they were still 'in the experience'. Far from seeing participation as a route to helping women regain control and confidence, workers in the field, ranging from refuge workers to statutory managers, often appeared to feel that the experience of men's abuse rendered women so vulnerable and in need of protection, from a range of outside influences as well as from their abusers, that they were usually not able to engage in consultative or participative processes, at least in the short term. Ways of expressing this view included 'survivors have enough to deal with already' and 'they should not remind themselves'. Some thought that participation was advisable 'once survivors have some distance from the experience', while others thought that survivors needed refuge workers to represent them because 'women are not strong enough while they are residents'. Officers in statutory agencies were often similarly reticent, most often citing lack of expertise among service users and ex-users and lack of resources as key factors in a regrettable situation.

The disempowering effect of constructing survivors in this way became clear in interviews and discussions with abused women, in which 81 percent thought that survivors should participate actively in domestic violence forums – but other survivors, not them. They were quick to talk of the disabling effects of experiencing abuse. While some had become strong and vocal, many spoke of having been adversely affected by the experience of abuse, and of the need to put the experience behind them and move on (see Box 8.2).

In broader discussions about user participation (including participation in the work of refuges) and the obstacles to it, most women service users echoed the 'not while in the experience' views of many agency and refuge workers, as illustrated in the following quotes from women who were resident in refuges: women 'need to get over problems first'; 'survivors are seen as "silly women"'; 'women should take part after they've gone through it all and things are a lot better'; 'women should be involved if they feel able to cope'; 'women would need a self-development course'; 'not a good idea to involve women who are still experiencing domestic violence'; 'there should be training and counselling for women who want to get involved'; and 'women are not strong enough'. Their words cover a combination of skills issues, emotional/adjustment concerns and discriminatory attitudes, which may require different approaches to overcome.

It is the case (as 71 percent of the survivors interviewed pointed out) that, in the early stages of trying to escape their abusers, the last thing that survivors need is to be asked to attend meetings and groups. The provision of focused and reliable, respectful support and unconditional help is invaluable in assisting survivors and should be the sole concern at this point. Nevertheless, there are difficulties with the kinds of explanation listed above for the absence of survivors from decision making. The view that underpins this blanket approach to survivor involvement could potentially exclude all women while they are still using services, and possibly beyond. Since many women live with the expe-

---

Box 8.2

- 40 percent of survivors said that they would rather move on and put the experience behind them;
- 33 percent said that the stigma attached to women who had experienced domestic violence would prevent their participation;
- 14 percent thought that confidentiality could not be assured;
- 13 percent gave other reasons.

rience of domestic violence and its aftermath for much of their lives, this could easily mean that survivors might never be perceived to be in the right frame of mind to participate.

Professionals' unwillingness to disclose abuse

While women labelled as 'survivors' are deterred from participation, it is clear from interviews and discussions with professionals throughout this study that survivors do in fact take part in forums and other initiatives to combat and respond more effectively to domestic violence but that they are there in other roles – notably as activists and workers in women's organisations and as professionals in a wide range of agencies. Very many women who have themselves experienced domestic violence, either as adults or as child witnesses, occupy professional positions and are members of domestic violence forums and other projects. One of the major findings of the study is the enormous role played by professionals who are survivors of abuse, both disclosed and undisclosed, throughout the development of domestic violence services over the last three decades, although this contribution has rarely been acknowledged or discussed.

Professionals who are also survivors often feel unable to declare such experiences, preferring to do what they can quietly, rather than risk embarrassment and possible pity, voyeurism or stigma from colleagues. Some of the interviews we conducted with workers in this position revealed that it is not so much experiencing domestic violence as disclosing it that disqualifies survivors from meaningful participation. By disclosing abuse, survivors risk being devalued or disbarred from participation in decision making, not only in relation to domestic violence projects but also in other areas of their lives. Professionals who are known to be domestic violence survivors risk having their objectivity and credibility called into question. As long as no one knows, job prospects are not blighted and they perform their roles perfectly adequately.

One way around the credibility gap in terms of job prospects for declared survivors appears to be to work in refuges for abused women or in related fields – to use the experience to make a career in domestic violence work, as described earlier in this chapter. There are significant numbers of survivors who return to work with abused women as volunteers in refuges, and various refuge organisations now work with local education providers to set up training courses for residents or ex-residents to facilitate this, with a view to career development. Some refuge and advocacy organisations have their own volunteer training programmes and criteria for involving residents and ex-residents, although, in some agencies in our study, it was unclear from discussions with the workers involved what criteria were used in recruiting survivors. Even here, there could be a tendency to value direct experience less highly than formal qualifications (in counselling, for example). In these examples, it was not at all evident what characteristics distinguished potential refuge workers from other survivors, or how it was established that they had moved on from the immediate trauma (a stated prerequisite). According to one declared survivor, who had spent time in a refuge as both a resident and a volunteer (but not as a paid worker), success by this route merely requires a readiness to exploit other survivors, to treat them as victims to be helped. Her view was that:

> Lots of survivors have got jobs in the voluntary sector in domestic violence – good jobs which they would not have got in any other circumstances. They turned their situation to their advantage – they rewrite their past, they're more powerful than they've ever been helping survivors of domestic violence. They get their strength from helping other women through but after they've served their purpose they're not interested.

The above respondent was not alone in this view but, equally, there were other interviewees who felt that, by volunteering and perhaps joining management committees or working with women and children in the refuge, they were 'giving back' for the assistance they had received to empower themselves and were attempting to help other women to do the same.

Many refuge organisations and other women's projects do have policies of involving women experiencing domestic violence in running the project and encourage them to join the management committee. Again, however, these policies normally prescribe that a specified period should elapse so that women ex-service users are only eligible if they have finished using services, if they have moved on beyond the immediate crisis, and if time for recovery has passed. While there is a certain wisdom in such policies in many circumstances, and in Women's Aid itself they have been carefully developed over many years, their blanket use could again be viewed as a potentially discriminatory and 'blunt instrument'. Procedures of this type need careful consideration because they can exclude women who want to be involved at an earlier stage and mute the raw power of many survivors' voices. They can also lead to personal experiences of responses to services being dismissed on the grounds of being outdated by the time they are shared.

None of the statutory or voluntary sector projects whose workers were interviewed in the study, excluding women's refuge, advocacy and support organisations, had policies in place as regards direct access to management or policy making. Although there were examples of good practice and of attempts to involve service users and ex-users in this way here and there, the overriding view in the statutory sector (with some exceptions, often local authority equality and other specialist officers and police domestic violence liaison officers) seemed to be that women who have experienced domestic violence deserve pity and protection rather than involvement and empowerment.

The message that disclosure of abuse rebounds negatively and affects other areas of life was not lost on the service users and refuge residents who took part in the study. Some had devised clear strategies in a bid to limit the impact of disclosure and to avoid being defined by men's abuse – strategies that have far-reaching consequences for those seeking to foster a more profound understanding of domestic violence. Many women described how, when they had no choice but to disclose abuse to get help, they censored their accounts and gave edited versions of their experiences: 'I didn't tell them it's domestic violence and they didn't ask'; 'I wanted to get a divorce by two years separation so as to gloss over the violence'; 'I wouldn't tell them the truth ... frightened of their reaction'; 'Women don't want people to know. If they know, they blame them'; 'I kept it quiet at the beginning'.

It was particularly the experience of some of the service users and ex-users interviewed that there were professionals for whom only experience characterised by physical, as opposed to sexual or emotional, violence was acceptable, and they tailored their accounts accordingly. Moreover, some women suspected officials they had encountered of having a prurient interest when they seemed to ask for excessive details of what had occurred, especially where this included sexual violence. Thus, not only the extreme personal embarrassment of disclosing sexual abuse but also the immediate stigmatisation and possible sexual innuendo that often accompanied it, among professionals as among the general population, were strong inhibiting factors.

Stigma and identity

Analysis of interviews with survivors, workers and professionals in this study suggests that the reconstruction of the identity of survivors as 'being in the experience' is one of the key unacknowledged barriers to their direct participation in service provision and policy making. This phrase is often used as a shorthand for the view that survivors of domestic violence are less competent than people who have not experienced – or, importantly, not disclosed – their experience of domestic violence. This stands in the way of an improved understanding of domestic violence and of an accurate picture of its extent. In this research, workers both in statutory agencies and in refuge and advocacy organisations often, either consciously or unconsciously, seemed to impose stereotypes on survivors in such a way that they absorbed a sense of themselves as helpless and unable to manage.

There are parallels in areas outside domestic violence, notably in the disability rights movement, where the extent to which 'pity oppresses' has now been made clear and challenged. Activists in this movement reject the 'poster child' image for its presentation of disabled people as being dependent and defined by their impairment (Wolf 1993: 228). Our study has also revealed views of domestic violence survivors that are similar to those encountered by researchers in the area of mental health, where service users, who may be defined as 'incompetent', face particular difficulties in getting their voices heard (Barnes 1999). Many respondents in our study, both workers and service users, assumed survivors of violence to be so adversely affected psychologically by their experience as to be incapable, at least temporarily, of participating in decision making. The consequences of being identified, or of identifying yourself, by the harm that has been done to you have long been recognised and were articulated by

survivors who took part in the study. These messages, relayed often unconsciously by agencies and conveyed by those in a position to offer services and
support, had various negative effects. Interviewees talked of low self-esteem,
apathy, damaged job prospects, not reporting abuse, and editing their experiences, especially where these were characterised by sexual abuse.

In this respect, it is plausible to argue that the identity of the survivors of
domestic violence is not only reconstructed but, to use the term first pioneered
by Goffman in the 1960s, is also 'spoiled' (1963: 19). In Goffman's analysis,
when evidence arises of someone possessing an undesirable attribute that makes
him or her different from others, this attribute is a 'stigma'. A stigma constitutes
'a special discrepancy between virtual and actual social identity ... that causes
us to reclassify an individual from one social category to another' (*ibid.*: 5). This
discrepancy, whether known about or visible, 'spoils his [sic] social identity; it
has the effect of cutting him off from society and from himself so that he stands
a discredited person facing an unaccepting world' (*ibid.*: 19).

Goffman's elaboration on the theme of spoiled identity resonates with the
reluctance of many survivors to participate in initiatives around domestic
violence when he asserts that someone with a stigma 'may perceive, usually
quite correctly, that whatever others profess, they do not really "accept" him
and are not ready to make contact with him on "equal grounds"' (*ibid.*: 7).
Furthermore, as Goffman notes, 'the standards he has incorporated from wider
society equip him to be intimately alive to what others see as his failing,
inevitably causing him, if only for moments, to agree that he does indeed fall
short of what he really ought to be. Shame becomes a central possibility, arising
from the individual's perception of one of his own attributes as being a defiling
thing to possess' (*ibid.*: 7).

The consequences of disclosure as experienced by domestic violence
survivors are also clearly covered by Goffman's thesis that we believe the person
with a stigma to be 'not quite human – we exercise varieties of discrimination
through which we effectively, if often unthinkingly, reduce his life chances ...
We tend to impute a wide range of imperfections on the basis of the original
one' (*ibid.*: 3) so that the individual can become 'reduced in our minds from a
whole and usual person to a tainted, discounted one' (*ibid.*: 5).

When the stigma is not immediately apparent – when there are no 'symbols'
or 'signs' of stigma that draw attention to a spoiled identity, for example, 'black
eyes when worn in public by females' (*ibid.*: 42) – the priority becomes the
management of undisclosed discrediting information about oneself. In other
words, the dilemma lies in the decision 'to display or not to display; to tell or
not to tell; to let on or not to let on; to lie or not to lie and in each case, to
whom, how, when and where' (*ibid.*: 45). Many of the abused women interviewed for this research had no choice but to disclose their experience of
domestic violence to get help. However, in so doing, they became in part
defined by men's abuse. Once labelled as 'in the experience', the survivors of
domestic violence seem to follow closely the process eloquently outlined by
Goffman. They are tainted and disqualified from full participation as active citi-

zens. Failure to involve them fully in representative forums can be seen to rest at least partly on this process, and the forums are rendered less effective as a result because they lack the ability of survivors to name immediate dangers and suggest routes to safety.

Conclusion

This paper has discussed briefly the way in which survivors of domestic violence – especially those who have used the services offered by statutory organisations, the voluntary sector and refuge, support and advocacy projects – are frequently constructed as being caught 'in the experience' and are being portrayed as unreliable informants and decision makers as a result. This often also applies to professionals who are declared survivors of domestic abuse. Goffman's discussion of spoiled identity and stigma has some direct relevance to women survivors of abuse by men, who are then often defined by that abuse and diminished by it. Many negative aspects of this type of view can be seen in the domestic violence field, only a few of which have been discussed here.

The extent to which survivors may be affected detrimentally by these processes needs to be recognised and addressed in future developments in the field, since it is a significant impediment to service improvements and has major implications for the safety of abused women. Many governments across the world assert that they are committed to such improvements and to challenging domestic violence against women effectively, yet the issues raised here are rarely addressed and obstacles to such developments remain. While these issues are clearly very complex, agencies, services and policy makers need to take them on board if future development is to occur. Consulting with, and listening to, the survivors of domestic abuse more carefully and systematically, with attention to issues of diversity and difference, would be an important first step forward.

Note

1   The apparent invisibility of survivors 'in their own issue' was the starting point for the research project, entitled 'Abused Women's Perspectives', on which this paper draws (ESRC Award no. L133251017). The study was a team effort involving both the Domestic Violence Research Group at the University of Bristol, which coordinated the project overall, and the Centre for the Study of Safety and Well-being at the University of Warwick. It was one of twenty funded as part of the ESRC Violence Research Programme directed by Professor Betsy Stanko.

References

Anderson, J. (1996) 'Yes, but is it empowerment?' in B. Humphries (ed.) *Critical Perspectives on Empowerment*. Birmingham: Venture Press.
Barnes, M. (1999) 'Users as citizens: collective action and the local governance of welfare', *Social Policy and Administration* 33(1): 73–90.

Berger, P. and Luckman, T. (1967) *The Social Construction of Reality*. Harmondsworth: Penguin.

Croft, S. and Beresford, P. (1992) 'The politics of participation', *Critical Social Policy* 35: 20–44.

Garfinkel, H. (1974) '"Good" organizational reasons for "bad" clinic records', in R. Turner (ed.) *Ethnomethodology*. Harmondsworth: Penguin.

Goffman, E. (1963) *Stigma: Notes on the Management of Spoiled Identity*. Englewood Cliffs, NJ: Prentice Hall.

Hague, G. Malos, E. and Dear, W. (1996) *Multi-agency Work and Domestic Violence: A National Study of Domestic Violence Inter-agency Initiatives*. Bristol: Policy Press.

Hague, G., Mullender, A., Aris, R. and Dear, W. (2001) *Abused Women's Perspectives: Responsiveness and Accountability of Domestic Violence and Inter-agency Initiatives. End of Award Report to the ESRC. Award No: L133251017*. Bristol: University of Bristol, School for Policy Studies.

Humphreys, C., Hester, M., Hague, G., Mullender, A., Abrahams, H. and Lowe, P. (2000) *From Good Intentions to Good Practice: Working with Families where there Is Domestic Violence*. Bristol: Policy Press.

Mullender, A. (1996) *Rethinking Domestic Violence: The Social Work and Probation Response*. London: Routledge.

Mullender, A. and Hague, G. (2001) 'Women survivors' views' in J. Taylor-Browne (ed.) What Works in Reducing Domestic Violence?: *A Comprehensive Guide for Professionals*. London: Whiting and Birch.

Pahl, J. (1985) 'Refuges for battered women: ideology and action', *Feminist Review* 19 (March): 25–43.

Ramcharan, P. (ed.) (1997) *Empowerment in Everyday Life*. London: Jessica Kingsley.

Smith, D.E. (1978) 'K is mentally ill: the anatomy of a factual account', *Sociology* 21: 23–53.

Smith, L.J.F. (1989) *Domestic Violence: An Overview of the Literature* (Home Office Research Study 107). London: HMSO.

Weider, D. (1974) 'Telling the code', in R. Turner (ed.) *Ethnomethodology*. Harmondsworth: Penguin.

Wolf. N. (1993) *Fire with Fire*. London: Chatto & Windus.

Women's Unit of the Cabinet Office (1989) *Living Without Fear: An Integrated Approach to Tackling Violence against Women*. London: Cabinet Office.

9 Bouncers and the social context of violence

Masculinity, class and violence in the night-time economy

Simon Winlow, Dick Hobbs, Stuart Lister and Phil Hadfield

Perhaps the most pervasive stereotypical view of bouncers is of a bunch of bow-tied, muscle-bound, simian thugs, devoid of social skills, oozing aggression and itching to deploy staggeringly proficient violence on anyone whom they deem to have violated their archaic and incomprehensible code of reason and ethics. As is the case with many stereotypes, this representation tells us as much about ourselves as it does about the focus of our analysis. Bouncers are not, for the most part, the creatures of this stereotypical image. To simplify the occupational role of bouncers, they are paid to control and constrain a group of consumers often hell-bent on carnivalesque abandon, and for this reason if nothing else, bouncing represents perhaps one of the most problematic occupational spheres in post-industrial Britain. In this chapter, we intend to offer a tentative look at the night-time economy as an economic and cultural environment, with the hope of contextualising both the violence that occurs there with alarming regularity and the occupational role of bouncers employed to police this environment.

The research on which this chapter is based was originally concerned with producing an analysis of the role and behaviour of bar and nightclub security, or 'bouncers', in post-industrial Britain. We were keen to explore an occupation based around the control of violence and the controlled delivery of violence, and we sought to understand the social, cultural and economic organisation of what we regarded as an inherently problematic profession. In order to do so, we employed a range of qualitative research strategies with the hope of producing a richness of data that we felt the subject matter merited. As our research developed, we embarked upon a number of important tangential enquiries, but our commitment to understanding this occupation from the viewpoint of those employed in it remained central to our project. We travelled the country conducting a large number of in-depth interviews, making contacts and gathering data, but perhaps most importantly, we were able to establish a member of the research team in a covert role, working as a bouncer (see Winlow *et al.* 2001 for a broader description of our research experiences). This enabled us to witness the behaviour of a social group unaware that they were being researched, and to form personal relationships and gather knowledge that would otherwise have remained hidden (see Liebow 1967; Whyte 1993). Our covert ethnography also allowed us a perfect vantage point to observe at first hand Britain's burgeoning nightlife; we watched as thousands upon thousands of young people engaged with the peculiar brand of excess and hedonism that represents a crucially seductive and sustaining element of the night-time economy, and from this vantage point we also saw the downside of this developing economic and cultural arena. With the drunkenness and mass intoxication, with the social competition and apparent abandonment of normative behavioural protocols, with the hyper-reality, peculiarity and developing forms of cultural expression comes an increase in situations that may produce conflict and violence (see Hobbs *et al.* 2003). Whether we like it or not, violence is manifestly a part of Britain's night-time economy, and over the course of our research we witnessed violence with alarming regularity, and occasionally with astounding ferocity (see, for example, Winlow *et al.* 2001).

As we began to gather together empirical findings from our interviews and ethnography, it became apparent that the nature of the contemporary night-time economy would be a crucial starting point from which we could begin to construct and contextualise viable theories that informed the violence we found in the night-time economy generally, and violence involving bouncers specifically. This after-dark leisure environment, based largely around drinking and hedonistic excess (see Hobbs *et al.* 2000), is crucial, as it frames not only the behaviour of consumers but also the occupation and occupational culture of the 'door supervisors' employed to keep order. From this starting point, we began to look at masculinities, class and habitus; self-identity; the economic and cultural foundations of violence involving bouncers (see Winlow *et al.*, forthcoming); the structure and form of bouncers' occupational culture (Hobbs *et al.* 2003); issues of policing, order, regulation and the state (see Lister *et al.* 2001; Hobbs *et al.* 2000); and a number of associated issues, ranging from deindustrialisation and economic and cultural change to policy initiatives aimed at reducing violence (see, for example, Hadfield *et al.* 2001). Despite the diversity of our concerns, the economic and cultural context of the night-time economy remained crucial.

When the research began, Britain's night-time economy appeared to be growing in both economic and cultural significance, and our first tentative hypotheses regarding bouncers and the social organisation of their profession were based around social, economic and cultural change, class, and masculine identity. The night-time economy had grown as British society had moved rapidly towards a new post-industrial consumer capitalism, and memories of heavy industry slowly receded as industrial capitalism was consigned permanently to history (for accounts of the impact of this economic and cultural change, see Lee and Turner 1996). Leisure time was on the increase (Rojek 1985, 1989), the never-ending treadmill of consumerism was consolidating its grip on the nation's psyche (Miles 1998), and conspicuous consumption was an increasingly crucial part of mass culture and individual self-identity (Featherstone 1990, 1995). Traditional class-based employment had all but disappeared, yet here, it seemed, in the night-time economy, was perhaps a developing occupational role for the seemingly extinct working-class man. Those with the necessary skills, connections and desire could use the forces of their bodies to secure employment and express the robust physicality of traditional working-class culture at the same time. This hypothesis slowly began to gather strength and refinement as we dug deeper and our empirical work began to bear fruit. The full complexity of the social change that had given rise to the expansion of the night-time economy had also provoked the development of the contemporary occupation of door supervision, defined its character and culture, and informed its strategies and protocols (see, for example, Monaghan 2002). Social change also altered labour markets and class culture, modified the foundations of identities and transformed the role and meaning of leisure and work. Faced with these powerful theoretical yet palpable forces, the situation seemed to necessitate macro-theories of social and economic change, class and gender (see Winlow 2001). The starting point may have been a seemingly micro-study of the social organisation of bar and nightclub bouncers, but if we were to understand the position and viewpoint of these groups fully, we were going to have to start by addressing the historical, economic and cultural context of the environment in which they work.

Social class and habitus

Over the course of our research, we were forced to wrestle continuously with class. Were the men we studied representative of the changes forced upon the working class in contemporary society? Is it overly deterministic to refer to an entire occupational group, especially this occupational group, as emanating from the same class origins? Furthermore, as so much of our empirical data seemed to indicate the profusion of postmodern cultural forms in the night-time economy, was it apt to refer back to forms of class analysis that seemed to contrast so starkly with our hyper-real research environments (Kumar 1995; Lash 1990)? While these debates lurked under the surface for some time, our empirical data, especially those emerging from our ethnography, seemed to indicate that social class was not something that could be ignored.

Postmodernism, especially in the work of Baudrillard (1993) and Lyotard (1984), has clearly posed serious questions about the continued relevance of class analysis in contemporary society, reflecting wider historical controversies about the place of culture in relation to the economy and the nature of contemporary forms of cultural and individual identity (Bauman 2001; Pakulski and Waters 1996). Sociologists such as Giddens (1991, 1994), and more directly Beck (1992), have argued that class and class consciousness have lost their viability as analytical tools in addressing contemporary social and cultural forms, as individualised cultures increasingly become 'the reproduction unit of the life world' (*ibid.*: 98). The epochal shift that has produced this engaging challenge to traditional social analysis has also produced a situation in which sociology (Lash 1990; Morgan and Stanley 1990; Owen 1997) and criminology

(South 1997; Sumner 1994) find themselves under attack from critics like Baudrillard and racked with internal debates about their relevance in both contemporary society and academia (Beynon and Glavanis 1999; see Bauman (1992) for a judicious riposte to these challenges).

Although other examples exist (for example, Scase 1992; Westergaard 1995), it is perhaps Bourdieu who has persevered most notably with the concept of class and an 'enclassed' society, but he has used class analysis primarily as a tool to identify and account for class-specific cultural practices (Bourdieu 1987, 1993), and this is our basis for using the term here. Our ethnography revealed that the habitus of bouncers is strongly linked to modifying working-class culture, and that while class becomes an increasingly vague characterisation in many people's lives (see Eder 1993; Emmison and Western 1990; Reddy 1987), it still represents a crucial source of knowledge about cultural meaning and understanding (see Milner 1999). Modifying working-class culture still provides a framework for understanding the objective logic of social and cultural conditions and their reproduction, and it provided us with a means of contextualising the social and cultural engagement of bouncers (see Winlow and Hall, forthcoming). As Bourdieu (1993) has argued, habitus is less about the regimented class analysis of Marx or Weber and more about a 'feel' for social life and social understanding. It provides the rules and parameters of social life, but it also draws in the richer context of cultural knowledge and understanding. Our empirical findings forced us to address social class, but our understanding of contemporary social class is firmly attached to contemporary culture and remains as fluid and changeable as that culture.

Social class, bouncers and the night-time economy

As we began our research we intended to focus our attention upon the work-based personas presented by bouncers, but as our research progressed we came to place the roots of their behaviour, and the meaning and understanding they employed to make sense of their social world, firmly within contemporary working-class culture. We acknowledge that making reference to 'the working class' immediately creates definitional problems (see Bradley 1996), especially given the scale of de-structuring that has gripped the British class system, and society generally, in the last 20 to 30 years (see, for example, Hoggart 1995; Wright 1989), but we will push on with this term as, if nothing else, it grants us a measure of generalisation that is not entirely unwelcome.

During the research, it became apparent that the overwhelming majority of bouncers had working-class origins, and it was this fact that prompted us to address the massive economic, social and cultural transformation seen in Britain in recent years in more detail. It also became apparent that the occupational culture of many bouncers drew significantly on forms of social understanding that members brought with them independently upon entering the occupation. These forms of understanding were then revalidated by the culture and remoulded to fit the environment and experience. A solidarity of social understanding and organisation existed that reiterated cultural practice and belief, and although commitment to the standard cultural practice of the habitus differed, it offered a means of making sense of their job and the situations they faced while at work and in their lives generally. The celebration and reaffirmation of these forms of cultural knowledge and individual and group identity took place in a number of highly diverse ways and could be drawn from the cultivation of body shape (see Monaghan 2001a, 2001b) to mutual congratulatory conversation (Spangler 1992; Winlow 2001).

The rapid economic dissolution of the old working class has obviously coincided with significant de-structuring in other areas of social life, and indeed it is this economic change, seen most obviously in the waves of deindustrialisation that occurred throughout the 1970s, 1980s and 1990s (Martin and Rowthorn 1986; Piore and Sabel 1984), that has provoked the transformation of society and culture and created the necessary circumstances for the creation and continued modification of the night-time economy (see Hobbs *et al.* 2000; Horne and Hall 1995). Not only have we seen the downward mobility of the lower working class, in contemporary society transformed into a socially excluded urban underclass (Bauman 1998a; Byrne 1999; MacDonald 1997a), but we have also seen all but the most resolute of traditional working-class occupations disappear, only to be replaced by a mass of unstable and often poorly paid jobs linked to the constantly shifting consumer and service sectors (Byrne 1989, 1993). The virtual disappearance of the practical point of their existence as contributors to profit making at an economic level and the increasing dispersal of their mutual interests at a political level clearly inform debates about contemporary working-class formation and solidarity (Horne and Hall 1995).

In a more general sense, society appears to have lost the solidity and clarity that characterised the modern social world (Bauman 1992). Now, 'to the individual, culture appears as a pool of constantly moving, unconnected fragments' (*ibid.*: 31), and as Hobsbawm has observed, recent history appears to be 'that of a world which has lost its bearings and slid into instability and crisis' (1994: 403). As the economy and culture have changed, so the nature of social engagement and incorporation has also changed. 'A disintegration of the old patterns of social relations' (*ibid.*: 15) is clear, and the speed with which these changes have occurred may well have been too much for society to easily 'come to terms with it' (*ibid.*). However, the working class has not necessarily disappeared; nor has it simply abandoned all aspects of social incorporation for a life of welfare, daytime TV and immediate gratification. Those elements of the working class best situated to do so have rolled with the punches and adapted to developing forms of economic engagement. We do not see this as a display of classic liberal self-determination but rather as a manifestation of the structural demands of contemporary capitalism. The gradual breakdown of the nine to five working day, the virtual disappearance of stable employment (see Hall and Jacques 1990) and the attractions of the grey and black economies (Hobbs 1988, 1995) continue to be negotiated daily.

What remains significant is that working-class culture, while it has been subjected to radical change over the last two or three decades, has not necessarily disappeared into the ether like its traditional occupational base. Working-class lives are still lived amid a range of meanings and understandings, which reflect the remnants of traditional working-class culture and its amalgamation with a range of new concerns created by changing economic and social circumstance (see Swyngedouw 1992; Winlow 2001; Young 1999). In our opinion, it is from this continually transforming working-class culture that most bouncers emerge. Their 'feel' for social life is directly informed by this habitus (Bourdieu 1993; Jenkins 1992). The foundation of their occupational culture owes much to the fact that their concerns about autonomy, respect, masculinity, violence, friendship, the future, women, work, money and leisure reflect wider contemporary working-class male culture. Their 'feel' for the social world, and their place within it, is unavoidably linked to the social, cultural and economic relationships that produced them.

However, the men that enter this occupation also display significant subcultural characteristics, constituting a particular strand of cultural understanding that differs from the contemporary mainstream working class. Yet this occupational culture is crucially informed by traditional and contemporary working-class concerns, and although it makes sense to regard these cultural characteristics as an accentuation of general (contemporary) working-class male values and concerns, the result of this accentuation is a remoulding and recontextualisation of key aspects of cultural practice. This progression is further quickened through the nature of interaction with colleagues, who confirm and reiterate the value order.

The occupational culture and mutual experience of the night-time economy as a working environment forces both practical and ideological modifications upon the cultural knowledge generated by contemporary working-class culture. The most pressing example here is the place of violence within the occupational culture of bouncers and, more practically, within the night-time economy they are paid to police. While 'hardness' (Willis 1977) has always been a part of working-class life, to these working-class men this particular masculine ideology and its forms of expression have altered to accommodate social and economic change, especially in light of recent 'challenges' to masculinity (Brittan 1989; Connell 1995; MacInnes 1998). Here 'hardness' is still a crucial component of self-identity and still finds its root in working-class culture, but expression is cast in relation not just to other men (Brittan 1989; Seidler 1997) and mutual understanding of context (Hobbs et al. 2003) but also in terms of their commercial role. The meanings, uses and significance of violence alter to accommodate the environment, culture and commerce of the night. These men are paid to be hard, to intimidate and control, and they would not have entered the occupation if they did not feel able to respond to the unmistakable challenge presented by the disorder that emerges within their enacted environment (see Winlow et al. 2001 for a discussion of the recruitment of bouncers).

Toughness has long been considered a crucial concern and ideal within working-class masculinities (see, for example, Miller 1958; Willis 1977). Historically, the lower classes have always felt the forces of violence most discernibly (Elias 1994; Hall 1997), and the most informed academic analyses of violence have addressed class as a central tool in understanding both the social and cultural causes of violence, and its meanings to participants (see Jones 2000). We are arguing that violence possesses a multiplicity of meanings within working-class culture, which elevates its importance in everyday life. Working-class men are more likely to be socialised with a form of cultural capital that places violence central to concepts of the male self. Violence is often treated as a resource that informs and advises social interaction and performance. We do not suggest that all working-class men are violent, or that all working-class men appreciate violence; they are simply more likely to be knowledgeable about its meanings and outcomes, as well as its pervasive influence upon their culture. While a diversity of men are likely to be socialised with attitudes likely to provoke competition and conflict, it is working-class men specifically who are more likely to internalise the meanings of actual physical violence. In many cases, violence simply is treated not as a blight upon everyday life but as a form of social behaviour to be treated with solemnity and gravitas (see, for example, Thompson 1994). All working-class people do not become violent: they may in fact despise violence in all its forms. Rather, we suggest that violence is often an aspect of their cultural environment, especially of male working-class culture, and consequently it influences their social and cultural understanding of everyday life (see Winlow 2001).

Bouncers and occupational culture

It is worth noting at this juncture that the practicalities of many bouncers' working environments and the jobs they undertake, in conjunction with their gendered cultural socialisation, often lead to a heightened sense of violence. Violence is virtually a continuous concern for many bouncers, and it is the reason why many of them are there in the first place. Violence is a form of social interaction in which they specialise; they are bouncers not just because they feel they are up to the job because they possess violent skills, but also because they are knowledgeable about the vague micro-intricacies of contemporary urban violence: they know, perhaps in part subconsciously, the complex reasons that lie behind the immediate causes of male violence and can often tell who is most likely to be violent, spot potentially dangerous situations and decide on the best way to tackle aggressive and potentially violent situations. As they become increasingly conversant with their working environment, new strategies are formulated for how to conduct violence successfully, and it is these practical occupational considerations that amalgamate with violence as a cultural focal concern and force violence to the core of both the individual and the subculture itself. Aside from actual violence, presenting a tough, no-nonsense persona for display (Goffman 1967, 1971) becomes an important aspect of maintaining an element of order within the wider disorder of a bar or nightclub. The body and demeanour become crucial devices in deterring violence and disorder. Being a bouncer is truly a career in toughness *par excellence*.

The practicalities of the occupation reinforce the importance of violence to the self and to the group; they both set in motion occupational strategies and bolster the idea of a robust and dominant masculinity. This form of hyper-masculinity is certainly not restricted to those who work in the profession (see Winlow 2001) but is exhibited by many men who work as bouncers (see Monaghan 2001a for associated discussion). Central to this form of masculinity are concepts of toughness, autonomy, vitality and power, dominance and hier-archy, respect, honour and pride, and of course violence. Clearly, these concerns are not exhaustive, but they do provide a framework that enables us to begin to think analytically about the masculine concerns of bouncers.

As many of these men have been taught from an early age, violence is impor-tant: it defines the self, places you in the context of the wider culture and community and provides a contextual framework for concepts of honour, respect and pride (see also Armstrong 1998). Upon entry to the occupation these men have often already inculcated an understanding of the import of violence into their own assessment of self. It often defines the way they think about themselves as men, and as they find themselves faced with the violence inherent in the night-time economy, it increases the importance of violence both to the self and to the culture exponentially.

Our ethnography and interview data revealed a range of men to whom violence was important for a variety of reasons: men who were the victims or victors of violence at an early age; men who had established reputations as successfully violent men; men engaged in combat sports; and men who had rarely experienced violence at first hand but had long looked on and acknowl-edged the cultural outcomes of violence. Largely, these were men whose concepts of self would not allow them to walk away from a violent encounter, and this knowledge of culture and self provided the primary skill, and indeed the starting point, for bouncing as an occupation.

In the environments in which bouncers move, pride, honour and respect remain bound up with concepts of 'maintaining face' (Goffman 1967, 1971) and represent a powerful motivation in all forms of interaction. As Bourdieu (1979: 115) has pointed out, perceptions of honour are strongest in those who see themselves through the eyes of others, and this appears to be particularly apt with regard to bouncers, given their working profile in the night-time economy and concerns regarding a reflexive and robust masculinity (Kimmel 1987; Mac an Ghaill 1996). Our ethnography revealed that this occupational concern metamorphosed into a number of forms: body size and shape would be accentu-ated; and stance, clothing, facial expression and general demeanour would often be tailored to display the mental and physical toughness of a no-nonsense gate-keeper and arbiter (see Winlow 2001; Monaghan 2002). For the most part, bouncers considered it imperative not to display signs of weakness, fearing that the slightest lapse would be seized upon and result in either some minor infrac-tion of night-time protocols, or even violence itself.

While the violence of the night-time economy and the occupational role of bouncers may seem unappealing to many men, for some men the occupation carries significant benefits (see Winlow et al. 2001). On occasion, the job can simply involve standing around talking and having fun, sexual opportunities are increased, and there is the general tumult of a busy bar scene to keep you occupied. Our ethnography also revealed that many of these men possess a potent form of bodily and cultural capital that carries with it a significant amount of status within the environs in which they move. These men possess power, and while this power may appear to be trifling in the wider scope of economic relations and general society (see Hall 2002 for associated discussion), within the night-time economy and the wider cultural background that frames their actions, such power can be all-encompassing, a reason to get out of bed in a morning and of central concern during waking hours. Here, standing on the door of a popular pub, bar or nightclub, they have significant cultural power, power that goes far beyond the simple ability to refuse admittance.

The night-time economy and contemporary youth culture

Clearly, the nature of contemporary youth culture has changed significantly in recent years, notably since the advent and proliferation of global cultural forms and their increasing influence upon the world economy (Featherstone *et al.* 1995; Robertson 1992) and contemporary culture and society (Bauman 1992; King 1991). The complexities of incorporation and differentiation, and defining the parameters of self, now appear to have lost the solidity we might once have used to anchor some kind of analysis of youth culture (see Epstein 1998; Wallace and Cross 1990). A powerful mass youth and young adult culture now exists in Britain alongside the vagaries of fashion, changing youth subcultures and lifestyles. The 'drinking culture', and the fashions, music and behaviour that sustain it, is closely linked to the mass consumerism that dominates all forms of contemporary culture (see Miles 1998, 2000) and is rapidly becoming the standard form of youth incorporation in contemporary Britain. The pursuit of inebriation and drug experiences, sexual fulfilment and adventure, dance and fashion, group belonging and self expression has become the standard way of defining expressive adulthood and cultural knowledge, both to the self and to the watching masses. This is not to say that a mass youth culture has not existed before, or that the forms that youth culture takes are not linked to dominant economic structures. Rather, we suggest that the way in which this dominant drinking culture interacts with other aspects of the economy and society is something new. More than at any point in recent history, this form of youth cultural expression reflects the dominant capitalist principle of consumerism, and this has fundamentally affected the way that many young people make sense of their lives (Lee 1993; Miles 1998).

The abandonment of conventional daylight comportment and expectation and the celebration of leisure and excess have long been central to the definitions of youth and self (Miles 2000; Skelton and Valentine 1998), but never before have they gripped the psyche of public culture with such force. Rampant consumerism and commodification have forced the pursuit of leisure and pleasure to centre stage, not just within the confines of consumer capitalism but also in the very nature of self-identity. We are increasingly what we consume rather than what we produce, and nowhere are these trends more patently exhibited than in the night-time economy.

This 'drinking culture' is indicative of wider society and culture at this point in history, and as such it provides a particularly useful means of analysing contemporary forms of youth self-identity and their relationship to consumerism and the market. Certainly, the prevailing arguments about the market as a bastion of consumer choice and self-expression need to be placed in a wider structural context reflecting global and local economic circumstances and the possibility that the lionisation of this consumerism and the market may actually accentuate social divisions and consequently prove to be increasingly problematic for society (Bocock 1993; Lee 1993). As Rojek (1989) has noted, the prevailing idea that leisure is inherently liberating may be well off the mark. The pressure that young people face to consume conspicuously, and to do so without offending the fickle vagaries of fashion, may indeed be inherently restrictive and reflect the ongoing demands of the capitalist economy (see Horkheimer and Adorno 1973).

We use the term 'drinking culture' in a general sense to describe the customary forms of inebriated leisure that dominate our city centres after dark – a comprehensive succession of theme bars, fun pubs and nightclubs and their knock-on commercial endeavours. As we have stated elsewhere, Britain's night-time economy is primarily sustained by money generated from alcohol sales and associated leisure provision (Hobbs *et al.* 2000), and the amount of money generated is becoming increasingly important to the British economy (*ibid.*). For the most part, despite the best efforts of city planners and local councils, our cities have failed to develop an air of European cosmopolitanism and have instead remained stoically British yet peculiarly postmodern (Hadfield *et al.* 2001; Winlow 2001). Drinking, hedonism and behavioural emancipation are the order of the day; and the violence we see in the night-time economy is in many respects directly related to this loosening of social control.

'Going out' at the weekend has been a part of youth leisure for generations (see Mungham 1976; Parker 1974), and although the bars and clubs, the music they play and the fashions that predominate, are often very much the same across the country, it is the underlying culture that is significant. As Presdee (2000) has pointed out, we all have to desire to consume to survive socially, and perhaps this pressure is most keenly felt by young people (see also Griffin 1993). The promise of hidden pleasures draws young people towards the night-time economy like iron filings to a magnet; they feel not only the individual desire for personal contentment but also the social and cultural pressure to be seen to be a participant in this commodified hyper-reality, to consume and consume correctly, to be culturally adroit (see Miles 2000: 92–104, for associated discussion). In a consumer culture that needs to be in almost constant motion to prevent stultification (see, for example, Veblen 1994), the social and cultural pressures can be considerable, and involvement for many is almost obligatory. They have to go. Upon arrival, they may find that the blunt realities of our night-time economy do not measure up to the subconscious advertising, but that in no way diminishes the power of the message. For when next weekend rolls around, the magnet clicks into effect and the cycle begins again (see Horkheimer and Adorno 1973). To be young and reflexive with this form of consumer culture represents the cultural compulsion that resides at the alcohol-soaked heart of this environment. Sitting on the sidelines as conformity and rebellion, homogeneity and heterogeneity, and culture and subculture merge and re-emerge in the night-time economy can be a frustrating and alienating business that young people feel compelled to negotiate as incorporation and integration grow in importance to concepts of self-identity (see Taylor 1999: 27–34, for discussion on the crisis of inclusion and exclusion).

The erosion of clearly structured, class-based life patterns has fundamentally altered the nature of contemporary leisure. While once lives were often lived almost in parallel with contemporaries (those whom you grew up with, went to school with, went to work with, associated with outside of work, saw married, etc., – a process that was often intergenerational), lives are now increasingly disjointed, and there is little certainty of having the same shared experiences and outlook as workmates and colleagues. Mutual experience seems to be less and less a tie that binds social groupings. The continued trend towards community dismemberment, transience and mobility (Bauman 1998b), linked to the decline of traditional labour and the continued growth of cities as sites of mass consumption (Wynne and O'Connor 1998) rather than of industrial production, commerce or high culture, has served not only to force instrumentality to the core of self-identity (Simmel 1950; Wirth 1938) but also to create an increasingly individualised culture and society (Bauman 2001). Work may be necessary, but for many it is simply a means to other ends, something to be completed and then forgotten; it is on a weekend that individuality and a sense of self are formed and camaraderie is moulded, along with other weekend leisure pursuits like the football match (see Armstrong 1998), rather than on the factory floor (Willis 1990; Winlow, 2001). Our investigations uncovered a sphere of youth experience that was often depersonalised and instrumental. Groups of young people who would 'go out' together on a weekend often knew relatively little about the intricacies of the lives of other members of the group; where they worked, and what they did at work, was often hazy, as were family relationships, schooling, and the like. Here, as much as in any other area of contemporary culture, was a clear manifestation of the break between modern capitalist society and the culture of contemporary consumer capitalism. What these young people knew, and knew in detail, were the leisure characteristics of their friends: how they would behave when drunk; embarrassing moments and amusing anecdotes from the past; sexual histories and futures; fashion and music sense and appreciation; favourite fast food, and so on.

As we investigated further, it became apparent that many of these young people often lived for the weekend (see Miles 2000: 87–106, on the hedonism of contemporary youth culture). Work was often treated as a means to an end, a way of financing the often expensive excursions into the night-time economy.

This was to be expected, but we also noticed that the self-identity of young people who spent leisure time in these environs related increasingly closely, and in some cases almost exclusively, to their 'going out' selves.

Missing a night out would be a huge disappointment, not because of all the fun that can be had on a night out but because young people *feared missing something*. 'Youthful insecurity and risk' (Taylor 1999: 71–7) was clearly a marked aspect of the culture. This was, after all, where it was happening; this was the social arena that mattered most to them.

The night-time carnival

Increasingly, public culture generally has become keenly aware of the seductiveness of transgressing (Presdee 2000), and nowhere is this more clearly seen than in the carnivalesque world of the night-time economy. Attempts have been made to contain elements of working-class festivities throughout the period of industrial capitalism (Fiske 1991), and in contemporary society this appears to be only partly curtailed by economic concerns. Not only is this a world in which the black and grey economies thrive (see Winlow 2001), but a powerful atmosphere of dangerous adventure also exists, suffused with suggestions of the illicit. Violence and disorder are in fact regular fixtures in our night-time economy (see, for example, Hutchison *et al.* 1998), and this is increasingly the stadium of drug experimentation and the amphitheatre of sex. As has been noted throughout history, carnivals revel in abuse, violence, sex and carnality (Bakhtin 1984; Presdee 2000), and its contemporary incarnation is no different. Drugs here are not signifiers of isolation and exclusion; indeed, the situation seems to indicate the contrary. Little, if any, attention is paid to the ordered world of daylight, and that is the reason the night-time economy is so attractive to contemporary youth (Malbon 1999). Identities become malleable, and the character you choose to play is only restricted by your imagination and the depth of your pocket.

In its present form and displaying such a significant impact upon youth culture and identities, the night-time economy is now the primary site for carnivalesque social forms. It is here that the promissory experience of a 'time out of time' (Presdee 2000: 33) exists, a break from all that disappoints and frustrates us with normative daylight reality. Leisure and excess become not some distant experience that we must strive for but a growing daily need. It is now less a gift we grant ourselves after a hard week's work but more a necessary form of everyday existence, a functional respite of carnival to prepare us for what lies ahead. The forms that this carnival takes in contemporary Britain are indicative of wider social, cultural and economic concerns; our night-time economy offers us an evidentiary snapshot of our economic, social and cultural life at this point in history, and the most dominant aspect, the most useful tool in attempting to analyse this peculiarly carnivalesque world, is consumer capitalism.

Consumer capitalism lies at the very core of our night-time economy and can be observed at every turn. In the night-time economy, the spoken word is being relegated in significance; this is a fast-paced world of loud music and instrumental concerns, and messages need to be easily sifted and sorted to allow for the effortlessly accessible meanings sought by participants. Commodities and their consumption offer direct signification of the self-created persona (see Horkheimer and Adorno 1973 on 'pseudo-individualization'). Who you are, or rather who you want other people to think you are, can be passed on easily through designer fashions, body language and attitude, which circle of friends you stand with and which nightclub you attend. And this cultural atmosphere is driven forward by the foibles of the market: wearing the wrong designer label in the wrong bar can generate sly mockery; the wrong haircut and you may not make it into your nightclub of choice (Chatterton and Hollands 2001: 54). The key to cultural belonging lies in the ability to consume both regularly and knowledgeably (McDonald 1997a; Purcell 1997), because centres of high culture have long constructed images of heavy-drinking barbarians at their frontier, yet the pleasure one feels at acceptance are inevitably encouraging and temporary, as the vagaries of market-led fashion are consistent only in their ability to continually mutate.

Alcohol, culture and the night-time economy

Assorted issues of postmodern youth culture, self-identity, and contemporary consumerism and carnival within the night-time economy cannot adequately be addressed without mention of alcohol as a consequential constitutive part. As we have described elsewhere (Hobbs *et al.* 2001), the night-time economy is awash with alcohol. A visit to our city centres in the early hours of a Sunday morning will etch this fact vividly into the mind of the reader. The after-effects of the night lie everywhere – drunken youths collapse, vomit and urinate in doorways; couples kiss and fornicate; fights break out; and empty lager and alcopop bottles, pizza boxes and kebab wrappers lie strewn around the pavement as, slowly but surely, by way of either a drunken and noisy walk or the perilous taxi rank, the young consumers make their way home (Tomsen 1997).

Alcohol consumption in the night-time economy is the necessary lubricant that aids the slide of young people into this carnivalesque and consumer-oriented world. Alcohol is the night-time economy's capitalistic *raison d'être* (Hobbs *et al.* 2000) and the focal point for the night-time economy in its present form (Hadfield *et al.* 2001). Additionally, alcohol is the commodity that supports the cultural attractions that draw people into our city centres after dark and consequently sustains associated markets (e.g. fast-food outlets, late-night restaurants, taxis). In cultural terms, it provides an accepted means of altering the mundane, pressurised, regimented and occasionally unattractive world of daylight comportment; of realigning meaning and understanding to fit a more seductive and alluring world of hedonism and carnival. The cultural expectation of alcohol's 'disinhibitor effect' (Room and Collins 1983) helps consumers to abandon their regulated daylight personas and allows them to become immersed in the seemingly chaotic culture of the night-time economy. It provides a culturally accepted way of altering behaviour, and it is this fact, in conjunction with the connected influences of postmodernism, carnival and consumerism, that renders the night-time economy so attractive to young people. Without this cultural acceptance of certain night-time forms of disorderly drunken behaviour, drunken conduct would result in significant social disapproval, and consequently the night-time economy would be less alluring to contemporary youth. It provides an excuse to 'overstep the mark,' to 'stop being sensible' and to abandon oneself to behaviour that would otherwise be socially constrained (see Foucault 1977 on 'power-knowledge', 1980 on sexual expression). Indeed, rather than alcohol consumption revealing a culture-free 'natural' self, drunken behaviour is learned behaviour like any other (MacAndrew and Edgerton 1969).

Alcohol and its consumption have always been inherently cultural matters (McDonald 1997b: 15; Heath 2000), and this remains true in the contemporary night-time economy. Despite society's general assumption to the contrary, 'the behaviour which alcohol induces is a cultural matter rather than a question of the inevitable or natural consequences of ethanol entering the bloodstream' (McDonald 1997b: 13); an analysis of society, culture and the economy provides us with the tools to understand the structure of, and behaviour in, the night-time economy in its contemporary form.

Our study focused on bouncers, and the basis of their occupational culture relates closely to individual, subcultural and environmental meanings and understandings of violence. The excesses of drunken behaviour, and its culturally prescribed meaning, have led to staggering amounts of violence within our night-time economy (Hutchinson *et al.* 1998), and it is often violence that is the bouncer's primary occupational concern (Hobbs *et al.* 2003). It is also worth noting that the link between alcohol and violence is not at all universal (Heath 1975) but is socially constructed (Riches 1986) and reflects incisive economic, social and cultural factors that are beyond the remit of this chapter. We do not claim that alcohol has no bearing upon incidents of violence (see Gottfredson 1984; Hodge 1993; Mott 1990). Rather, we suggest that wider structural and agentic influences lie behind apparently alcohol-related violence.

Commercial imperatives and order after dark

The maintenance of order among young people often hell-bent on disorder, and willing to pay for the privilege, is the conundrum faced by entrepreneurs and leisure corporations. On the one hand, they are commodifying carnival and excess: advertising, sometimes literally, drunkenness, debauchery, sex and abandon. On the other hand, they are faced with the real possibility of this excess being vented through violence, and this is deemed to be bad for business. The majority of consumers do not want to be subjected to unfettered aggression; they want to get drunk and party, deal with the hangover and find their way to work on Monday free from significant facial scarring. They want their hedonism to be unrestrained, yet they do not want to be the subject of someone else's unrestrained hedonism. Violence, especially when it occurs regularly in the same venue, dissuades regular customers and can in fact breed further violence (Winlow 2001). It may also lead to increased police attention, with the ultimate sanction being the revocation of the licence to sell alcohol – or more practically, being put out of business (Lister *et al.* 2001). Thus the solution, in the form of the bouncer, can be seen supervising admissions to bars and nightclubs across the country – regulation through private security, monitoring with the threat of sanctions, deterring violence with a highly complex mixture of signifying threat, and social and cultural knowledge and understanding.

As the police and state yield ground to significant levels of violence and disorder in the night-time economy (Hobbs *et al.* 2003), private industry is given the task of dealing with the problems it creates, while retaining commercial viability.

Yet these are problems that are not easily dealt with. Regulating and deterring violence is fraught with difficulties (Hobbs *et al.* 2002). Consumers need to be persuaded to come; they need to believe that a world completely divorced from daylight personas and experience awaits them, an unregulated world of hedonism. Yet when they arrive in this economically, socially and culturally constructed world, regulation is what they receive, at least some of the time. Their hedonism needs to be sanitised to fit in with the business imperatives and the moderation of the masses – hedonism, yes, but within limits. Their carnival needs to be monitored, and while this is no easy task, it is the requisite practice of capital and social control – take the leisure and cultural practices of the masses from the masses, change it slightly, and sell it back to them (Elias and Dunning 1993). This is apparent in the shift from the 'illegal' DIY raves of the early 1990s to the corporate and heavily branded and commodified 'superclubs' of today.

Within the night-time economy, many people can and do choose to discard normative behaviour in a number of problematic ways, and they do not take kindly to being told that some forms of their hedonistic excess are inappropriate. Within this context, the police presence is often minimal and restricted to public spaces; business interests therefore need to hire their own 'specialised forces' in order to preserve commercial viability and deal with aggression and violence.

Concluding remarks

The emergence of bouncers as a powerful literal and symbolic force relates closely to the development and commodification of the night-time economy as a central site for contemporary carnivalesque social forms, and the incursion of leisure cultures into the void left by industrialism has profound implications for ongoing debates about social control, youth, inclusion and exclusion, and forms of contemporary identity. Bouncers, using powerful remnants of industrial working-class culture, offer violence and threat as a commercial device in an emerging marketplace of non-state authority, indicating a crisis not of capitalism but of governance, as under shadow of the night, the muscular physique of the private sector replaces the state's puny, debilitated body.

References

Armstrong, G. (1998) *Football Hooligans: Knowing the Score*. Oxford: Berg.

Bakhtin, M. (1984) *Rabelais and His World*. Bloomington: Indiana University Press.

Baudrillard, J. (1993) *Symbolic Exchange and Death* (translated by I.H. Grant). London: Sage.

Bauman, Z. (1992) *Intimations of Postmodernity*. London: Routledge.

Bauman, Z. (1998a) *Work, Consumerism and the New Poor*. Buckingham: Open University Press.

Bauman, Z. (1998b) *Globalization: The Human Consequences*. Cambridge: Polity.

Bauman, Z. (2001) *The Individualized Society*. Oxford: Basil Blackwell.

Beck, U. (1992) *Risk Society: Towards a New Modernity*. London: Sage.

Beynon, H. and Glavanis, P. (eds) (1999) *Patterns of Social Inequality*. London: Longman.

Bocock, R. (1993) *Consumption*. London: Routledge.

Bourdieu, P. (1979) *Algeria 1960*. Cambridge: Cambridge University Press.

Bourdieu, P. (1987) 'What makes a social class? On the theoretical and practical existence of groups', *Berkeley Journal of Sociology* 32: 1–17.

Bourdieu, P. (1993) *Sociology in Question*. London: Sage.

Bradley, H. (1996) *Fractured Identities: Changing Patterns of Inequality*. Cambridge: Polity Press.

Brittan, A. (1989) *Masculinity and Power*. Oxford: Basil Blackwell.

Byrne, D. (1989) *Beyond the Inner City*. Milton Keynes: Open University Press.

Byrne, D. (1993) 'De-industrialisation, planning and class structures: a study in the effects of social policy and social structures', unpublished Ph.D. thesis, University of Durham.

Byrne, D. (1999) *Social Exclusion*. Buckingham: Open University Press.

Chatterton, P. and Hollands, R. (2001) *Changing our Toon*. Newcastle: University of Newcastle.

Connell, R.W. (1995) *Masculinities*. Oxford: Basil Blackwell.

Eder, K. (1993) *The New Politics of Class*. London: Sage.

Elias, N. (1994) *The Civilising Process*. Oxford: Basil Blackwell.

Elias, N. and Dunning, E. (1993) *Quest for Excitement: Sport and Leisure in the Civilising Process*. Oxford: Basil Blackwell.

Emmison, M. and Western, M. (1990) 'Social class and social identity: a comment on Marshall *et al.*', *Sociology* 24(2): 241–53.

Epstein, J.S. (ed.) (1998) *Youth Culture: Identity in a Postmodern World*. Oxford: Basil Blackwell.

Featherstone, M. (1995) *Undoing Culture*. London: Sage.

Featherstone, M. (ed.) (1990) *Global Culture*. London: Sage.

Featherstone, M., Lash, S. and Robertson, R. (1995) *Global Modernities*. London: Sage.

Fiske, J. (1991) *Understanding Popular Culture*. London: Routledge.

Foucault, M. (1977) *Discipline and Punish*. New York: Pantheon.

Foucault, M. (1980) *The History of Sexuality*, Vol. 1. New York: Vantage.

Giddens, A. (1991) *Modernity and Self-Identity*. Cambridge: Polity Press.

Giddens, A. (1994) *Beyond Left and Right*. Cambridge: Polity.

Goffman, E. (1969) *The Presentation of Self in Everyday Life*. Harmondsworth: Penguin.

Goffman, E. (1971) *Relations in Public: Microstudies of Public Order*. London: Allen Lane.

Gottfredson, M.R. (1984) *Victims of Crime: The Dimensions of Risk* (Home Office Research Study No. 81). London: HMSO.

Griffin, C. (1993) *Representations of Youth: The Study of Youth and Adolescence in Britain and America*. Cambridge: Polity Press.

Hadfield, P., Lister, S., Hobbs, D. and Winlow, S. (2001) 'The "24 Hour City" – condition critical', *Town and Country Planning* 70(11) (November): 300–2.

Hall, S. (1997) 'Visceral cultures and criminal practices', *Theoretical Criminology* 1(4): 453–78.

Hall, S. (2002) 'Daubing the drudges of fury: men, violence and the piety of the hegemonic masculinity thesis', *Theoretical Criminology* 6(1): 35–71.

Hall, S. and Jacques, M. (eds) (1990) *New Times: The Changing Face of Politics in the 1990s*. London: Lawrence & Wishart.

Heath, D. (1975) 'A critical review of ethnographic studies of alcohol use', in R. Gibbins *et al*. (eds) *Research Advances in Alcohol and Drug Problems*, Vol. 2. New York: John Wiley & Sons.

Heath, D.B. (2000) *Drinking Occasions: Comparative Perspectives on Alcohol and Culture*. Hove: Brunner/Mazel.

Hobbs, D. (1988) *Doing the Business*. Oxford: Oxford University Press.

Hobbs, D. (1995) *Bad Business*. Oxford: Oxford University Press.

Hobbs, D., Hadfield, P., Lister, S., Winlow, S. and Hall, S. (2000) 'Receiving shadows: governance and liminality in the night-time economy', *British Journal of Sociology* 51(4): 701–17.

Hobbs, D., Hadfield, P., Lister, S. and Winlow, S. (2002) 'Door lore: the art and economics of intimidation', *British Journal of Criminology*.

Hobbs, D., Hadfield, P., Lister, S., Winlow, S. (2003) *Night Moves: Bouncers: Violence and Governance in the Night-time Economy*. Oxford: Oxford University Press.

Hobsbawm, E. (1994) *The Age of Extremes*. London: Michael Joseph.

Hodge, J. (1993) 'Alcohol and violence', in P. Taylor (ed.) *Violence in Society*. London: Royal College of Physicians.

Hoggart, R. (1995) *The Way We Live Now*. London: Chatto & Windus.

Horkheimer, M. and Adorno, T. (1973) *Dialectic of Enlightenment*. London: Allen Lane.

Horne, R. and Hall, S. (1995) 'Anelpis: a preliminary expedition into a world without hope or potential', *Parallax* 1: 81–92.

Hutchinson, I.L., Magennis, P., Shepherd, J.P. and Brown, A.E. (1998) 'B.A.O.M.S. United Kingdom Survey of Facial Injuries, part 1: aetiology and the association with alcohol consumption', *British Journal of Oral Maxillofacial Surgery* 36: 3–13.

Jenkins, R. (1992) *Pierre Bourdieu*. London: Routledge.

Jones, S. (2000) *Understanding Violent Crime*. Buckingham: Open University Press.

Kimmel, M.S. (ed.) (1987) *Understanding Men: New Directions in Research on Men and Masculinity*. London: Sage.

King, A.D. (ed.) (1991) *Culture, Globalisation and the World-System*. Basingstoke: Macmillan.

Kumar, K. (1995) *From Post-Industrial to Post-Modern Society*. Oxford: Basil Blackwell.

Lash, S. (1990) *Sociology After Postmodernism*. London: Routledge.

Lee, D. and Turner, B. (eds) (1996) *Conflicts About Class*. London: Longman.

Lee, M. (1993) *Consumer Culture Reborn: The Cultural Politics of Consumption*. London: Routledge.

Liebow, E. (1967) *Tally's Corner*. Boston: Little, Brown.

Lister, S., Hadfield, P., Hobbs, D. and Winlow, S. (2001) 'Accounting for bouncers: occupational licensing as a mechanism for regulation', *Criminal Justice* 1(4): 363–84.

Lyotard, J.-F. (1984) *The Postmodern Condition: A Report on Knowledge* (translated by G. Bennington and B. Massumi). Minneapolis: University of Minnesota Press.

MacAndrew, C. and Edgerton, R. (1969) *Drunken Comportment*. Chicago: Aldine.

Mac an Ghaill, M. (ed.) (1996) *Understanding Masculinities*. Buckingham: Open University Press.

MacInnes, J. (1998) *The End of Masculinity*. Buckingham: Open University Press.

Malbon, B. (1999) *Clubbing: Dancing, Ecstasy and Vitality*. London: Routledge.

Martin, R. and Rowthorn, B. (eds) (1986) *The Geography of De-industrialisation*. London: Macmillan.

McDonald, M. (1997a) 'Drinking in the west of France', in M. McDonald (ed.) *Gender, Drink and Drugs*. Oxford: Berg.

McDonald, M. (ed.) (1997b) *Gender, Drink and Drugs*. Oxford: Berg.

Miles, S. (1998) *Consumerism as a Way of Life*. London: Sage.

Miles, S. (2000) *Youth Lifestyles in a Changing World*. Buckingham: Open University Press.

Miller, W.B. (1958) 'Lower class culture as a generating milieu of gang delinquency', *Journal of Social Issues* 14(3): 5–19.

Milner, A. (1999) *Class*. London: Sage.

Monaghan, L. (2001a) 'Regulating "unruly" bodies: work tasks, conflict and violence in Britain's night-time economy', paper presented to BSA Language Study Group Conference on Ethnography, Law and Crime, 20 September 2001, Buckinghamshire Chilterns University College.

Monaghan, L. (2001b) *Bodybuilding, Drugs and Risk*. London: Routledge.

Monaghan, L. (2002) 'Opportunity, pleasure and risk: an ethnography of urban male heterosexuality', *Journal of Contemporary Ethnography* 31(4) 440–77'.

Morgan, D. and Stanley, L. (eds) (1990) *Debates in Sociology*. Manchester: Manchester University Press.

Mott, J. (1990) 'Young people, alcohol and crime', *Home Office Research Bulletin* 28: 24–8.

Mungham, G. (1976) 'Youth in pursuit of itself', in G. Mungham and G. Pearson (eds) *Working Class Youth Culture*. London: Routledge & Kegan Paul.

Owen, D. (1997) 'The postmodern challenge to sociology', in D. Owen (ed.) *Sociology after Postmodernism*. London: Sage.

Pakulski, J. and Waters, M. (1996) *The Death of Class*. London: Sage.

Parker, H. (1974) *View from the Boys*. London: David & Charles.

Piore, M. and Sabel, C. (1984) *The Second Industrial Divide*. New York: Basic Books.

Presdee, M. (2000) *Cultural Criminology and the Carnival of Crime*. London: Routledge.

Purcell, N. (1997) 'Women and wine in Ancient Rome', in M. McDonald (ed.) *Gender, Drink and Drugs*. Oxford: Berg.

Reddy, W. (1987) *Money and Liberty in Modern Europe: A Critique of Historical Understanding*. Cambridge: Cambridge University Press.

Riches, D. (ed.) (1986) *The Anthropology of Violence*. Oxford: Basil Blackwell.

Robertson, R. (1992) *Globalisation*. London: Sage.

Rojek, C. (1985) *Capitalism and Leisure Theory*. London: Tavistock.

Rojek, C. (ed.) (1989) *Leisure for Leisure: Critical Essays*. Basingstoke: Macmillan.

Room, R. and Collins, G. (eds) (1983) *Alcohol and Disinhibition: Nature and Meaning of the Link*, NIAAA Research Monograph No. 12. Washington: US Government Printing Office (DHNS Pub. no. (ADM) 83–1246).

Scase, D. (1992) *Class*. Buckingham: Open University Press.

Seidler, V.J. (1997) *Man Enough*. London: Sage.

Simmel, G. (1950) 'The metropolis and mental life', in K.H. Wolff (ed.) *The Sociology of Georg Simmel*. New York: Free Press.

Skelton, T. and Valentine, G. (eds) (1998) *Cool Places: Geographies of Youth Culture*. London: Routledge.

South, N. (1997) 'Late-modern criminology: "late" as in "dead" or "modern" as in "new"?', in D. Owen (ed.) *Sociology after Postmodernism*. London: Sage.

Spangler, L.C. (1992) 'Buddies and pals: a history of male friendships on prime-time television', in S. Craig (ed.) *Men, Masculinity and the Media*. London: Sage.

Sumner, C. (1994) *The Sociology of Deviance: An Obituary*. Buckingham: Open University Press.

Swyngedouw, E.A. (1992) 'The mammoth quest: "glocalisation", interspatial competition and the monetary order: the construction of new scales', in M. Dunford and G. Kaftalas (eds) *Cities and Regions in the New Europe: The Global–Local Interplay and Spatial Development Strategies*. London: Belhaven.

Taylor, I. (1999) *Crime in Context*. Cambridge: Polity Press.

Thompson, G. (1994) *Watch My Back: A Bouncer's Story*. Chichester: Summersdale.

Tomsen, S. (1997) 'A top night: social protest, masculinity and the culture of drinking violence', *British Journal of Criminology* 37(1): 90–102.

Veblen, T. (1994) *The Theory of the Leisure Class*. London: Constable (originally published 1899).

Wallace, C. and Cross, M. (eds) (1990) *Youth in Transition*. Basingstoke: Falmer Press.

Westergaard, J. (1995) *Who Gets What? The Hardening of Class Inequality in the Late Twentieth Century*. Cambridge: Polity Press.

Whyte, W.F. (1993) *Street Corner Society*. Chicago: University of Chicago Press.

Willis, P. (1977) *Learning to Labour*. Farnborough: Saxon House.

Willis, P. (1990) *Common Culture*. Milton Keynes: Open University Press.

Winlow, S. (2001) *Badfellas: Crime, Tradition and New Masculinities*. Oxford: Berg.

Winlow, S. and Hall, S. (forthcoming) *Economic Change and Criminal Practice*.

Winlow, S., Hobbs, D., Lister, S. and Hadfield, P. (2001) 'Get ready to duck: bouncers and the realities of ethnographic research on violent groups', *British Journal of Criminology*, special issue: *Methodological Dilemmas of Research* 41(3): 536–48.

Winlow, S., Hobbs, D., Lister, S. and Hadfield, P. (forthcoming) *The Art and Economics of Intimidation: A Preliminary Look at the Social Organisation of Bar and Night-club Bouncers in Britain*.

Wirth, L. (1938) 'Urbanism as a way of life', *American Journal of Sociology* 44: 8–20.

Wright, E.O. (1989) *The Debate on Classes*. London: Verso.

Wynne, D. and O'Connor, J. (1998) 'Consumption and the postmodern city', *Urban Studies* 35(5–6): 841–64.

Young, J. (1999) *The Exclusive Society*. London: Sage.

10 Violence in a changing political context

Northern Ireland and South Africa

Colin Knox and Rachel Monaghan

Introduction

Northern Ireland and South Africa are moving from conflict to post-conflict societies. Both countries have new political dispensations and seek to eschew the legacy of bitter and bloody violence. However, the history of the political struggles has embedded a culture tolerant of violence characterised by descriptions such as 'an acceptable level of violence' or 'an imperfect peace'. Somehow, the threshold of violence is different/higher in these countries because of their transitional status.

This chapter will therefore explore how the meaning of violence is inextricably linked to the political context in Northern Ireland and South Africa. Specifically, it will examine the continuing role of violence meted out by paramilitary/vigilante groups to alleged wrongdoers within the communities in which they operate, the stranglehold that these groups exert and how, if at all, this is changing. The role played by the police and the criminal justice systems will also be discussed within the new era of established political systems that have replaced 'white rule' and 'direct rule' in South Africa and Northern Ireland, respectively.

Northern Ireland

Northern Ireland has entered a new political era. The Belfast Agreement of April 1998 heralded the end of a political, constitutional and security crisis lasting almost 30 years. Its signatories reaffirmed their 'total and absolute commitment to exclusively democratic and peaceful means of resolving differences on political issues' and their 'opposition to any threat of force by others for any political purpose' (Belfast Agreement 1998: 1 section 4). However, this agreement between the political parties did not, of itself, change the course of violent activity on the ground. In 1999/2000, for example, the number of deaths due to the security situation fell from forty-four in the previous year to a low of seven. This increased to eighteen deaths in 2000/01, all of whom were civilians. There has also been a substantial rise in the recorded number of security-related shooting incidents, from 131 in 1999/2000 to 331 in 2000/01. The number of casualties as a result of paramilitary-style attacks rose from 178 to 323 in the same year (Report of the Chief Constable 2000–2001). All this in an era of ceasefires, peace and political agreement.

While not oblivious to the ongoing and in some areas increasing violence, the government rationalises this as 'an imperfect peace', or what former Secretary of State Mo Mowlam described as 'an acceptable level of violence'. Quite how 'acceptable' is defined is unclear, but the notion that a society riven with violent conflict can be more tolerant of murder, shootings and bombings is the implication of this description, which can become self-fulfilling and encourage acquiescence in the *status quo*. Instead, the government argues that its role is to create the political context in which violence becomes a thing of the past and the aims of paramilitary groups have been superseded by political progress. The British government has attempted to do this in several ways:

- by securing the political institutions that are the democratic core of the Belfast Agreement – devolved government through the Northern Ireland Assembly and the Executive;
- implementation of the Patten Report on police reforms, including the introduction of legislation to amend the Police (Northern Ireland) Act 2000 to reflect Patten's recommendations more fully;
- implementation of the Criminal Justice Review so that the criminal justice system has the confidence of all parts of the community and delivers justice efficiently and effectively through a fair and impartial system that encourages community involvement, where appropriate;
- a progressive rolling programme of reducing levels of troops and military installations as the security situation improves; and
- further progress in implementing the Belfast Agreement's provisions on human rights and equality.

In practice, the government's attempts to deliver democratic stability have made faltering progress. The on–off nature of devolution (through suspensions of the institutions) demonstrates the fragility of the peace process and how contingent it is on the resolution of issues such as policing, decommissioning of weapons and demilitarisation. Some Unionists, for example, are challenging historic moves by the IRA to put a quantity of weaponry verifiably 'beyond use' as insufficient. The establishment of a new Police Service of Northern Ireland (replacing the RUC from November 2001) accountable to a Policing Board has not secured the agreement of Sinn Féin. Stable governance is far from secure. Dr John Reid (Secretary of State for Northern Ireland) declared:

> We are on a journey from violence to democracy. For those who are making that change from violence to politics, including Republicans, we have shown patience. We don't underestimate how far they have come. We understand the historical and ideological enormity [*sic*] of that challenge.

But ultimately we all face a stark choice. The ballot box, or bomb and the bullet. There is no mix 'n' match in a democracy.

(speech to Labour Party Conference, 3 October 2001)

However, the research in this chapter would contend that there *is* in fact a 'mix 'n' match' in the democracy that is Northern Ireland, but the government simply chooses to ignore it in the interests of what it perceives to be the broader collective good of securing a long-term political settlement. In other words, the meaning of, and tolerance towards, violence is inextricably linked to the political context of Northern Ireland. The most obvious manifestation of the parallel tracks of violence and democracy are paramilitary-style attacks or so-called 'punishment' beatings and shootings, which in 2000/01[1] were at an all-time high since figures for such attacks were recorded. We examine these in some detail.

South Africa

South Africa similarly has emerged from a bitter ethno-national conflict in which violence and crime characterised the transition to a peaceful political settlement. The collapse of apartheid in 1989, the lifting the 30-year ban on the African National Congress (ANC) and the subsequent release of Nelson Mandela created a climate for political negotiation and change in South Africa. This paved the way for an interim constitution, the first multiracial democratic elections in 1994 and led to the Government of National Unity. The ANC's success in the June 1999 elections gave the party an overwhelming mandate to accelerate Thabo Mbeki's programme of 'transformation' aimed at tackling the significant socio-economic problems facing South Africa: unemployment, AIDS, crime and education. The legacy of political resistance, often violent, deployed to make the townships ungovernable during apartheid has created a culture tolerant of citizens taking the law into their own hands. Although the number of political killings dropped sharply from about 2,500 in 1994 to fewer than 240 in 1999 (South African Institute for Race Relations 2000), in his inauguration speech Thabo Mbeki regretted that some South Africans were 'forced to beg, rob and murder to ensure that they and their own do not perish from hunger'. This is reflected in a rising tide of other kinds of violent crime. Rape, car-jacking, serious assault, housebreaking and common robbery have been increasing since 1996, and the trend has been sharply upwards since 1998. About a third of all reported crimes in 1999 were violent, and the number increased by over 9 percent on 1998. The savagery of the crime wave is captured in reports that one in every two South African women will be raped during their lifetime, the average South African is eight times more likely to be murdered than the average American, and one policeman is killed every day – 1,400 have died since the ANC came to power. Accordingly, the public response is that 'brutality should be met with brutality. The rich surround themselves with razor wire and private security guards, and the poor resort to vigilantism' (*The Economist* 1999: 23).

Given the rising levels of crime, politicians, judges and township residents alike have begun calling for the reintroduction of the death penalty and corporal punishment. Indeed, Pan-Africanist Congress president Bishop Stanley Mogoba called for criminals to have their limbs chopped off: 'It is our view that we must start taking the war to criminals and if it means we have to use the method of dismembering them, we will do it' (quoted in Lekota 1999: 3). More recently, senior provincial government ministers in KwaZulu–Natal have called for the castration of rapists and the return of the death penalty for serious crimes such as murder.

What these accounts illustrate is that there is a disjuncture between political settlements in Northern Ireland and South Africa and the transition to peaceful democracies at grass-roots level. This is perhaps unsurprising given that the 'political struggles' in both countries have involved the use of violence to achieve constitutional change. When political objectives have been met, there is a blurring of the boundaries between political acts of violence and criminality. In both countries, a sharp decline in political violence has given way to a surge in non-political organised crime, using similarly violent methods. We now consider two particular forms of violence prevalent in the changing political contexts of Northern Ireland and South Africa: paramilitary-style attacks and vigilante activity, respectively.

Intra-community violence

Paramilitary-style attacks

The informal or alternative criminal justice system has evolved in its current form since the beginning of 'the Troubles' (1968) in Northern Ireland.[2] This system involves a graduated series of 'punishments' carried out by paramilitaries, including threats or warnings, public humiliation, curfew, exile, beating or shooting and, in exceptional circumstances, 'execution' (Thompson and Mulholland 1995). In theory, the more serious the 'crime' the more severe the penalty imposed – a crude tariff system is in place (Silke 1998). In practice, 'being connected' through kinship or friendship to the paramilitary hierarchy can be used in mitigation or to evade 'punishment'. Kennedy (1995: 69) describes the system as a range of punitive measures against individuals 'who violate some community norm, as defined by the paramilitary grouping'. Typically, this includes petty criminals allegedly involved in burglary, car theft and joy-riding, vandalism, muggings and more serious accusations against drug dealers and paedophiles. 'Punishment' is inflicted through baseball bats spiked with nails, hammers or power tools used on bones. Assaults are aimed directly at bones to cause multiple fractures, shots are directed at the elbows or hands and knees/ankles to exact maximum damage. This crude emulation of the formal criminal justice system ignores due process and shows contempt for the human rights of those who stand accused. Hence there are cases of mistaken identity, attacks on children as

young as 13 years old, and personal grudges over money, personal relationships and control of drug territory, all masquerading as paramilitaries
protecting their communities.

According to police statistics (see Figure 10.1), between 1973 and the end of
2001 there were 2,563 paramilitary 'punishment' shootings (an average of
eighty-eight per year), 45 percent of which were perpetrated by loyalists and 55
percent by republicans. From 1982 to the end of 2001 there were 1,833 beatings
(an average of ninety-six per year), 47 percent of which were carried out by
loyalists and 53 percent by republicans. Statistics on paramilitary-style attacks
were not collated before 1973 in the case of shootings and 1982 for beatings,
and police admit that official figures may underestimate the true extent of the
problem by as much as 30–50 percent, because victims are reluctant to report
incidents for fear of paramilitary reprisals.

The figures show that there was a significant increase in beatings and a
concomitant decrease in shootings following the ceasefires of August and
October 1994.[3] This reflected moves by paramilitaries not to implicate their
political representatives in claims that their ceasefires had broken down, particularly on the republican side with their public avowals of non-violent

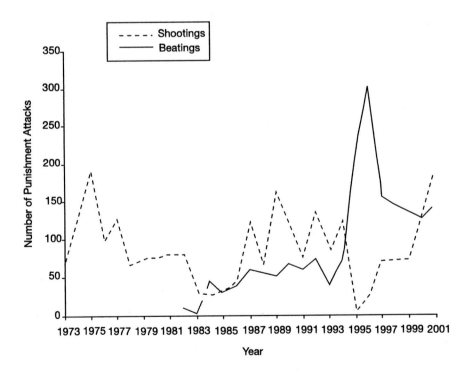

Figure 10.1 Paramilitary-style attacks

Source: Police Service of Northern Ireland (2001 figure provisional and subject to change)

alternatives. Since 1996, beatings have decreased but still remain higher than pre-ceasefire levels, and shootings are escalating year by year. In short, the situation is getting worse. There is no information available on charges brought against perpetrators. Offenders are charged with crimes such as common assault, grievous bodily harm and actual bodily harm, hence it is impossible to ascertain successful police prosecutions. The Chief Constable of the Police Service of Northern Ireland has confirmed that the Provisional Irish Republican Army (IRA), the Ulster Defence Association (UDA) and the Ulster Volunteer Force (UVF) all of which have declared ceasefires, are behind many of these attacks.[4] He highlighted the distinction that they make between 'a cessation of military operations and some distorted view that this sort of barbarity doesn't come within these terms' (MacKay 1999: 351, quoting the Chief Constable). In October 2001, the government concluded, in the wake of violence in the North Belfast area, that the UDA, the Ulster Freedom Fighters (UFF) and the LVF were no longer maintaining their ceasefires and specified these organisations.[5] The central role played by paramilitaries in these attacks is cynically demonstrated by their complete cessation (on the republican side) during the Clinton visits to Northern Ireland in 1994 and 1998 and the Mitchell review on the implementation of the Belfast Agreement in November 1999.

Vigilante attacks

Likewise in South Africa, alternative forms of justice can be found in the black townships. During the apartheid years, township inhabitants developed informal criminal justice mechanisms to deal with crime in their community. These mechanisms were developed, in part, from traditional rural practices such as the *lekgotla*,[6] which emphasised the restoration of harmony and the reintegration of offenders into the community. Sentences handed down to those found guilty included fines, corporal punishment and community service. Neighbourhood patrols and street committees were also established in an attempt to deal with 'normal' crime, for instance robbery, theft and rape. With the emergence of politicised youth, or 'comrades', people's courts were established in the townships and residents were encouraged to take their problems to the 'comrades'. These courts were seen as part of the political struggle against apartheid as they represented an alternative to the state structure and dealt with both 'normal' and 'political' crime. Gradually, these courts, which numbered about 400 by 1987, began to acquire the reputation of 'kangaroo courts' (Brogden and Shearing 1993; Minnaar 1995). Such courts were characterised by their predetermined assumption of guilt of the accused and instant redress, and they often engaged in human rights abuses. In some cases, the people's courts of the 'comrades' meted out beatings and whippings with a *sjambok*, with sentences of up to 300 lashes. On some occasions a death sentence was passed. By the mid-1980s, individuals accused of 'political' crimes such as collaboration, informing or being a 'sell-out' (working as a councillor or a police officer) were being 'necklaced' for their alleged crimes. The necklace method involved the placing of a petrol-filled tyre around the accused person's neck, which was then set alight. Estimates suggest that between 1985 and 1990 350 to 400 people were killed by this method of execution, with a further 500 necklaced between 1990 and 1994 (Minnaar 1995).

The advent of a negotiated settlement to the political conflict and the holding of multiracial elections have not resulted in the disappearance of retributive informal justice in the 'new' South Africa. The 'comrades' are no longer involved in such justice, but new groups have emerged, including the Peninsula Anti-Crime Agency (PEACA)[7] in the Western Cape and *Mapogo a Mathamaga*[8] (hereafter referred to as *Mapogo*) in the Northern Province. The taxi associations in some townships have been willing to become involved in crime solving for a fee. All of these groups stand accused of using corporal punishment and violence in responding to crime. Indeed, *Mapogo*'s leader, John Magolego, asserts that public flogging 'is the African way of stopping crime. The criminal must lie on the ground, and we must work on his buttocks and put him right' (cited in Soggot and Ngobeni 1999). Alleged suspects are usually beaten until they confess or provide information as to the whereabouts of stolen goods. *Mapogo* has also been accused of throwing suspects into crocodile-infested waters, while taxi drivers in Guguletu are implicated in dragging alleged criminals behind vehicles.

Furthermore, in some cases spontaneous mobs form to mete out justice to alleged criminals. In some instances, those present convene kangaroo courts, but this is not always the case. The justice meted out is often of an extremely brutal nature, and deaths are common. Examples in the townships include the stoning to death of a motorist after he had run over and killed a 2-year-old child in Carletonville (South African Press Association 1999); the necklacing of four immigrants accused of gangsterism in Ivory Park (Midrand) (Reuters 1999); and the beating to death of a suspected thief in Philippi East, just outside Cape Town (Le May 2001). In some cases, members of a suspected criminal's family or the family home are targeted. Their houses are either destroyed or burned, and often the families subsequently leave the area as a result of intimidation. In February 1997, the mother of an alleged criminal was stoned to death for the deeds of her son by a crowd of 4,000 in the township of Mamelodi, near Pretoria (Amupadhi 1997).

Community condonation

Northern Ireland

Paramilitaries claim to be responding to popular pressure from within their communities for instant retributive justice. This is borne out by Cavanaugh (1997) in an ethnographic study undertaken within both communities in Belfast, where she posits the community not as a passive entity but as integral to the analysis of political violence in Northern Ireland. She suggests that civil society in Northern Ireland is characterised by a strong sense of community, ethnic separation, and traditions of loyalism and republicanism in both its cultural and political forms. 'With basic security needs left unfulfilled and fear of identity loss prevalent in both republican and loyalist communities, strong intra-communal infrastructures have evolved which protect and promote community cohesion' (*ibid.*: 46). This strong community cohesion, she argues, demands social order and control constructed through 'alternative legalities to that of the state'. As Northern Ireland becomes more polarised, and segregated housing increases as a result of people feeling more secure 'living among their own', so too do the demands for social order.

That social order is exercised through paramilitaries, and communities argue that the need for their involvement exists for three principal reasons. First, particularly in republican areas, there is an absence of an adequate policing service. The RUC (now the Police Service of Northern Ireland (PSNI)) has no legitimacy among republicans, and their communities would not normally involve the police in dealing with crimes in their areas. Republicans claim that the PSNI is prepared to tolerate at best, or encourage at worst, crime in their communities as a way of undermining republicanism. Police are therefore willing to trade dropping charges for petty crime in return for low-level intelligence gathering. In loyalist areas, where the PSNI, given its composition, was once seen as 'their' police force, things have changed. Political developments have eroded Protestants' monopoly grasp on the state and its organs, creating a real sense of alienation. For example, police tactics in upholding the rights of Catholic parents to walk their children to school through loyalist areas in North Belfast (the Holy Cross dispute[9]) have reinforced antagonism towards the police. Loyalists want to keep the PSNI out of communities where drug dealing, racketeering and illegal drinking dens are commonplace. Second, levels of 'antisocial behaviour' and petty crime are rising, particularly in working-class areas. From police statistics, the levels of recorded crime, one-third of which is accounted for by common assault and criminal damage, have been increasing (Police Authority for Northern Ireland 2001: 53). In the absence, therefore, of a legitimate police force and/or because people are discouraged from seeking PSNI intervention, communities turn to the paramilitaries to secure a prompt, visible and, in their view, effective response to crime in their areas. Third, the formal criminal justice system in these communities is perceived as slow, ineffectual and soft on crime. In a society where violent conflict has been the norm for over 30 years, it is not surprising that the time taken to process offenders, the necessary safeguards in the legal system and the standard of proof required for conviction are seen as no match for summary justice meted out by paramilitaries.

Working-class communities in Northern Ireland that have been brutalised during the conflict have become desensitised to violent crime. Victims of crime reporting to paramilitaries almost certainly know the consequences of their actions for the alleged perpetrator. In a country that has witnessed over 3,600 deaths and numerous serious injuries, the emphasis is more on revenge than on justice (McKittrick *et al.* 1999). The nature of the conflict and the roles played by the protagonists are important in understanding the response to community crime. When the legitimacy of the state and the effectiveness and impartiality of its organs (security forces and legal system) are integral to the conflict, this forecloses recourse to the normal channels by which communities seek to tackle crime (Ní Aoláin 2000; Rolston 2000). Hence communities develop their own responses to crime through informal justice mechanisms, which will be significantly influenced by the violent environment in which they live. As one communitarian suggested: 'if you have a gripe with someone, the way to resolve it is to hit them a dig on the gob, if it was bigger than that, pull the paramilitaries in' (interview with loyalist community worker, 2000). All of this suggests that the meaning of violence in Northern Ireland, and the community response to it, is closely bound to the political milieu within which it takes place. Given this argument, it is obvious that attempts to tackle the informal criminal justice system have been politically laden. Similar community support/endorsement for informal 'justice' is also evident in South Africa.

South Africa

Vigilantes and vigilante groups such as *Mapogo* and PEACA argue that their activities, aimed at combating crime and maintaining 'law and order', are a direct response to community demands for action to be taken against criminals. Both groups point to continued community support and membership of their organisations as evidence of this. Indeed, people queue on a daily basis outside PEACA's offices in Khayelitsha, and *Mapogo's* supporters/members display the organisation's symbol in their homes, shops, businesses and cars as a warning to criminals not to target them. In addition to its crime-solving activities, *Mapogo* has moved into the area of crime prevention by offering services usually provided by private security firms, such as the protection of property and patrolling; takers have included schools and churches.

Like Northern Ireland, a number of principal reasons are cited by communities for the continued existence of the informal criminal justice system in the 'new' South Africa. First, although the South African Police Service (SAPS) is now regarded as the legitimate police service of the government, it is widely seen as being ineffective. According to recent research conducted by the Institute for Security Studies (cited in Meyer 2001), 'crime pays in South Africa' as the majority of criminals never get caught, and of those who are arrested, a mere 8 percent spend any time in jail. Of the 2.58 million cases that were reported to and/or recorded by the police in 2000, only 610,000 went to court, and of these only 210,000 ended in a conviction. Second, the formal criminal justice system is viewed as ineffectual, slow and soft on criminals. As one township resident explained: 'The law takes it very easy [on criminals] and the person gets out of jail easily' (community focus group participant, Khayelitsha, November 1999). Although mandatory minimum sentences for certain offences and tough bail laws have been introduced, this has not countered criticism levelled against the judiciary. Rape, for example, now carries a life sentence where the victim is raped more than once, is seriously assaulted, or is under the age of 16. Lesser sentences may be imposed if 'substantial and compelling' circumstances exist. In October 1999, Judge Foxcroft handed down a seven-year sentence to a man found guilty of raping his 14-year-old daughter. In his judgement, Foxcroft stated that this was 'not one of the worst cases of rape' and that the man's 'sexual deviancy' was limited to his own daughter (see Smith 1999 and South African Press Association 2001 for more details). Such a sentencing rationale does not inspire confidence in those communities most affected by crime and sends a message to the community. As Bronwyn Pithey, a Rape Crisis legal adviser explains: 'One can empathise with people who take the law into their own hands. With the Foxcroft judgment it is no surprise that people are acting like this' (Abarber 1999). In contrast, informal justice is quick and 'punishes' offenders there and then; in some cases, stolen goods and money are returned to their rightful owners. More often, alleged suspects are killed or end up in hospital in a critical condition. In a recent incident in a township in Cape Town, a mob began stoning a suspect in full view of the police. The police fired warning shots into the air; however, the crowd refused to disperse and threatened the police and ambulance staff (Le May 2001).

Indeed, commentators note 'as was the case with the conservative vigilantes of the apartheid era, it appears that those involved in vigilante action today are most unlikely to face legal consequences for their actions' (Bruce and Komane 1999: 41). Victims of vigilante attacks are reluctant to lay charges against their attackers. For example, a 16-year-old youth suspected of housebreaking was assaulted by three men in Vredehoek (Cape Town); although the attackers were known to the police, the youth declined to make a complaint against them (Kemp 2001). Since its inception, at least twenty people are thought to have been killed by *Mapogo*, although none of those initially charged has been convicted (Tromp and Gophe 2001). Although 607 members of the group were arrested between 1996 and 2000 and charged with a range of offences, including kidnapping, assault and attempted murder, only fourteen have been convicted of any offence (for more details, see Sekhonyane 2000). In August 2000, *Mapogo*'s leader, John Magolego, and eleven other members were cleared of murder and assault charges because witnesses were too frightened to testify against them. What then has been the response to dealing with communal violence associated with paramilitaries and vigilantes 'protecting' their communities against criminality?

The politics of resolution

Northern Ireland

Several examples illustrate how seeking to tackle paramilitary-style attacks has clashed with the 'high' politics of Northern Ireland. The response of statutory organisations to these attacks has been one of minimisation and indifference to the problem, or what Conway has described as 'reactive containment' (1997: 114). The police argue that many of the victims refuse to make a witness statement for fear of reprisals and that in the absence of forensic evidence or catching paramilitaries in the act, they have little chance of apprehending the perpetrators. However, participants in this research claimed that, while not openly encouraging the informal justice system, the police recognise its existence and perpetuate its use by referring some complainants to the paramilitaries. Their motives for doing so may be no more sinister than accepting that the informal system in particular circumstances such as a burglary may be more effective at retrieving stolen goods than the formal police and legal systems. At best, therefore, the police acquiesce in the *status quo*. Although the Northern Ireland Office (NIO) has responsibility for law and order, its response has been to see paramilitary-style attacks more within the framework of crime prevention and community safety that seek to address the causes of antisocial behaviour. It does not commit resources directly to the problem, and its interest in it appears to peak only when it is linked to the political agenda of the day. Hence when there was a parliamentary debate on informal 'justice'[10] initiated by the Conservative Party in an attempt to halt the early release of political prisoners under the terms of the Belfast Agreement, the Northern Ireland Office suddenly became interested in the research of the authors.

Moreover, criticism by the researchers of the lack of response by statutory agencies to paramilitary-style attacks was met with a political rebuttal. The Northern Ireland Office, stung by accusations that the government was adopting a 'see no evil, hear no evil' stance to ongoing beatings and shootings, responded with a statement denying its indifference and attacking the research findings (Knox 2002). It claimed that the research represented 'a series of unsubstantiated, generalised and politically tendentious assertions and successive Northern Ireland Secretaries and Security Ministers had consistently condemned the attacks and had called for those with influence to end them' (Breen 2000). The statement was issued before the NIO had asked for a copy of the research report from the authors! The research also became the subject of a Northern Ireland Assembly debate, with pro- and anti-Belfast Agreement politicians adopting positions on its findings. One pro-Agreement party argued that the report 'highlighted the strong support that there is for alternatives to "punishment" attacks (such as restorative justice) in the absence of a legitimate policing service' (Gildernew 2001: 31). Anti-Agreement parties claimed that paramilitary attacks had soared as a direct result of prisoner releases, and the research 'presented cogent evidence that the Good Friday Agreement is failing' (Paisley 2001: 47). Politicisation is an ongoing feature of the debate on this issue. The Sinn Féin Health Minister, Bairbre de Brún, is regularly asked for information in the Northern Ireland Assembly on how the immediate hospitalisation of those subjected to beatings and shootings is displacing patients on long waiting lists in need of orthopaedic surgery and trauma counselling. This is as much to embarrass and undermine the Sinn Féin minister as it is to highlight the plight of paramilitary victims.

All political parties call publicly for an end to paramilitary-style attacks, yet, given their lack of influence with paramilitaries, it is left to parties such as Sinn Féin and the Progressive Unionist Party to tackle the problem directly. They, in turn, are fighting against a history of summary justice in the areas they represent. Both have attempted to introduce and/or support alternative mechanisms for dealing with community crime. On the republican side, a number of community restorative justice projects have been set up as a means of addressing antisocial behaviour through mediated agreement, work with families, restitution, payment of damages, and referral to a programme or statutory agency and community service (Auld *et al.* 1997). On the loyalist side, the Greater Shankill Alternatives Programme has piloted a restorative justice approach that features offender/victim mediation, community service work for individuals under threat from paramilitaries, and intensive training and peer education groups focusing on behavioural problems (Winston 1997). Reactions to these schemes have been at best mixed and at worst dismissive. This is particularly true of republican initiatives, which exclude police involvement in the implementation of their programmes. The most recent government proposals for community restorative justice schemes contained in draft legislation (Justice (Northern Ireland) Bill 2001) emerging from the review of the criminal justice system suggest that referrals must come from a statutory criminal justice agency rather than from within the community. The police must be informed of all such referrals, and all schemes must be accredited and subject to standards (human rights, due process, etc.) laid down by the government (Northern Ireland Office 2001: 79). This is clearly a political and criminal justice response to existing community restorative justice schemes, about which there are legitimate fears for the rights of the accused and over paramilitary involvement. However, it ignores the legacy of community condonation of summary justice and the reality of living in working-class areas controlled by paramilitaries.

South Africa

Like Northern Ireland, a number of key responses were discernible across the range of statutory agencies and NGOs to the problem of vigilante attacks. First, there is condemnation of vigilante attacks by government ministers, politicians, NGOs and public prosecutors. For example, the former Minister for Safety and Security, Steve Tshwete, stated:

> We cannot and will not condone any action by vigilante groups as this can only contribute to crime. Merely resorting to vigilantism is not only unscrupulous, but an abdication of responsibility. Criminals don't stay on Mars, but in our communities.
>
> (Legget 1999: 8)

This view is echoed by police personnel in areas where vigilante groups operate and/or mob justice has occurred. In the Western Cape, which has seen seven suspected criminals killed in one month by mobs in townships in and around Cape Town, Provincial Police Commissioner, Lennit Max, issued a lengthy public statement saying that vigilantes will 'face the full brunt of the law'. The second response identified was that of toleration. On the ground, pockets of toleration, and in some cases support, for vigilantism were found within the ranks of the SAPS. Bruce (2001: 1) argues:

> Many rank and file members of the SAPS tacitly support vigilante justice, while some of them may even overtly encourage it. It is frequently the case that, when the police hear a report that an alleged criminal has been appre- hended and is being assaulted by members of the public, they deliberately delay their arrival on the scene. Sometimes this is because they wish to avoid the risky task of confronting an angry mob. At other times it is because they wish to allow the mob an opportunity to 'deal with the suspect' first.

Other research has found that some officers were tolerant of vigilantism (Bruce and Komane 1999). This toleration ranged from non-intervention in a situation where an alleged criminal was being attacked to openly expressing support for vigilante action and failing to take action against individuals involved in vigi- lantism. The reasons given for non-intervention included sympathy with the original victim of crime and a lack of confidence in the criminal justice system – a view not confined to community members. Community members involved in the research also perceived that there was police support for vigilante actions in Khayelitsha (Cape Town). Furthermore, a number of interviewees suggested that police officers were taking cases to PEACA to be dealt with, although an inspector at the Khayelitsha Police Station denied this. However, he did acknowledge that PEACA had provided accurate information concerning stolen vehicles in the area.

Other key responses by agencies to vigilantism can be described as both indifference and a disjointed approach to the problem. Historically in South Africa, the government has largely neglected victims of political violence and, indeed, crime. The work of the Truth and Reconciliation Commission was an attempt to address the plight of victims of political violence by piecing together a comprehensive picture of the human rights abuses of the apartheid era. Discussions about what should be done for victims of crime, which in theory would include victims of vigilante attacks, continue.

Unlike in the United Kingdom, systematic victim support services do not exist in South Africa. Moreover, very little financial support is available to victims of crime in the form of benefits from the Department of Welfare. Social security benefits are open to all South African citizens who meet the eligibility criteria but are very limited in terms of financial assistance and the types of benefit offered (see Liebenberg and Tilley 1998 for details). Victims of crime, including vigilante attacks, are not eligible for any special grants or awards and can only apply for those grants already offered. At present, no compensation fund exists for victims of crime. Furthermore, there is no statutory duty to provide housing in South Africa: 'There is no provision which requires you to be housed by anybody' (interview with a representative from Black Sash,[11] November 1999). Thus, if a person's house or shack is burned down as a result of a vigilante attack, then that person has no access to state social welfare.

Some non-governmental organisations (NGOs) are beginning to offer services to victims of crime – those subjected to vigilante attacks are incorporated into the general client portfolio. On speaking to a number of NGOs, it was difficult to ascertain if any victims of vigilante attacks had ever availed themselves of the services on offer or if they had, what sort of numbers were involved. NGOs rely, in part, on donations from domestic and international donors in order to carry out their work. Many have found that since the establishment of a democratically elected government, international governments and funders have donated money directly to government coffers. Subsequently, NGOs have felt a financial squeeze, and this has affected their ability to run programmes, offer services and address issues. Thus, organisations offering support services to victims of crime add to the disjointed nature of such service provision. Given the precarious nature of NGO funding, the long-term needs of victims of crime, including those who have been attacked by vigilantes, are not being addressed.

Conclusions

Both the legacy of political violence and the changing constitutional and security context significantly condition the meaning of violence in Northern Ireland and South Africa. In the case of Northern Ireland, as the state and its organs were (are) pivotal stakeholders in the cause and resolution of the conflict, they have a crucial role to play in defining the parameters of what is 'an acceptable level of violence' in the context of 'an imperfect peace'. The boundaries are determined by the wider political agenda of the British government and its search for a lasting settlement to the Northern Ireland conflict. This has resulted in its resignation, or at the very least quiet indifference, to paramilitary-style attacks that would simply be unacceptable in other parts of the United Kingdom. This happens in the interests of a wider collective good – long-term peace. When violent acts become part of the political equation, the government through its response has defined that such beatings and shootings do not constitute a breach of the principles of democracy and non-violence, core tenets of the Belfast Agreement. It is noteworthy that the most recent proposals on the full implementation of the Agreement, involving the British and Irish governments (the Weston Park discussions) make no mention of the worsening problem of paramilitary shootings or ways of tackling this problem. It must therefore be concluded that these shootings and beatings come within the purview of 'an acceptable level of violence' and, while it is distasteful for the government, little can be done to address the problem other than condemnation. More worrying are the reasons why communities condone these attacks and subscribe to the paramilitary 'policing'. The lack of confidence in the police and formal criminal justice systems has not been adequately addressed from their perspective. Sinn Féin has not endorsed the new Police Service of Northern Ireland and refuses to take its seats on the new oversight Policing Board. Similarly, the response by the criminal justice review process to community-led restorative justice projects has been so heavy-handed that few could comply with the formal requirements contained therein. All of this adds up to the pessimistic prospect of a continuing role for paramilitaries in meting out their own form of summary justice.

In South Africa, when discussing community support and/or use of violence directed at criminal elements within their own community, it is important to remember that recourse to violent action outside the formal institutions of the state is a well-established principle. Indeed, a 'culture of violence' can be said to exist in which society endorses and accepts violence as an acceptable and legitimate means of not only resolving problems but also achieving goals (Hamber and Lewis 1997). The Reverend Frank Chikane wrote in 1987 that 'the most tragic reflection of [the] war situation in which South Africa finds itself is that it faces the years to come with children who have been socialised to find violence completely acceptable and human life cheap' (quoted in Mehlwana 1996: 31). In the period before the unbanning of the ANC and the lifting of the state of emergency (February 1990), much of the conflict and violence was driven by township residents' opposition to apartheid and their attempts to make the townships ungovernable. This included rent, services and consumer boycotts, worker stay-aways, protest marches and mass mobilisation. The government responded by imposing a state of emergency and clamping down on overt political activity, thus leading to confrontation between township residents and the security forces. The period leading up to democracy (1990–1994) was characterised by both inter- and intra-community violence, facilitated by the deregulation of the repressive state security forces and the legitimation of violence by all political groupings prior to the 1990s (Hamber 1998). In the democratic South Africa, violence is endemic and can be found in almost all parts of social life, including attacks against illegal aliens and xenophobia, campus violence, domestic violence, minibus taxi 'wars' and violent crime (Minnaar *et al.* 1998). Thus the *sjambokking* of 'skollies' (local hoodlums) by organised groups such as *Mapogo* or the coming together of concerned community members like taxi drivers or ex-combatants has become commonplace in the townships in the 'new' South Africa despite the state's attempts to reform and legitimise the criminal justice system.

This chapter has attempted to demonstrate that the meaning of violence is closely bound to its social context. Where that context has overt political and security manifestations, ways of understanding and dealing with violence are conditioned by, in this case, the failure of the formal police and justice systems to tackle the problem effectively. Hence, direct involvement by paramilitaries and vigilantes in addressing community crime is a legacy of failed political systems. However, the corollary, that a political settlement somehow changes the ways in which communities respond to crime, cannot be assumed. Political settlements do not of themselves immediately impact on communal violence. New political dispensations must, over time, demonstrate that reformed policing and criminal justice systems have secured sufficient community confidence in their impartiality and efficacy that these communities can give their allegiance to the very institutions of the state that they previously distrusted. In the short to medium term, 'tried and tested' instant retributive 'justice' meted out by paramilitaries and vigilantes will continue with community support, and the glib descriptions 'imperfect peace' and 'acceptable levels of violence' will apply.

Notes

1   The only year in which shootings and assaults were higher was 1996/97, in which 332 casualties of paramilitary-style attacks were recorded by the police.
2   Informal justice systems have historical antecedents in Ireland in the eighteenth- and nineteenth-century revolutionary agrarian societies, which were concerned with protecting tenants, smallholders and labourers who worked on the land from arbitrary acts by landowners. See, for example, Alter (1982), Bell (1996) and Monaghan (2002).
3   The IRA ended its ceasefire on 9 February 1996 with the Canary Wharf bombing and restored it on 19 July 1997.
4   The UVF is a loyalist paramilitary group that was formed in 1966. It has been responsible for a large number of murders, mostly of innocent Catholics, in Northern Ireland. The UVF became part of the Combined Loyalist Military Command in 1991. In 1996, a number of disaffected 'maverick' members broke away to form the Loyalist Volunteer Force (LVF). The UDA was, and remains, the largest loyalist paramilitary group in Northern Ireland. It was formed in 1971 from a number of loyalist vigilante groups, many of which were called 'defence associations' – one such group was the Shankill Defence Association. Since 1973, members of the UDA have used the cover name the Ulster Freedom Fighters (UFF) to claim responsibility for the killing of Catholics. The Ulster Democratic Party, which earned a place at the multi-party talks following the Forum elections in May 1996, represented the UDA until November 2001 but has since dissolved as a political party over disagreements about the UDA's lack of support for the Belfast Agreement.
5   Results of specification include measures such as prisoners associated with the UDA, UFF and LVF who have been released early being liable to having their licences suspended and being returned to jail if they are believed to continue to support their organisation. And any UDA, UFF or LVF person found guilty of a scheduled offence that took place before the Belfast Agreement cannot qualify for early release provisions. The Real IRA, Continuity IRA, Red Hand Defenders and Orange Volunteers have already been specified.
6   The *lekgotla* is a court comprised of elders of the community who convene a meeting to listen to disputes and problems within the community and pass judgment. The *lekgotla* emphasises a conservative moral code, including respect for elders, the importance of kin and patriarchal authority (the plural of *lekgotla* is *makgotla*).
7   PEACA is based in Khayelitsha, a township near Cape Town. It was formed in August 1998 by ex-combatants of the liberation struggle and local residents who had come together to fight crime. Its members number about 1,500.

200 *Colin Knox and Rachel Monaghan*

8   *Mapogo a Mathamaga* was established in August 1996 and has 50,000 members, who pay a monthly subscription to the organisation in return for protection against crime.

9   A picket was set up in June 2001 to protest against Catholic children who attended the Holy Cross Primary School walking through a Protestant estate in the Ardoyne area of Belfast. Ugly scenes of sectarian chants and taunts by Protestants aimed at the schoolchildren and their parents were broadcast around the world. North Belfast was once a Unionist stronghold with a low-income Catholic minority. The demography has changed with the flight of middle-class Unionists from the area. Protestants now see themselves as a besieged minority and react with anger to what they perceive as increasing territorialism by Catholics.

10 House of Commons debate, 27 January 1999, 'Terrorist mutilations (Northern Ireland)', *Hansard*: 347–98.

11 Black Sash is a national NGO that monitors infringements of political and socioeconomic rights, monitors how the rights of women are affected, engages in para-legal work that strengthens people's capacity to understand and claim their rights, and campaigns for justice in legislation and state administration.

References

Abarber, G. (1999) 'Rape fury surges into vigilante violence', *Cape Times* (Cape Town), 12 October.

Alter, P. (1982) 'Traditions of violence in the Irish National Movement', in J.M. Wolfgang and G. Hirschfield (eds) *Social Protest, Violence and Terror in Nineteenth Century Europe*. London: Macmillan.

Amupadhi, T. (1997) 'Police worried about the rise in mob action', *Weekly Mail and Guardian* (Johannesburg), 14 February.

Auld, J., Gormally, B., McEvoy, K. and Ritchie, M. (1997) *Designing a System of Restorative Community Justice in Northern Ireland: A Discussion Document*. Belfast, published by authors.

Belfast Agreement (1998) *The Agreement Reached in the Multi-Party Negotiations*. Belfast: Northern Ireland Office.

Bell, C. (1996) 'Alternative justice in Ireland', in N. Dawson, D. Greer and P. Ingram (eds) *One Hundred and Fifty Years of Irish Law*. Belfast: SLS Legal Publications.

Breen, S. (2000) 'London indifferent to attacks – study', *The Irish Times* (Dublin), 28 November.

Brogden, M. and Shearing, C. (1993) *Policing for a New South Africa*. London: Routledge.

Bruce, D. (2001) *Problem of Vigilantism Raises Key Questions About community Involvement in Policing*. Johannesburg: Centre for the Study of Violence and Reconciliation [www.wits.ac.za/wits/csvr/articles/].

Bruce, D. and Komane, J. (1999) 'Taxis, cops and vigilantes: police attitudes towards street justice', *Crime and Conflict* 17: 39–44.

Cavanaugh, K.A. (1997) 'Interpretations of political violence in ethnically divided societies', *Terrorism and Political Violence* 9(3): 33–54.

Conway, P. (1997) 'Critical reflections: a response to paramilitary policing in Northern Ireland', *Critical Criminology* 8(1): 109–21.

The Economist (1999) 'Mandela's heir', 29 May: 19–25.

Gildernew, M. (2001) '"Punishment" Beatings', Northern Ireland Assembly debate, 23 January, *Hansard*.

Hamber, B. (1998) ' Dr Jekyll and Mr Hyde: problems of violence prevention and reconciliation in South Africa's transition to democracy', in E. Bornmann, R. van Eeden and M. Wentzel (eds) *Violence in South Africa*. Pretoria: Human Sciences Research Council.

Hamber, B. and Lewis, S. (1997) *An Overview of the Consequences of Violence and Trauma in South Africa*. Johannesburg: Centre for the Study of Violence and Reconciliation.

Kemp, Y. (2001) 'Vigilante attack gets the thumbs-up', *Cape Argus* (Cape Town), 19 April.

Kennedy, L. (1995) 'Nightmares within nightmares: paramilitary repression within working-class communities', in L. Kennedy (ed.) *Crime and Punishment in West Belfast*. Belfast: Summer School, West Belfast.

Knox, C. (2002) 'See no evil, hear no evil: insidious paramilitary violence in Northern Ireland', *The British Journal of Criminology* 42(1): 164–85.

Legget, T. (1999) 'Mr Fix-it tackles crime: an interview with Steve Tshwete', *Crime and Conflict* 17 (Spring): 5–8.

Leibenberg, S. and Tilley, A. (1998) *Poverty and Social Security in South Africa*. SANGOCO Occasional Publication Series No. 7. Braamfontein: South African National NGO Coalition.

Lekota, I. (1999) 'Mogoba confirms PAC will dismember', *The Sowetan* (Johannesburg), 19 February.

Le May, J. (2001) 'Mob justice claims two more victims', *Cape Argus* (Cape Town), 17 November.

MacKay, A. (1999) House of Commons debate', 27 January, 'Terrorist Mutilations (Northern Ireland)', *Hansard*: 347–98.

McKittrick, D., Kelters, S., Feeney, B. and Thornton, C. (1999) *Lost Lives: The Stories of the Men and Women who Died as a Result of the Northern Ireland Troubles*. Edinburgh: Mainstream.

Mehlwana, A.M. (1996) 'Political violence and family movements: the case of a South African shanty town', in L. Glanz and A. Spiegel (eds) *Violence and Family Life in Contemporary South Africa: Research and Policy Issues*. Pretoria: HSRC Publishers.

Meyer, J. (2001) 'SA's criminals are getting away with murder', *Daily News* (Johannesburg), 11 December.

Minnaar, A. (1995) 'Desperate justice', *Crime and Conflict* 2: 9–12.

Minnaar, A., Pretorius, S. and Wentzel, M. (1998) 'Political conflict and other manifestations of violence in South Africa', in E. Bornmann, R. van Eeden and M. Wentzel (eds) *Violence in South Africa*. Pretoria: Human Sciences Research Council.

Monaghan, R. (2002) 'The return of "Captain Moonlight": informal justice in Northern Ireland', *Studies in Conflict and Terrorism* 25(1): 41–56.

Ní Aoláin, F. (2000) *The Politics of Force: Conflict Management and State Violence in Northern Ireland*. Belfast: Blackstaff.

Northern Ireland Office (2001) *Criminal Justice Review: Implementation Plan*. Belfast: Stationery Office.

Paisley, I. (2001) Northern Ireland Assembly debate, '"Punishment" beatings', 23 January, *Hansard*.

Police Authority for Northern Ireland (2001) *Listening to the Community, Working with the RUC*, Annual Report 2000/2001. Belfast: PANI.

Report of the Chief Constable 2000–2001 (2001) Belfast: Royal Ulster Constabulary.

Reuters (1999) 'Witnesses silent on lynch mob killings', *The Citizen* (Johannesburg), 12 February.

Rolston, B. (2000) *Unfinished Business: State Killings and the Quest for Truth*. Belfast: Beyond the Pale Publications.

Sekhonyane, M. (2000) 'Using crime to fight crime: tackling vigilante activity', *Nedbank ISS Crime Index* 4 (July–August).

Silke, A. (1998) 'The lords of discipline: the methods and motives of paramilitary vigilantism in Northern Ireland', *Low Intensity Conflict and Law Enforcement* 7(2): 121–56.

Smith, A. (1999) 'Father gets 7 years for raping daughter', *Cape Argus* (Cape Town), 5 October.

Soggot, M. and Ngobeni, E. (1999) 'We must work on their buttocks', *Weekly Mail and Guardian* (Johannesburg), 14 May.

South African Institute for Race Relations (2000) *South African Survey 1999/2000.* Johannesburg: South African Institute of Race Relations.

South African Press Association (1999) 'Man stoned to death', *The Sowetan* (Johannesburg), 15 February.

South African Press Association (2001) 'Court reserves judgment in rapist dad's case', *Independent Online* (South Africa), 5 November [*www.iol.co.za*].

Thompson, W. and Mulholland, B. (1995) 'Paramilitary punishments and young people in West Belfast: psychological effects and the implications for education', in L. Kennedy (ed.) *Crime and Punishment in West Belfast.* Belfast: Summer School, West Belfast.

Tromp, B. and Gophe, M. (2001) 'Mapogo vigilantes to "clean up" the Cape', *Cape Argus* (Cape Town), 11 September.

Winston, T. (1997) 'Alternatives to "punishment" beatings and shootings in a loyalist community in Belfast', *Critical Criminology* 8(1): 122–8.

Part IV

Violence, meaning, and institutional contexts

11 Institutional violence

Prison conflicts in context

*Kimmett Edgar, Carol Martin
and Ian O'Donnell*

The Conflicts and Violence in Prison project team (CVP) examined interpersonal violence – that is, fights, assaults and other forms of deliberate harm – among prisoners. The prison context is a specialised area within which to study violence because of the unusual characteristics of prisons as total institutions (Goffman 1961). However, the innovative contribution that the CVP makes to research into violence is to examine violent incidents in the context of conflicts.

This chapter[1] is based on data gathered in four prisons in England: a young offenders' institution, a local prison, a female establishment and a high-security prison. The CVP surveyed 590 prisoners about prison violence. In addition, it interviewed 209 of the prisoners surveyed, all of whom had recent experience of disputes. Some of these prisoners had reported in the survey that they had recently been involved in a fight or assault. Others were recruited to the study following disciplinary hearings adjudicated by the prison governor. Still others (forty-one) were interviewed about disputes that they said had been settled without physical violence. In total, the in-depth interviews covered 141 disputes, ninety-seven of which had resulted in a fight or assault.[2]

The CVP worked from an understanding of conflict as any situation in which the interests of two or more parties clashed. The 209 accounts of conflicts were analysed according to a framework based on the six dimensions shown in Figure 11.1.

These dimensions help to describe the way in which the CVP defined conflict. The purposes of setting violence in the context of conflict are:

- to explore the pathways to violence, the ways in which disputes escalate to a point at which one party (or both) deliberately harms the other;
- to demystify violence, so that the reasons for its occurrence become clear; and
- to identify points at which the paths to violence can be diverted so that deliberate harm can be prevented.

Prisoners' accounts of violent incidents

The meanings that participants in prison conflicts assign to violence can be understood by tracing their accounts of actual incidents. After presenting two

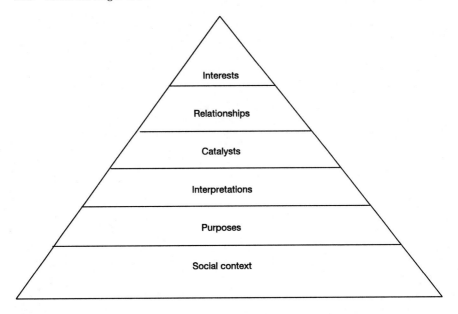

Figure 11.1: The conflict pyramid

prisoners' accounts of a fight, we illustrate each of the dimensions of conflict shown in Figure 11.1. Fulford[3] described his difficult relationship with his cell-mate, Reeth:

> I moved in the cell, got on with him for a bit. He shouts out the window. We were having conflicts about some of the things he did. I asked the officers for a move. They said, 'You'll have to wait till a single cell becomes available'. The night before it happened, he was slagging me off to the nextdoor neighbour, calling me a dickhead. I called him a div [fool] and said we'd fight if he didn't shut up.
>
> [The next day] when Reeth came in he was looking at me. That really upset me and I said, 'What you fucking looking at?' I was sat on my bed reading a letter and felt him looking at me and he was staring at me and his face was all twisted up and I lost it and said, 'What you fucking looking at? Don't look at me like that'. He said, 'Don't talk to me like that', waving his finger. He come up to me and grabbed my throat. I got up and threw his hand off. He picked up the coffee jar and threatened me with it. I jumped up and said, 'Look, Reeth, I'm not going to lose days for you but if we'll have it [fight] then we'll have it'. I lost my head. I threw him on the bed. I had hold of his head and told him to stop struggling. He tried to hit me and I lost it and banged him in the face a couple of times. I was screaming at him and he was shouting back. I heard the screws [officers] coming, and as they got closer I jumped off and sat on my bed.

Fulford's story provides an incomplete picture of the episode. Conflicts are interactions between at least two parties. The inherent partiality of each person's perspective means that the violence can be fully understood only if we have heard both sides of the story. Thus far, the situation has been constructed upon only one account. How can Reeth's view further explain how violence resulted? Here is Reeth's description of the dispute:

> We were pad mates. Things were okay to start with, but banged up 23 hours together ... I thought I must be going mad. I went to Education in the morning and when I came back my mail had been moved around. I didn't realise to start with, but it kept happening. I left it for a couple of days but it kept happening so I realised he must be reading it. I started to be less friendly and stopped having conversations with him. I told him and I told officers that I wanted to move cells. I wanted a single cell.
>
> The next day I came back from exercise and a letter I had been expecting wasn't there. I said to him, 'I should have got mail today'. At tea time I saw my letter on his cupboard and I took it and said, 'Why is it on your side?' He said he didn't know. I pressed the bell straight away. I was going to move or go to the block. I didn't want to lose days, though. Next thing, he hit me on the back of the head and we had a fight.

Fulford's explicit *interest* was to restore his reputation, having been humiliated by the remarks that Reeth had made to their neighbour. Asked what he wanted to achieve, Fulford stated, 'He was calling me a dickhead and hurting me. I wanted to show him not to do that'. Reeth's *interest* was to move to a different cell, but he was motivated by a need for his cellmate to respect his privacy. Hence, for Reeth, the *social context* from which the violence emerged meant not only that he was forced to share personal space with someone he would not have chosen but also that his privacy was being invaded to an intolerable degree. The situation shows that neglect of prisoners' need for privacy increases the likelihood that violence will arise.

Both prisoners made it clear that their *relationship* was aggravated by the pressures of being forced to live together. But the interviews also revealed tensions over superiority. Fulford said that he disliked Reeth 'deep down' because Reeth was 'always bigging himself up and bragging'. Reeth confirmed that he felt superior. He commented: 'He's got nothing. I let him use everything – toiletries, everything'. His *interpretation* of their relationship was that Fulford was dependent on him ('I felt a bit sorry for him').

How did these prisoners deal with the tensions between them? What tactics were they using that functioned as *catalysts* for violence? Fulford stated that Reeth was 'slagging him off' (insulting him) to the nextdoor neighbour ('calling me a dickhead'). The tactic of deriding Fulford demonstrates an interaction of two of the dimensions of conflict: relationships and catalysts. Fulford felt that Reeth was acting like he was superior, and Reeth's behaviour, making insulting remarks about Fulford to other inmates, aggravated the problem. Fulford reacted to the insults with a threat ('I said we'd fight if he didn't shut up'). When the tension had built up to breaking point, Reeth began to stare at Fulford, a hostile gesture. Fulford also *interpreted* the staring as a sign of contempt, inferring that Reeth was showing him disrespect ('He looked at me as though I was nothing'). When Fulford felt threatened and demeaned by Reeth's glaring, his response was to challenge Reeth. Fulford asked him: 'What are you looking at?' Faced with this challenge, Reeth was obliged either to stand up to the implied threat or to back down. The challenge closed off the options of both cellmates, defining their exchange as a win or lose competition. Reeth reacted by standing up to the challenge with an accusation ('Don't talk to me like that!')

According to Reeth, when he first became aware of their conflict, he tried to show his displeasure through avoidance: 'I stopped having conversations with him'. This response blocked off communication and gave Fulford no indication of the reason for the change of behaviour. When Reeth confirmed, to his satisfaction, that Fulford was reading his mail, he accused him ('I saw my letter on his cupboard and said, "Why is it on your side?"'). Accusations place full responsibility for a problem on the other party, driving them towards a defensive position. However, perhaps the most provocative way that Reeth dealt with the problem was to press the cell bell – in effect bringing officers to the cell to enquire what was going on. Reeth had said nothing to explain to Fulford what his intentions were in seeking an officer. Reeth stated in his interview that he wanted to demand a single cell, but from Fulford's perspective, Reeth's purpose could as easily have been to inform on him, bringing the sanctions of the prison authorities down upon him.

Their conflict was exacerbated by the *social context*. As a result of the clashes between them they had asked the staff for a cell change but were told they would have to wait until a spare cell became available. The prison regime could not exercise the flexibility required to separate them. Unusually, no other inmates were in a position to witness the encounter, and thus peer pressure played little part in the actual fight. Nonetheless, the origins of the conflict go back to the way Reeth publicly insulted Fulford. In this way, the influence of peers compelled Fulford to find some way to restore his reputation.

Fulford was asked, 'What was Reeth trying to achieve in the situation?' Fulford explained, 'He was trying to intimidate me'. He *interpreted* Reeth's behaviour as an attempt to dominate him. The immediate *purpose* of Fulford's use of force was apparently self-defence, as – in his account – Reeth precipitated the fight by grabbing Fulford's neck. However, he continued to assault Reeth after he had gained the upper hand, suggesting that he also wanted to punish Reeth for insulting him.

The two stories were largely in agreement about the ways the conflict gradually escalated to a point at which physical violence erupted, but each party failed to mention how his own behaviour had contributed to the tension. Reeth did not say that he had insulted Fulford to the neighbour; Fulford did not mention reading Reeth's letters. Nonetheless, their fight – analysed in terms of interests, relationships, catalysts, interpretations, purposes and social context – provides a demonstration of the power of a conflict-centred approach to clarify how conflict can lead to violence. In the next section, we describe each of the dimensions of conflict in more detail, adding illustrations from prisoners' accounts where relevant.

Six dimensions of conflict

Interests

Conflicts often began in a clash of interests over what each party wanted out of the situation. Contrary to a widely held belief, the majority of fights and assaults were not about material goods, such as tobacco, phone cards or even drugs. Typically, conflicts that began over some material interest escalated as values, such as self-image or fairness, grew in importance. In most of the conflicts, prisoners felt that the other person was trying to intimidate, exploit, threaten or wrong them, or that their beliefs or image were being challenged.

John Burton (1990) distinguished between interests and needs. Interests refer to the aspirations of individuals or groups, encompassing material goods and social roles. Interests generate competition, but they are also negotiable. Needs are basic to human development and are not negotiable. The denial of basic needs generates conflicts. Burton's distinction was played out in the conflicts between prisoners, as disputes that began over a material good deepened when the focus shifted to each party's needs. For example, what was at stake for Reeth was first his letters, and then, at a deeper level, his privacy. Fulford's initial desire was to change cells; his deeper need was respect, as he felt underestimated by Reeth.

Another of the 141 incidents examined showed a similar distinction between material interests and deeper needs. Drebly was in the queue to change his kit. He had lost one of his towels in the shower, and he now wanted the kit change orderly to give him another two towels. One of the kit change orderlies, Meltham, refused, stating the rule that kit is exchanged on a one-for-one basis. Drebly explained that he wanted a second towel because one of his had been stolen. Meltham again refused to give him a second towel. Drebly appealed to an officer, but still Meltham refused to grant his request. The other kit change orderly, Poynton, intervened. Poynton described what happened next:

> I leaned down on the table to say, 'Look, bugger off!' As I leaned towards Drebly, he slapped me on the face and ran off. The screw went and grabbed hold of him and took him straight down the block.

Drebly explained why he slapped Poynton in a dispute that began over a second towel:

> I was intimidated by the way he leant towards me. I knew he was going to say something smart. I didn't want him to put me down. I don't like that. You can't allow it in here – you really can't. It causes bullying and everything.

The story illustrates how a dispute, initially over a material interest, deepened as questions about domination and respect were brought to the surface by the way in which the prisoners involved handled their conflict.

Relationships

Social distance is one way in which relationships influenced the development of conflicts. Conflicts between strangers tended to spring from tensions that arose spontaneously in impersonal situations, such as waiting to use the telephone or for food. Two parties who saw each other as anonymous faces on the wing were liable to clash over misunderstandings. They did not know each other well enough to predict how the other would react. People who said they associated with each other fell into dispute over trades, contested ownership of goods or issues of loyalty.

Relationships exercised a deeper influence on the course of conflicts through the power balance between the parties. All conflicts include some calculation of the power each party has or is willing to use. Dominance can lead to violence when the more powerful prisoner uses force to rob or otherwise exploit a weaker victim. A power disadvantage can lead to violence when a vulnerable prisoner assaults a stronger prisoner to demonstrate to others that he is tough. In many prison conflicts, however, the question of the power balance was undecided. When a dispute over interests became centred on the power balance, the conflict was transformed into a contest of power.[4]

Contests of power arose when one or both parties defined their situation as a win or lose struggle. They were anxious about being dominated by their opponent and tested them to gauge their personal power. They espoused values that viewed compromise and non-violence as weaknesses. Intimidation was a common element in these conflicts, as both parties channelled their efforts into gaining supremacy over their opponent. The characteristic that most starkly defines a dispute as a power contest is revealed by the intended objective of the parties involved. Power in disputes can be defined as the capacity to determine the outcome. Over the course of contests, the two parties transformed the meaning of power from control of the outcome to power over the opponent.

Catalysts

The tactics that prisoners used to handle disputes escalated their conflicts and were a direct contributor to fights and assaults. Table 11.1 shows the number of times that each catalyst of violence appeared in the sample of 141 incidents. Every incident featured more than one catalyst.

We next describe four catalysts – accusations, threats, challenges and personal invasions – to show the impact of such tactics on a conflict, using material from the prisoners' accounts to illustrate each one.

Accusations place full blame for a problem on the other person, suggesting that they have sole responsibility for solving the problem between them.

Table 11.1 Reported presence of catalysts

Accusations	65
Threats	65
Verbal challenges	59
Invasions of space/privacy	45
Insults	44
Commands	43
Undermining behaviour	40
Verbal abuse	38
Invitation	37
Hostile gestures	34
Harassment	27
Spreading of rumours	21
Deception	20

Number of incidents, multiple counting (n 141=incidents)

Blaming language closes off discussion, rather than opening the conflict to creative solutions.

For example, Urmston was a remand prisoner. On returning from court, she heard a rumour that in her absence a young inmate, Truro, had propositioned her girlfriend. Urmston found Truro and said: 'What's this I hear? You were trying to chat up my missus' and immediately head-butted her. Urmston was not interested in waiting for an explanation – the accusation was assumed to be accurate. Accusations clearly increase the tension between parties to a dispute.

Threats draw their power from the unpredictable consequences that the use of physical force could bring. They are often intended to coerce the other person into doing something they do not want to do. Threats also introduce the possibility of harm into a situation, impeding non-violent solutions.

For instance, Hatton stated that Midgley had tried to frighten him into taking the blame for something that Midgley had done. But Hatton resisted. Midgley reacted by threatening him in a way that led Hatton to decide to get to him first:

> I said I wasn't going to take the rap. He then started to threaten me through the pipe .... He threatened to cut me up and throw hot water at me if I didn't agree. I became paranoid about it. I waited till dinner time when we were unlocked and then I hit him.

Challenges convey aggression and underlying threat, as these quotations from prisoners illustrate:

- 'What's your problem?'
- 'What are you looking at?'

- 'What the fuck are you doing?'
- 'Are you calling me a liar?'
- 'What are you going to do about it?'

Challenges stake a claim of superiority over another person, demanding that they adjust their behaviour to the challenger's desire. They are a form of ultimatum, suggesting that if the person continues in their behaviour they risk harmful consequences. Any challenge will aggravate a conflict by limiting the options of both parties. The person who is challenged may feel that if they ignore it or give in, they will show that they are afraid. Equally, if the challenge is not respected, the challenger must take forceful action. Hence, when someone rebels against a challenge, violence is the likely outcome.

Personal invasions include physical and symbolic incursions, such as that experienced by Reeth when Fulford read his personal letters. Prisoners were sensitive to body language or gestures that could be seen as invasions of their privacy or attempts to intimidate them. Actual physical contact, when one prisoner shoved another, was less common than hostile gestures, such as staring at someone.

> In education, Skelton stared at me for a long time. It was the way he was looking at me – trying to intimidate me. I said, 'What are you looking at?' Skelton swore at me. I walked towards him with the intention of a fight. He took a swing at me but missed. I gave him about five blows – I can't remember if he hit me back.

Anyone who has spent time in a penal institution knows that prisoners routinely insult, threaten and challenge each other. The CVP demonstrates how catalysts work together, aggravate disputes and drive them towards violent outcomes. Catalysts tend to close off options, driving prisoners to believe that there is no alternative but to fight. Each in its own way violates the other person – each has the power to be degrading, intimidating, humiliating and distressing.

Interpretations

The relationships between the parties, the knowledge one has of the interests of the other, the use and impact of catalysts – all are mediated through interpretation. Prisoners in conflicts used interpretation to assess the situation on three levels:

1   Each person interpreted the specific actions of their counterpart. For example, had Hatton (above) not perceived that Midgley's threat was genuine, had he interpreted it as empty or in jest, he would not have had reason to assault Midgley. The catalysts exacerbated the disputes as each person interpreted the other's behaviour as provocative.

2   Each person built up a picture through the other party's actions of the other's overall objectives:

I know he had something against me. He just kept on at me all the time.

Throughout the day she had been trying to boss me about.

He was trying it on, testing me. He's quite a predatory guy. He wanted to find out how strong I was.

3 Each person also defined their situation in terms of the reactions of onlookers or the wider prison culture:

> As the door opened, there were loads of heads there and that must have made him change his mind. He started saying, 'Get out, what you doing there, you little monkey', and he started pushing me. He threw me out like I was a rag doll, and I thought that was humiliating, so I retaliated by punching him in the face.

The potential influence of peer pressure meant that any particular interaction took on long-term implications. Prisoners did not want to be seen by others as soft:

> I was sat at the table with all the girls and they were all winding me up so much. 'Chicken, you're not going to do anything.' They were really winding me up, so I walked down to the table and called her a grass and then I just punched her in the face 'cos I was so wound up.

Thus particular interactions were also understood in the light of the person's view of prison life in general. For this reason, prisoners maintained a wariness towards others:

> You don't really know no one in jail. If they can take what's yours without you knowing, they'll take it.

When prisoners perceived the prison setting as a place of danger, their interpretation of the social context was one factor that drove the dispute towards a violent outcome:

> If I got into a fight here, I'd use a weapon. You have to use violence in prison to survive. The first person to take a liberty with you needs to be sorted out or they all do it.

The ways that prisoners responded when conflicts arose were aggressive, manipulative, humiliating and undermining. Their choice of tactics reflected their interpretation that the opponent meant to take advantage of them. Prisoners in conflict were caught up in dynamic loops of challenging actions, suspicious interpretations and aggressive reactions, which often culminated in physical harm but which began with deliberate social or psychological harm.

Purposes

The major reasons why prisoners decided to use injurious force in responding to conflict were:

- punishment
- retaliation
- to demonstrate their toughness
- self-defence
- to settle differences between them.

Here, we focus on self-defence and punishment because these purposes in particular raise important questions of definition for the concept of violence.

Prisoners interpreted *self-defence* in two ways: either they believed that they were in imminent danger of physical assault and they used force to repel the threat in a pre-emptive strike; or while they were being assaulted, they used force to stop the physical harm. Prisoners who believed they had acted in self-defence espoused particular values. They believed they had been right to use force, but they also felt that they had not been violent.

Prisoners sometimes reacted to an assault upon them by trying to stop their opponent. But, during the episode, some found that a motivation to do harm to the other took hold. In these cases, one can speak of 'reactive force' – the force used was more than was strictly needed to repel the threat of physical harm.

For example, Eaton was in the shower when Bower came in swinging a pool ball in a sock. Eaton grappled with Bower, eventually taking the weapon from him. Then he gained the upper hand, so that the option to leave the area was available to him, but he persisted in fighting.

Prisoners who acted purely in self-defence followed a different pattern. They tended to use the minimal force required to stop their opponent. Then, when the attack was finished, they ceased using physical force.

For instance, Crediton was challenged to a fight by Portishead. He ignored the challenge and continued talking to a mate. Portishead pursued the matter, entering the cell to try to force Crediton into a fight. Crediton tried different responses to bring the assault to an end:

> Portishead came in and punched me on the head. I jumped up and pushed him. He slipped and fell sideways out the door. I stepped over him and went out into the middle of the landing 'cos I knew the officers were there. I thought it would stop him. He came towards me. I started backing round the table tennis table. The officers were coming down. Just before they got there, he threw a punch. I grabbed hold of his arms and we both fell on the table.

Some claims of self-defence were self-justifying when considered in retrospect. To determine whether there was any basis for the claim, the CVP had to judge:

1 whether there was a genuine risk of physical harm;
2 whether force was necessary to avoid being harmed; and
3 whether the amount of force used was reasonable in the circumstances.

This last criterion was the most delicate, as the amount of force needed to escape varied, depending on the particular circumstances of the assault. In some cases, although prisoners who were being assaulted used sufficient force to cause an injury, their intentions were clearly not to harm the opponent but merely to escape the danger.

For example, Selby was unexpectedly assaulted while in the food queue by Leith, who used a weapon. Selby described the assault and his response:

> We were in the queue and suddenly I heard, 'Selby, look out!' and I felt the blow to the side of my head. I looked up and saw him swinging a sock with a glass jar in it. I tried to get away but there were too many people in the way. He kept hitting me with the jar. I tried to keep him away with kicks while he's still hitting me. I managed to get my head through the doorway and as he tried to swing it again it caught the bars and the jar broke and cut my hand. Normally there are officers but I couldn't see any at all when I was being attacked. Once I got through the gate I saw officers who accused me of fighting and said they didn't see the attack. They pushed me against the wall and said I had been kicking him. Blood was dripping from my hand. I tried to tell them what happened, and they kept saying, 'But you were kicking him'.

Selby's kicks, which appeared to the officers to be aggressive, seemed to be required by the situation in which he found himself. Although a kick could deliver injurious force, in this case these kicks seemed to have been used in self-defence. The distinction between sufficient and reasonable force (self-defence) and excessive, aggressive force (violence) is analytically clear. But it is not surprising that the fine balance is not easy to determine by prisoners when they are being assaulted.

The use of force as *punishment* presented a very different set of circumstances and motivations. Physical assaults as punishment were used to deter undesirable behaviour; to set boundaries of tolerable conduct (denunciation); or to gain satisfaction for some wrong (retribution). The CVP distinguished between retaliation and punishment by limiting the latter to behaviour that was widely recognised as a transgression of the norms of prison society. These included insulting or exploiting others, bullying, making a noise and informing. Three cases will illustrate the use of punishment to draw boundaries, to deter others and to gain retribution:

1 Ventnor and Plumpton learned that Morland had informed on them. Ventnor threatened Morland; then, later, Plumpton assaulted her. Ventnor explained their motives:

>   She'd grassed people up. She broke the worst rule ever. If you let someone get away with it, it is telling others it is no problem. You got to be seen doing something. She has got to pay for it.

2   Ripon believed that Checkley was ridiculing her. She walked up to her, grabbed her by her throat and pushed her back into her cell. She explained that she had not used her full strength in attacking Checkley. Asked what she wanted to achieve, she explained her use of force as a deterrent:

>   Just to warn her to back off, or I would seriously hurt her.

3   Lechlade and Clapham went to Sunderland's cell determined to assault him. Clapham explained that Sunderland had broken the rules by exploiting them, taking what was rightfully theirs. The previous night, their mate on a higher landing had offered them two bottles of hooch [illicit alcohol]. There was a logistical problem: he wanted to send them the bottles on a line hung from the window, but it wouldn't reach their cells. So they agreed to use Sunderland as the middle man. Their mate would drop the bottles down to Sunderland's cell, then Sunderland would take the line and swing it to Lechlade's cell. The first stage went according to plan. Then Sunderland drank the hooch. Clapham commented:

>   I don't know why he drunk it 'cos he knew he would get a beating.

Clapham viewed the assault as inevitable, a fundamental requirement of prison justice:

>   If someone takes the piss, you do them, full stop. They've done you a wrong 'un; so you've got to do them a wrong 'un.

The CVP found that the prisoners who used force had their reasons, even if their explanations did not justify hurting another person. If prisoners felt forced into situations in which they believed that violence was necessary, it was partly due to the tactics they used in conflict, the catalysts that tended to close off options that could otherwise have led to non-violent solutions.

Social context

The conflict-centred approach to prison violence developed by the CVP analysed interactions between prisoners from the perspective of those most directly involved. The study was not intended to determine how prison settings fostered potentially violent situations. Nonetheless, the interview data provide indications of the ways that prisoners interpreted their social context in making decisions about how to handle their disputes.

Hans Toch (1992) argued that the deprivations of prison life aggravate inter-actions between prisoners, increasing the likelihood that conflicts will arise. He listed seven areas of primary concern for prisoners: privacy, safety, structure, support, emotional feedback, activity and freedom. In a similar vein, John Burton (1990: 29) believed that a full understanding of conflict requires atten-tion to the underlying human needs:

> Do we assume that conflicts are due to human aggressiveness requiring and justifying authoritative political structures and processes of punishment and containment as the means by which to control conflict; or do we assume that there are inherent human needs which, if not satisfied, lead to conflictual behaviors?

The work of Toch and Burton provides insights into ways that a prison commu-nity can slide into cycles in which conflict is pervasive and violence becomes routine. In a prison with high rates of assault and threats of violence, the human needs for personal security, rationality and a sense of control are unful-filled. Prisoners in such a setting might grasp violence as a means of reasserting some control over their circumstances, if they assume that potential predators will respect shows of force. This cycle of violence is shown in Figure 11.2.

High rates of theft and robbery signal a failure to uphold prisoners' needs for distributive justice, consistent responses and personal security. The norm-enforcing violence identified by Hans Toch (1969) would lead some prisoners to manage these risks by inflicting punishment on suspected thieves. This cycle is shown in Figure 11.3.

A final example of a cycle of violence would begin with a lack of useful activity. Prisoners in such a setting are deprived of adequate stimulation, but, more importantly, they may lose a sense of role and feel that they have little control over their future. The lack of incentives that jobs otherwise provide – improved standards of living, time out of cell, opportunities for the prisoners to prove that they can be reliable – means that prisoners may feel that they have little to lose if they resort to violence.

Toch listed privacy among the human needs that prisons by their nature neglect. When invasions of privacy (rub-downs and cell searches) are combined with the damaging impact of imprisonment on family relationships, it is unsur-prising that conflicts result. When two prisoners get into a fight over access to a telephone, the background circumstances to the violence reflect the depriva-tion of intimacy imposed by the prison. As one prisoner told us: 'Letters and phone calls are time bombs here – if you muck about with people's letters or phone calls, it is serious'.

The social construction of the meanings of violence in prison

How do prisoners understand violence? Some evidence suggests that violence is the norm in prison. O'Donnell and Edgar's victimisation survey of 1,566

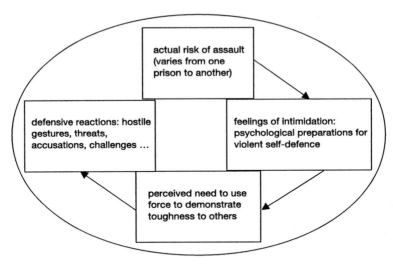

Figure 11.2: Cycle 1: force begets force

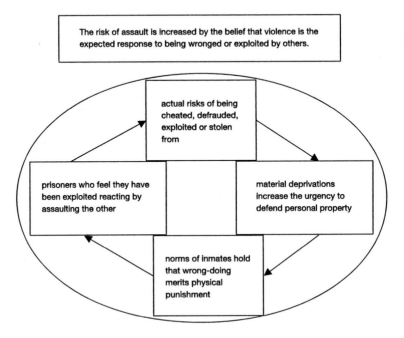

Figure 11.3: Cycle 2: exploitation fosters retribution

prisoners (1996: 1) found that 46 percent of young offenders and 30 percent of adult males had been assaulted, threatened with violence or robbed in the previous month. In the CVP study, 89 percent of 590 prisoners surveyed (and 88 percent of fifty-eight prison staff interviewed) agreed with the statement: 'violence in prisons is inevitable'. In this attitude at least, the prison societies explored in the CVP accepted that violence was part of everyday life.

Richard Sparks and his colleagues (1996: 119) defined social order, in part, as the absence of violence:

> an orderly situation is any long-standing pattern of social relations (charac-terized by a minimum level of respect for persons) in which the expectations that participants have of one another are commonly met, though not necessarily without contestation. Order can also, in part, be defined negatively as the absence of violence, overt conflict or the immi-nent threat of the chaotic breakdown of social routines.

Thus, one way to characterise violence is as disruption to social order. But there are at least three other possible links between violence and social order. Violence can also be seen as:

1 A *regulating device*: violence is used to stop the descent into chaos, to restore equilibrium, at which point the need for harming someone is ended (violence as a regulator).
2 *Order itself*: human existence is 'naturally violent'; violence is the expecta-tion that each party has of everyone else (violence as convention).
3 A *form of rebellion*: harm is used by one side in a conflict to resist the 'order' imposed by the stronger party (violence as rebellion).

How do prisoners understand violence? Whether it was considered disruptive, a regulating tool, convention or rebellion depended on the circumstances in which the harm was inflicted. The CVP found strong differences in the meaning of violence in the four types of prison studied.

Among male young offenders, fights were widely viewed as an appropriate means of settling differences. One in five of the young offenders who used inju-rious force did so with the purpose of settling a dispute. The tendency of young offenders to enter into fights by prior agreement provides strong evidence that they viewed violence as a response expected by their counterparts (conven-tion).

In contrast, female prisoners almost never turned to violence to resolve differences (only one woman – 2 percent of the female sample – used force for this purpose). Women prisoners tended to disapprove of the use of injurious force. Prisoners who intended to commit an assault sometimes took the prior step of announcing to the wing that they would attack their intended victim, justifying the assault in terms of a transgression committed by the victim. Among the women prisoners, therefore, violence was acceptable at a reasonable level if used as a punishment for widely despised behaviour. Although an assault was sometimes used to regulate interactions (for example, to enforce a debt), this was set against a backdrop in which violence was considered disruptive.

The least likely purpose of violence among the short-term and remand male prisoners in the local prison was to defend their honour or reputation. The high turnover of inmates in this population is sometimes linked to high rates of assault because of the instability it fosters. Thus, violence can be said to disrupt an already fragile social order. The CVP also found that prisoners in this setting were less likely than other prisoners to feel that they needed to defend their reputations, or to use violence as a punishment, perhaps because the men in the local prison had little emotional investment in the standards or stability of their (prison) community.

The prisoners who used injurious force in the high-security prison comprised a much smaller sample – only twelve – and it is therefore difficult to draw reliable conclusions about their reasons for resorting to violence. Nonetheless, it was clear that they tended to recognise potentially violent conflicts earlier than the other prisoners. Their interest in a stable social environment probably led many of them to see violence as disruptive – or, at best, a rarely required regulator of interactions – rather than as an everyday phenomenon of prison life.

The violent nature of the prison world can be overstated. Looked at in another way, O'Donnell and Edgar's findings show that over two-thirds of young offenders and more than four in five adult males surveyed had not been assaulted in the previous month. They also found that most prisoners felt safe from assault most of the time and that significant numbers of young offenders believed that other prisoners would intervene if they were being picked on (1996: 2). The CVP found that many prisoners expressed values that supported non-violent methods of dealing with conflict. Only 10 percent agreed with the statement: 'prisoners who won't fight back are weak'. The prisoners' accounts of the disputes included practical examples of methods that contributed to the resolution of conflict and reduced the likelihood of violence. Violence between prisoners was not inevitable.[5]

The punitive use of assaults to enforce debts, deter others from using verbal abuse or to gain retribution after a cell theft suggests that violence was used as a regulating tool, in part because turning to the authorities to arbitrate in conflicts was not viewed as a viable option. When violence is used to regulate inmate interactions, its capacity to disrupt the social order depends largely on whether particular instances can be justified to one's inmate peers. A punishment beating that witnesses perceived had been unnecessary or excessive would damage the social order in ways that punishment judged to be appropriate and measured would not.

Links between punishment and violence

Prisoners who used injurious force as retribution justified their behaviour as a fitting response to those who had transgressed prison norms. This rationale may reflect the prisoners' experience of retributive harm in the form of the punish-ment they receive from the state. Equally, a punitive ideology reflects values imported into prison life from the wider culture outside. State-sponsored punishment, like the sanctions prisoners inflicted on each other, also inflicts deliberate harm, albeit in non-physical forms. Examining the ways that society justifies its punitive ideology can shed light on the reasons why prisoners perceive it to be right for them to punish wrongdoers.

Punishment by prisoners is certainly not officially recognised as a legitimate use of force, yet just under half of the prisoners who used injurious force believed that they had been violent and that their violence was justified.[6] At a theoretical level, the distinction between the actions of these prisoners and wider society is clear: society imposes deliberate harm through a legitimate authority. Prisoners who take it upon themselves to assault wrongdoers have no formal, legal authority to do so, although their actions might find widespread approval among the prison community.

René Girard argued that the distinction between private vengeance and public justice is essential to the maintenance of social order. He contrasted the ways in which pre-industrial societies respond to the threat posed by violence by banishing a sacrificial scapegoat with the methods used by modern society (1979: 15):

> For us the circle has been broken. We owe our good fortune to one of our social institutions above all: our juridical system, which serves to deflect the menace of vengeance. The system does not suppress vengeance; rather, it effectively limits it to a single act of reprisal, enacted by a sovereign authority specializing in this particular function.

Girard added (*ibid.*: 23) that the punitive function of banishing offenders has a cost: the reprisal that the sovereign authority carries out is legitimate delib-erate harm – violent, except for the fact that it is imposed by a legitimate state authority: 'The procedures that keep men's violence in bounds have one thing in common: they are no strangers to the ways of violence'.

Despite the possibility that prisoners who use assaults to punish are mimicking their own treatment by the state, there are two important differences between the injuries they inflict and the deliberate harm inflicted through public vengeance.

First, imprisonment is enacted through a legitimate political authority. The prisoner might refuse to recognise its legitimacy, but the harm that governments use to draw boundaries, to deter others or to exact retribution is legitimate because of this authority, so long as the harm is not excessive.

Second, punitive assaults committed by prisoners inflict physical injury. The pain caused by imprisonment is often intangible. Corporal punishment is largely in the past. Whether prisons harm people in less measurable ways is debatable. A statement by the American Friends Service Committee (1971: 33) reframes the question of whether imprisonment constitutes deliberate harm:

The basic evils of imprisonment are that it denies autonomy, degrades dignity, impairs or destroys self-reliance, inculcates authoritarian values, minimizes the likelihood of beneficial interaction with one's peers, fractures family ties, destroys the family's economic stability, and prejudices the prisoner's future prospects for any improvement in his economic and social status.

These harms are not measurable in the same way as a punch on the nose. There are differences between the violence that prisoners commit when they assault those among them who have broken the code and the retributive punishment the state inflicts through the deprivation of liberty. But they hang on the legitimacy of the state and the perceived proportionality of harm, which cannot be measured.

Legitimacy must be earned by demonstrations of fairness, not power (see Sparks and Bottoms 1995). The use of force or punishment by prisons to counter the punitive violence of prisoners raises two fundamental problems. First, in using force or punishment, the prison reinforces the message that these are legitimate methods of responding to conflicts. Second, as Sparks and Bottoms pointed out, the use of force by the prison is a test, not a guarantor, of the legitimate authority of the prison. Thus, the state's use of force or punishment cannot establish the distinction between legitimate state punishment and illegitimate punishment by an inmate.

Concluding thoughts

Robben and Nordstrom (1995: 6) wrote:

> There is no fixed form of violence. Its manifestation is as flexible and transformative as the people and cultures who materialize it, employ it, suffer it, and defy it .... Violence is not reducible to some fundamental principle of human behaviour, to a universal base structure of society, or to general cognitive or biological processes.

These words of caution apply to the conflict-centred approach. Not all conflict features deliberate harm, and neither can every violent episode be traced back to an identifiable conflict. However, the CVP demonstrates the value of setting prison violence in the context of conflict. On a practical level, the CVP's analysis of fights and assaults in terms of the conflict pyramid shows that violence is neither arbitrary nor purposeless. The diverse catalysts that prisoners used exhibit a vast range of behaviour by which humans can deliberately harm others. Positioned as a dimension of interpersonal conflict, the use of deliberate harm by prisoners often emerged as the behaviour of people who believed they had run out of options. More theoretically, when violence is contextualised in conflict, the ways in which situations gradually take on violence-prone connotations become clear. Violence becomes meaningful, although not condoned.

Notes

1 We benefited from comments on earlier drafts of this paper by the editor of this volume, Elizabeth Stanko, and also by Roger Hood, Director of the Centre for Criminological Research.
2 For further details about the methodology, see Lee and Stanko (2002).
3 All surnames are fictitious, taken at random from a list of English towns. The use of pseudo-surnames facilitates cross-references to particular stories and does not depersonalize the people interviewed in the way that 'Prisoner A' and 'Prisoner B' would do.
4 For a detailed elaboration of the role of power in prison violence see Edgar, O'Donnell and Martin et al. (2002).
5 For further evidence that prison conflicts can be resolved non-violently, see Edgar and Martin (2002: 4).
6 Sixty-eight percent of the prisoners who resorted to force (90/132) saw their behaviour as 'violent'; 73 percent felt they had been right to use force; and 46 percent (61/132) said both that they had been violent *and* that they had been right to use force.

References

American Friends Service Committee (1971) *Struggle for Justice*. New York: Hill & Wang.
Burton, J. (1990) *Conflict: Resolution and Provention*. Basingstoke: Macmillan.
Edgar, K. and Martin, C. (2002) *Conflicts and Violence in Prison*, Violence Research Programme research findings. London: Economic and Social Research Council.
Edgar, K., O'Donnell, I. and Martin, C. (2002) *Prison Violence: The Dynamics of Conflict, Fear and Power*. Devon: Willan Publishing.
Girard, R. (1979) *Violence and the Sacred*. London: Johns Hopkins University Press.
Goffman, E. (1961) *Asylums*. New York: Anchor Books.
Lee, R.M. and Stanko, E.A. (eds) (2002) *Researching Violence: Methodological Issues and Ethical Dilemmas*. London: Routledge.
O'Donnell, I. and Edgar, K. (1996) *Victimisation in Prisons* (Home Office Research Findings No. 37). London: Home Office Research and Statistics Directorate.
Robben, A.C.G.M. and Nordstrom, C. (1995) 'The anthropology and ethnography of violence and sociopolitical conflict', in. Nordstrom, C. and A.C.G.M. Robben (eds) *Fieldwork under Fire: Contemporary Studies of Violence and Survival*. Berkeley: University of California Press.
Sparks, R. and Bottoms, A. (1995) 'Legitimacy and order in prisons', *British Journal of Sociology* 46: 45–62.
Sparks, R., Bottoms, A. and Hay, W. (1996) *Prisons and the Problem of Order*. Oxford: Clarendon Press.
Toch, H. (1969) *Violent Men*. Chicago: Aldine.
Toch, H. (1992) *Living in Prison: The Ecology of Survival*, revised edition. Washington: American Psychological Association.

12 Violence, fear and 'the everyday'

Negotiating spatial practice in the city of Belfast

Karen Lysaght and Anne Basten

Introduction

> I mean it's not just you're a Catholic, it's that they think you're a Catholic and that's what fears me.
>
> (Catholic female, thirties)

Violence, segregation and the spatialised nature of fear in Northern Ireland

The paramilitary ceasefires of 1994–97 and the attendant 'peace process' have brought significant change to everyday life in Northern Ireland. However, sectarian violence remains an aspect of daily reality for many people. High levels of residential segregation in urban areas show few signs of diminishing. Segregation is most pronounced in districts that are working-class in composition. While neither the intensity of sectarian violence nor segregation is uniform across Northern Ireland, they continue to form the social and spatial parameters within which many people's everyday lives take place.

Discourse on sectarian violence in the general population tends to emphasise violent incidents, victim profiles, individual perpetrators and their respective paramilitary organisations. While these themes are significant, they tend to ignore the wider societal implications of fear of sectarian attack. Just as violent attacks do not occur in a social vacuum but are conditioned by a web of social relations that stretch beyond the individual, their repercussions transcend the individuals involved to affect society at large. Incidents are 'digested' by communities and translated into narratives, which, in addition to personal experience, provide pivotal sources of subjective local knowledge. Such bodies of information form the building blocks with which individuals construct their perceptions of safety and danger in relation to their environment. However, the resulting constructs are not monolithic; rather, they resemble a mosaic in which various emotions of varying intensity are attached to different places that – in their entirety – make up an individual's environment. Fear, in other words, is highly spatialised. Perceptions of relative threat inform decisions on spatial behaviour. People do not merely exist fixed in a single location; instead, they engage in a multitude of productive and consumptive activities as they go about their daily lives. This necessitates moving outside the boundaries of their own ethnically exclusive neighbourhood and criss-crossing the territory of the 'other'. In consequence, many individuals have to negotiate the spatial realities of violence and fear daily, and they develop appropriate coping strategies to offset potential danger.

This chapter seeks to address the relative lack of attention given to the mundane implications of sectarian violence in socio-political as well as academic discourse in Northern Ireland. In particular, it wishes to draw attention to the experience of fear of sectarian violence and how it shapes spatial practice. In pursuit of this objective, we shall first review the current Northern Irish research landscape on the topic, before proceeding to examine spatial practices in working-class districts of Belfast. The analysis focuses on the movements by local residents into both the territory of the 'other' and into public space bordering their residential neighbourhoods. The paper explores the specific factors that local people take cognisance of in their daily spatial negotiations. The final section draws together the findings and draws conclusions with respect to some of the effects of political violence on everyday life.

Spatialised fear, coping strategies and the Northern Irish research landscape

Sectarian violence and segregation have for many years drawn the attention of academics with an interest in Northern Ireland. Studies of the impact of violence have traditionally followed one of two lines of investigation: either the largely positivist analysis of lethal incidents or the socio-psychological examination of the effects of violence on surviving victims or witnesses of attacks.

The first of these is comprised of the work of a range of scholars, geographers and political scientists in the main, who focus almost exclusively on fatal attacks, individual perpetrators (or their respective paramilitary organisations) and the characteristics of the victims involved (Fay *et al.* 1999; Murray 1982; O'Duffy 1995; O'Duffy and O'Leary 1990; Poole 1983, 1990; White 1993). Their main interest lies in measuring violence over time and in identifying patterns with regards to victims and locations in which violent incidents occur. For example, Murray (1982), analysing data on victims of killings and explosions between 1969 and 1977, identified gender and age as significant variables. Moreover, he detected specific spatial patterns, pointing to five regions displaying high levels of violence in Northern Ireland: Belfast, Derry/ Londonderry, south Armagh, the Fermanagh and Tyrone border areas, and mid-Ulster. Finally, Murray identified various factors to explain these spatial patterns, predicting that the ethnic composition (a great majority of Catholics), high levels of segregation, a history of resistance and specific environmental properties of a place (terrain containing targets such as specific people or buildings and/or providing cover and escape routes) are conducive to high levels of violence. More recently, Fay *et al.* (1999) have followed a similar approach. Compiling and analysing a comprehensive database on killings, the authors set out to construct a profile of victims and the geographical variation of violent incidents, based on quantitative analyses.

What is characteristic of this first kind of research is its focus on the primary effects of violence, with the analysis most commonly restricted to lethal incidents. While these analyses provide indispensable insights into patterns of violence, the wider social repercussions of such deaths are beyond their scope. Furthermore, this research is characterised by a specific conceptualisation of the role of space in relation to violence: geography features as location, as objective coordinates of violent attacks. In contrast, the examination of secondary effects relates to both the construction of mental maps as a mediated result of violence and its impact on spatial behaviour.

Sociologists and psychologists have examined violence in Northern Ireland from an alternative angle. Their main interest relates to individuals who have survived or witnessed violent incidents and how they have coped with these traumatic experiences (Smyth and Fay 2000). Frequently, the emphasis is placed on children and young people. Some studies have widened their focus to look at the broader impacts on socialisation processes, asking whether the experience of violence during the Troubles has produced a generation that is more violence-prone. Cairns (1987) reviewed existing (quantitative) studies on individual coping strategies (such as denial and habitualisation), on the extent of psychological disorders among children in Northern Ireland and on children's moral development (regarding both moral standards and behaviour). He concluded that in spite of the immense suffering of some, the majority of children have shown a remarkable resilience to the experience of violence. Moreover, he saw little evidence of a detrimental effect on children's moral standards. Smyth (1998), drawing on Cairns' work, dealt with both children who have survived attacks themselves and children whose parents have gone through traumatic experiences. She has vividly illustrated the effects of such experiences and the resulting coping strategies (e.g. displacement of memories, silence and non-communication within families, substance abuse).

The merit of this research in relation to violence lies in widening the study of its effects to the living, escaping the focus on killings that marked the first group of writers. The prevailing emphasis is on traumatic experiences and the fear that develops from such occurrences. The insights gained from this research lead on to further questions as to the wider socio-psychological implications of individual trauma: those processes that may engender perceptions of fear among whole communities. Moreover, it then becomes important to draw attention to the way fear permeates people's perceptions of space, the manner in which space becomes mentally tagged with attributes of 'safety' or 'danger'.

The importance of space in relation to violence is addressed by the literature on residential segregation in Northern Ireland (Boal 1978, 1981, 1982, 1987, 1993, 1994; Boal and Livingstone 1983; Boal *et al.* 1976; Doherty and Poole

1995; Poole and Doherty 1996). The literature is predominantly concerned with either examining the wider functions of segregation or measuring its scale. The former is most clearly addressed in the work of Boal, who identifies four main functional aspects: defence, preservation of one's own culture, avoidance of contact with the 'other' community, and providing a base for attack on the opposition. Doherty and Poole (1995) serve as an illustrative example of the second of these endeavours. The authors calculated a number of segregation indices for data on Belfast's population. The study of segregation scales over time, in conjunction with an analysis of historical sources on riots in the city, led them to conclude that segregation must be seen as the spatial outcome of violence, echoing earlier claims by Boal *et al.* (1976). Residential movements are thus interpreted as a behavioural response to violence.

Studies of residential movement implicitly suggest that individuals cope with fear of sectarian violence through a one-off decision: through moving house, into an area that is perceived to be safe. In many ways, however, coping is an ongoing process. Since the majority of urban communities in Belfast are not self-sufficient, residents need to negotiate their spatial practices on a continuous basis. Coping, in other words, is very much a feature of daily life. In addition, the existing literature does not distinguish between segregated space (based on residential housing) and sectarianised space (based on behaviour and perceptions of behaviour). In short, the (differential) *experience* of residential segregation by different communities and residents is beyond the scope of these studies, which is largely a result of the positivist approach they adopt.

With one notable exception, the relationship between residential and activity segregation has not been the focus of the literature to date. The exception is Boal's earliest work (1969), in which he conducted a quantitative analysis of activity patterns in the area surrounding Cupar Street in West Belfast. Based on a survey of residents, he examined spatial movements to bus stops, grocery shops and social visits and detected clearly demarcated activity spaces between Catholic and Protestant residents. Whereas the former showed a distinct orientation of movements towards the (Catholic) Falls Road area, the latter's activities are almost exclusively directed to the (Protestant) Shankill Road.

Boal's study, which predates the Troubles, is seminal in drawing attention to the daily spatial movements of residents and in casting light on discernible patterns therein. The outbreak of the Troubles and the attendant steep rise in the level of violence and segregation have underlined the importance of fear in relation to spatial behaviour. Accordingly, important questions emerge concerning the decision-making processes that lead to specific behavioural patterns and, more importantly, the daily negotiations that this entails.

Darby took the examination of violence and residential segregation a step further (1971, 1986, 1990; Darby and Morris 1974). He applied a multi-method research design, using both quantitative and qualitative elements in the analysis of intimidation and residential movement. Darby (1986) provided an ethnographic description of the way in which fear of violence induced large-scale residential de-mixing in the early 1970s. Like Doherty and Poole (Doherty and Poole 1995; Poole and Doherty 1996), Darby focused on residential movement as one specific behavioural response to fear. His contribution lies in providing an in-depth analysis of the underlying socio-psychological processes. More importantly, Darby also turned his attention to the evolution of relationships between neighbouring communities after de-mixing. Based on the analysis of social contacts (personal friendships and interactions between community groups), the author contended that communities adopted two main behavioural patterns after times of violent confrontation: avoidance of contact and partial interaction (restricted to clearly defined contexts such as the pursuit of common material interests).

In the course of his analysis, Darby devoted some attention to daily activities and the spatial movements involved once residential relocation has taken place; however, the issue was addressed only as a minor part of his investigation. Darby's main interest lay in the link between violence, segregation and community relations rather than in the implications of segregation and violence for the everyday life of individuals as members of these communities. He was concerned with the nature of intergroup relations, not with individual practice. Darby's interest did not pertain to the intricate ways in which the use of space shapes and is shaped by social relations.

The research rationale

The present project thus builds on this existing valuable research on violence in Northern Ireland and attempts to address certain significant gaps. It aims to cast light on the daily negotiations of spatial practice, which are induced by fear of sectarian violence and informed by subjective constructions (perceptions of 'safety' and 'danger') of objective realities (violence and segregation). It takes a microscopic view of spatial behaviour, drawing attention to the various coping strategies that individuals employ as members of one or other of the two main 'ethnic' communities in Northern Ireland. The study reaches beyond the most immediate and visible effects of sectarian violence in Belfast to its wider social impacts, which are no less 'real' or significant even if less tangible.

Individuals' negotiations of spatial practice are by definition highly subjective and, as a result, the examination calls for a qualitative approach in order to unravel the perceptions and rationales underlying behaviour. Accordingly, in-depth and focus group interviews were chosen as primary methods.[1] In total, approximately eighty residents were interviewed during the period May 2000 to May 2001. Access was gained to these individuals through various neighbourhood-based organisations such as residents groups, community centres, youth clubs, church groups, schools and political parties. Given the close association of violent incidents and residential segregation with working-class areas, detailed ethnographic work was undertaken in working-class, segregated, inner city areas in East and South Belfast.[2]

Quantitative data (see Table 12.1) underlines the deprived character of these communities. They display strong patterns of residential segregation, high

Table 12.1 A demographic and socio-economic profile of the five study areas

Indicator	Belfast urban area	Area 1	Area 2	Area 3	Area 4	Area 5
Population	475,903	7,352	2,449	1,140	1,308	1,043
Population (1999)	495,691	6,174	2,913	1,266	1,440	1,796
% Catholic	33.95	00.16	94.56	07.09	85.37	96.44
% age 0–15	23.59	21.44	32.99	19.04	29.05	27.80
% age 0–15 (1999)	23.01	21.42	31.55	20.47	29.99	26.16
% pensioners	17.43	23.01	13.47	27.89	09.25	17.26
% pensioners (1999)	19.64	24.35	15.38	23.80	15.26	17.66
% households without car	45.95	82.30	77.88	76.65	69.94	81.25
% owner-occupied housing	57.39	22.44	08.22	13.89	39.80	07.02
% public housing	35.64	64.49	90.69	84.49	41.02	90.23
% unemployment	18.48	35.36	48.17	31.67	36.48	50.40

Source: figures calculated from 1991 census data unless otherwise stated; 1999 figures calculated from data supplied by the Northern Ireland Statistics and Research Agency (see *http://www.nisra gov.uk*)

proportions of public housing and unemployment, and low car ownership. However, their demographic dynamics differ, Catholic districts (areas 2, 4 and 5) being characterised by a relatively young population, while Protestant districts (areas 1 and 3) show high levels of elderly residents. The contrast between the 1991 and 1999 figures illustrates contracting populations in some Protestant areas and growing populations in Catholic districts.

Spatial practices in working-class areas of Belfast

In the city of Belfast, day-to-day reality in segregated working-class districts builds upon a paradox. Although regular reference is made to the fact that there is little or no contact with neighbouring districts, residents often speak of those from neighbouring areas by name. Despite the existence of walls and fences dividing some districts from one another, mechanisms are at work whereby people have quite detailed information about one another, derived from moving in the same narrow spaces. It is not only the names of leading paramilitary figures from beyond the divide that are common knowledge; the identities of less high-profile individuals are also familiar. Contact and knowledge often result from cross-community schemes, school programmes, engagement in recreational rioting or involvement in the occasional examples of cross-community dating or marriage.

Certain forms of routine contact have a ritualised nature, where playful acts of competition and conflict are enacted between neighbouring groups:

When Rangers [Protestant-supported Glasgow football team] and Celtic [Catholic-supported Glasgow football team] play, and when Celtic win you will get phone calls to the Brighton Rock Bar [Protestant bar] from the Blackthorn, the White Lion [Catholic bars] and the Flying Fox [city-centre mixed bar] asking what was the score, they ask for people by name. When Rangers win we would ring the White Lion and the Blackthorn. And we would all gather around the phone and start singing. It happens every Celtic and Rangers match. They slam the phone down. It is getting to the stage if Rangers get beaten, you don't answer the phone, because you know who it is.

(Protestant male, thirties)

Such ritualised acts of conflict between neighbouring districts take on a more territorial form at interfaces. Boundary spaces are treated by some as zones of confrontation and identity performance, particularly in the shape of rioting (throwing stones, bottles and paint bombs, breaking windows). Many of those involved are young people, who often choose to wear their Celtic or Rangers football shirts as they engage in displays of territorialism on their neighbourhood boundaries. In addition, involvement in bands and fraternal organisations who parade along local thoroughfares and interfaces means that participants are identifiable even when not clothed in organisational regalia. Ritualised expressions of conflictual relations between groups ensure that people become aware of their neighbours' identities. Moreover, mere exiting and entering of ethnically exclusive neighbourhoods marks ethnic identity.

A whole range of sources therefore provide knowledge about residents in neighbouring districts. This has crucial implications for life 'on narrow ground'. Given that ethnically distinct communities coexist in a limited geographical area, reducing visibility in boundary areas proves difficult. As a result, people travelling in the vicinity of their local community cannot assume that they are unrecognisable.

The communities live cheek by jowl and people get to know your face.

(Catholic male, forties)

They would know you because you were on the interface [rioting and posturing]. You get to know people and faces and names.

(Protestant male, thirties)

They know where you're from. I mean I can look at somebody in the town and I'd say they're from the Prendergast Road [a main thoroughfare linking Protestant and Catholic districts]. 'Cause I know their faces, we're so close.

(Protestant female, forties)

As a result of these various forms of interaction, it proves practically impossible for residents to mask their religious identities within the local area and its surroundings.

Behaviour in neighbouring 'hostile' territory

This belief that group identity is highly visible impacts on how people use space outside their own residential areas. Individuals adopt strategies that allow them to regulate the relative visibility of their daily movements. One strategy that is employed is that of completely avoiding neighbouring districts that are ethnically different and hence perceived to be hostile. The following examples point to such a coping mechanism:

> There's a lot of people up there [registered with a doctors' surgery located across an interface] … what we actually do, it's illegal, but we get them to ring our prescriptions down to our pharmacy. You don't have to go up … they're not supposed to do that, but they do, because they know people are nervous and they're quite accommodating.
>
> (Catholic female, thirties)

> I had to do a project for school so I was going up to get books on it and my Daddy left me up to the library and he came back to collect me in 10 minutes so I was sitting there looking for books and asking the woman and there was this crowd of wee girls and wee boys sitting in the corner going 'you're a Fenian [historical term used as a derogatory word for a Catholic] aren't you?' I didn't know what to do. I just stood there beside the woman and they started calling me 'Fenian'. What am I to do for books now if I have to do a project or anything? So we're scared to go up to the library, so we've nothing to do for books now.
>
> (Catholic female, teens)

Frequently, parents impose their own mental maps of 'no-go' areas. Adults commonly speak of their fear for the safety of their children and young people, and the need to impose micro-geographical boundaries on their movements.

> I think the people who worry most are the parents. They probably don't worry so much about themselves, as they do about their children. I say to my kids 'These are no-go areas, don't go into town, don't go here and there. If you go anywhere, stay deep inside [your own area]'.
>
> (Protestant male, forties)

While using an avoidance strategy is commonplace, access to shared services makes it necessary for many people to enter 'other' neighbouring districts regularly. It may be possible not to use a library, but other daily activities are essential and leave people with little choice. In these cases, individuals use a range of coping strategies designed to reduce the visibility of their ethnic identity. While parents impose spatial rules as to where young people are allowed to venture, they are also realistic about the need for children and young people to leave their local neighbourhoods, whether for school or leisure pursuits. In such cases, parents try to impose restraints on their children's choice of dress or use of language.

> My ones are mad into Celtic and if they're going somewhere, into the town or the doctors or hospital appointments … I'd say 'don't put that [football shirt] on you … if you've to go to the city' … I'd be nearly having a heart attack.
>
> (Catholic female, thirties)

> I remember one time my son used to think that British was a bad word. He heard that many people shouting 'you dirty British [bastard]', but he thought that British was the bad word so we were walking up Gordon Road [Protestant area] and it was coming up to the 12th [of July, climax of the marching season] and all the flags were out, and there used to be a toy shop on the corner and he wanted a toy in it and I just hadn't got the money to buy it for him. So he says 'you dirty British', he shouted at me, and I ran up the street, it was just to get my hand over his mouth, you know, before he said it again.
>
> (Catholic female, thirties)

Restraints are associated not only with the use of clothing and language but also with the number of individuals venturing into neighbouring districts in a group. Large groups are perceived as likely to cause provocation:

> You might get two friends going up but you wouldn't get the crowd of girls that would roam the streets. You wouldn't catch them all saying 'let's go up to Parkfields [shopping centre located in a neighbouring Protestant district]'. You know on foot, two girlfriends taking a walk. But you wouldn't catch a crowd of them. When I say a crowd I mean about four or five.
>
> (Catholic male, twenties)

Safety measures are not only imposed by parents; children and young people independently adopt strategies designed to offset threat:

> My youngest daughter is 9 and her name is Ciara [Irish name associated with the Catholic population] and I have never ever said to her that she had to take her school uniform off or explained it but she always knew that if she was going to Parkfields Shopping Centre with me she couldn't say her name was Ciara and she had to put a coat over her to cover her school uniform. I didn't even notice it until about four weeks ago, we went to a shopping centre on the Clifford Road [Catholic district] instead of Parkfields and she said to me 'Mummy do I not need to put my coat on here'? And I said 'no, you're all right'. She said 'why, do they like Irish people up here'?
>
> (Catholic female, forties)

As the quotation above demonstrates, people employ several important coping strategies in their everyday spatial negotiations. The first of these involves the practice of not using or changing certain names: Irish first names such as Mairead and Séan identify people as Catholic, just as English names such as Sammy and Billy are more commonly Protestant. These names rarely cross the religious divide. Hence the act of changing or not using names in particular spaces can be seen as a deliberate strategy to offset the possibility of ethnic identification. Similarly, in order to reduce the chance of being associated with families known to be politically active in neighbouring districts, people refrain from divulging surnames. This is a particular concern in the case of cross-community projects with neighbouring districts, where such knowledge would be available. A second coping strategy that the quotation vividly illustrates arises from the connection of schools with particular religious groups, and the resulting ease with which an individual's religious affiliation can be identified by the uniform worn. Respondents refer to covering uniforms, wearing jackets and removing ties as measures designed to reduce potential threat when moving in mixed city spaces.

Crucially, what all of these strategies seek to address is the overriding need to avoid attracting attention to one's ethnic identity, the paramount need to avoid provoking a negative reaction to presence within the territory of the other community.

> I wouldn't walk down Pleasance Road [Protestant district], past Moville Heights [Catholic district] with my uniform on. I would get the feeling that I would be provoking them or something, if I was going down I would take my blazer off and only wear my skirt and jumper. Everyone knows it is the Arlington [Protestant school] blazer.
>
> (Protestant female, teens)

Coping strategies relate not only to people's behaviour in the public realm but also to their use of space, in particular when accessing services. As the catchment areas of schools are spread across wide geographical areas in a city characterised by residential segregation, it is necessary for many young people and their parents to negotiate a complicated mosaic of territories in their movement to and from school.

> My kids go to school up the road and I won't go up to the school the same route every day. I change routes, different streets, to make sure that I'm not seen because I've had remarks made to me when my kids have had their school uniform on and they've recognised the uniform.
>
> (Catholic female, twenties)

Just as it is imperative for individuals to avoid incensing those in 'hostile' areas, they must also seek to ensure that they do not present an easy target. Residents aim to reduce the possibility of an attack by choosing to vary their routes. This coping mechanism is not restricted to travelling to and from schools. It is equally employed when travelling to the post office, shopping centre, unemployment exchange or the workplace. They avoid adopting a 'same time, same place' predictability in their daily movements. Such strategies are informed by experience and reinforced by wider family and community valuations of 'intelligent' spatial behaviour. Remarks such as 'what was he/she doing there?' and 'walking there was asking for it' and 'working there was stupid' are value judgements that serve to impose community norms with respect to spatial practice. In summary, residents regulate their behaviour to reduce both provocation and predictability, in order to manage their relative (in)visibility in 'hostile' territory successfully.

Travelling through 'no man's land'

Not only are movements into the 'other's' territory inevitable, residents must also undertake journeys that bring them into areas that cannot initially be defined as belonging to either group. This includes main roads without adjacent residential housing, motorways and flyovers, green spaces, bridges, railway stations, and industrial or waste ground. Despite their supposed non-segregated and indeed non-political nature, these spaces become sectarianised through use. Spatial practices in 'no man's land' are highly patterned, primarily by the need to reduce the threat of potential attack. As when moving through the 'other's' territory, spatial choices are arguably dictated by the maxim 'become invisible'. People walk on specific sides of the street that are viewed as alternatively Protestant or Catholic. They follow predefined routes, crossing roads at particular traffic lights or junctions.

> That's how you know, see when people's walking up and down the Prendergast Road [main thoroughfare linking Protestant and Catholic districts] if they're on the side of the post office they're not Protestants and that's how we've always known.
>
> (Protestant female, teens)

> If we were walking into town it would be on the side opposite [to the Catholic district] so we would be nowhere near them. I would have stayed on that side until I got to the train station and then I would have crossed over so I wasn't walking on the same side as the Beeches [Catholic estate next to the station]. At night, I would probably get a taxi but if I were to walk at night I would walk that way because I wouldn't stay on the other side just in case anyone was to say anything. I remember when I was younger walking home from the train station and it was late at night and I was walking on that [Protestant] side and there were ones on the other side and they threw stuff [bottles] over. They were running across the road and throwing them.
>
> (Protestant female, teens)

Using the predefined 'Protestant' side of the street is part of a silent contract by which non-residential space is territorialised into areas that are alternatively 'ours' or 'theirs'. Such non-verbalised agreements effectively produce and define micro-geographies. This 'contract' appears to offer the possibility of dividing sectarianised space into zones of possible use. If adhered to, there is a lack of interest in this routine; presence effectively becomes unremarkable, even invisible.

However, sectarianised spatial practices entail an essential ambivalence. The young woman's reference to the difficulties in using these predefined routes at night clearly illustrates that while this arrangement allows a division of territory into relatively 'safe' spaces, it also marks out people's ethnic identity. For those intent on finding a target for their violence, patterned spatial practices provide the means for easy identification, particularly for night-time attacks.

While thoroughfares are functional spaces, other places could be more accurately described as 'void' spaces. Such areas are characterised by their lack of immediate function, especially at night. Here, fear of an imminent attack is often the result of the dominance by one group of a particular space. It is through certain leisure activities of young people that public space of this type can become sectarianised. Those engaging in underage drinking or making unacceptable levels of noise in their local districts may choose to gather at (or be instructed by paramilitaries to move to) open spaces where they can indulge in their leisure pursuits without fear of harassment from the police, paramilitaries or indeed parents. Drinking gangs habitually gather on vacant land: under flyovers, on playing fields and other green spaces, behind railway stations, and by the river. These young people are viewed by some as marking space as sectarianised by their sheer presence. Their actions ensure that others perceive the locality as threatening regardless of the actual intentions of the young people involved:

> When they built those new roads [flyovers] they put in a green area underneath, with flowerbeds and stuff, and they decided to put seats in there, which they thought was a good idea at the time. But of course there was nowhere for the young ones in Moville Heights to go. They didn't want their parents to see them drinking, so under that flyover they knew there was a row of seats and flowerbeds. Perfect spot, nobody could see you and you could see who was coming. The Protestants wouldn't walk on the far side of the road where Catholic territory was, they walked, because they felt safe, on their side of the road but, of course, there the Catholics were sitting with their drink. After a long number of years and some serious incidents they removed them [the seats], which actually, believe it or not, made a hell of a difference.
>
> (Protestant male, forties)

The research therefore reveals that space outside segregated residential areas is as equally sectarianised as that within. Although particular places may be contested, and usage may shift over time, these spatial practices and the perceptions that underpin them are clear-cut in the main, reproduced in the daily negotiations of those who share this body of knowledge.

Tacit agreements between communities

Whether or not sectarianised space is identified by group emblems and markings (and thus visible to the uninitiated), local people possess a complex body of knowledge about these locales and how they should be negotiated. This knowledge takes the form of a 'text of fear' or a 'boundary rulebook', imposing boundaries on personal behaviour within space. It provides a body of information on the appropriate use of sectarianised locales, which when properly employed acts to reduce the likelihood of violent assault. This common stock of knowledge is area-specific and deals with the micro-geographies of particular districts, whether individual corners, sides of the street, the place to cross the road, clumps of bushes, bus stops or bus routes.

Several factors are highly important in any risk calculation. Among these are social characteristics such as the age and gender of the individual concerned, temporal conditions, the wider political atmosphere, and socio-economic factors. Various stages of the life-cycle are reflected in spatial behaviour in sectarianised territory.

> I think when you're younger [there's more danger], if a 20-year-old is walking down the Prendergast Road and there's three or four 20-year-olds coming there is a good chance there would be a confrontation. But if there's a 45-year-old walking down and his hair going grey and he's got a jacket on and trousers, chances are that those 20-year-olds will walk past him and ignore him ... I think it is because when you are into middle age you're not sort of seen as a threat. A guy in a suit or in a pair of trousers and a jumper isn't seen as a threat where a young lad with maybe a short hair cut and a T-shirt and tattoos would be seen more as a threat ... Age has got a lot to do with it.
>
> (Protestant male, thirties)

In addition, spatial freedoms are clearly gendered, with men and women displaying different spatial practices.

> Men would be a natural target. I mean we're in a society where men were the main combatants more or less for thirty years and they were seen as the threat. Most men would probably see another man as a threat but you could have a woman who could do you ten times as much damage and be physically twice the size of the man but it's in your thinking. You're going to ignore her because she's a woman and you're going to concentrate on the man.
>
> (Protestant male, fifties)

In recent years there have been women intimidated off the roads, but as I say it has generally been the rule that women usually can have freer movements than the men.

(Catholic male, twenties)

The research reveals that men's activity spaces are severely curtailed, relative to women. Indeed, their movements are so restricted that they take place almost entirely within the boundaries of their own communities. The liberties that women possess represent an extension of the domestic sphere, allowing them to fulfil the tasks of everyday family management.

The boundary rulebook thus delineates a range of social characteristics that allow individuals a means of calculation as to whether they could potentially become the victim of a sectarian attack. These criteria are also used in order to assess the relative danger that others pose. While an elderly person is viewed as non-threatening, a young man is deemed more likely to pose a danger. Such common criteria for crediting threat and vulnerability demonstrate that an expectation of equivalence exists between the two groups. Despite limited interaction between neighbouring communities, there are clearly shared beliefs about appropriate behaviour. In many respects, the two communities view one another as mirror images of themselves.

Likewise, temporal factors play an important role in influencing the possibility of increased levels of sectarian tension. Miserable wet evenings and dark winter nights keep young people indoors and off the streets and interfaces, whereas bright summer evenings allow them to spend considerable amounts of time outside. Time-specific variations thus interplay with knowledge of the locality and its geographical referents to produce a patterned use of space within the city.

The Northern Irish 'marching season', from spring to early autumn, is associated with significant controversy and street disturbance. Cyclical in nature, the marching season represents a highly politicised period that impacts on the mundane features of daily life during the summer months. As one Protestant man noted: 'we're condemned to the politics of the marching season'. Other respondents echo this sentiment, speaking of the threat felt to be present in particular months of the calendar year:

I wouldn't mind working there [in a Protestant-dominated workplace in East Belfast] from September to May, but then once it comes after May, you don't know what's going to happen.

(Catholic female, thirties)

I suppose the doctors are either on the interface or across it. In the norm it doesn't really affect people but in tensions, round about the July time when you've got UVF flags flying at the top of the street and banners, it's intimidating for even fellas or young girls to go up because maybe there would be a crowd standing at the corner. You actually have to go round the corner

onto Pleasance Road for the chemist. So people might go to the doctor's
but they mightn't walk round to get their prescription.

(Catholic woman, thirties)

The wider political situation is in fact crucial among the various constraining or
enabling conditions for spatial practices. While individual movements can be
negotiated through an evaluation of one's social characteristics against the
existing temporal conditions, the wider political environment provides an all-
embracing atmosphere within which all spatial decisions are made.

The problem with these areas is that if there is an incident somewhere else
and it has nothing to do with you or anyone, if they are going to retaliate,
they pick on an easy target. Because it is easy and you are guaranteed to get
away. It is very difficult [to get a high-profile target] and it takes a lot of
time and preparation.

(Protestant male, thirties)

People's spatial behaviour is informed by such perceptions of fear. The parameters of perceived safety and danger shift in response to heightened tensions.
Movements into the territory of the other community are temporarily
suspended, only to be resumed after an appropriate cooling-off period.

While it is possible to find patterns in the use of space that are dictated by
such factors as age, gender, and temporal and political conditions, many people
negotiate their daily lives with much more ease. This is particularly the case for
those individuals with a higher level of disposable income or access to a car. For
those with access to a car, spatial divisions can be ignored and overcome.
However, with low levels of car ownership and dependence on public transport
in interface districts (see Table 12.1), most residents rely on services such as
doctors' surgeries, post offices, and shops being provided locally. This suggests
that the repercussions of sectarianised space are particularly significant to those
whose socio-economic position is such that they neither own cars nor have
sufficient funds to allow for private transportation. For these individuals, spatial
negotiations are even more intricate and constrained.

Conclusions

Fear of sectarian violence remains a highly significant feature of everyday life
for many residents in working-class areas of Belfast. It is mediated by the knowledge that acts of violence continue to be carried out almost daily, as well as by
residential segregation enforced by territorialism. This paper has sought to
address the effects on people's everyday lives that result from fear of sectarian
violence, examining how people manage their lives 'on narrow ground' and
negotiate sectarianised city spaces.

To date, research in Northern Ireland has devoted inadequate attention to
the impact of violence on daily spatial practices, focusing instead on violent

incidents, their psychological effects on victims and the relationship between communities. In a similar manner, literature on segregation in Northern Ireland does not cast light on these intricate spatial negotiations. Its concern with residential segregation conveys a static picture of life in the divided city of Belfast. It does not provide insights into the mundane activities of everyday living, which are dynamic and necessitate movement across diverse spaces and territories.

Spatial practices both in the territory of the 'other' community and in 'neutral' territory are highly rule-bound. An elaborate rulebook serves as a regulating mechanism. Its primary objective is to minimise risk. As a result of numerous contacts, whether formal (such as cross-community contact schemes) or informal (such as encounters of 'recreational' rioting), residents possess a substantial body of knowledge about neighbouring communities. Consequently, mutual recognisability is taken for granted. Masking one's own identity is impossible as members of one community enter a neighbouring community (in the course of undertaking fundamental daily activities). As a result, they seek to minimise the time spent in 'hostile' territory. More importantly, spatial practices are guided by two distinct strategies. First, it is essential not to attract 'unnecessary' attention to one's presence and not to 'provoke' those in the 'other' community. Second, the need to reduce the predictability of one's movements is paramount. If adhered to, these strategies effectively allow individuals to move into 'hostile' territory. In this sense, activity spaces are incongruent with residential spaces and activity patterns can be seen to challenge residential patterns. From this point of view, segregation is diluted on a daily basis through the sheer presence of the 'other' in supposedly segregated space. Ultimately, however, these movements are only possible if an individual complies with the unwritten rules imposed by the 'other' community and suppresses her/his own ethnic identity. By so doing, spatial divisions are reinforced and power relations reproduced.

An intricate text of norms likewise determines spatial practices in supposedly 'neutral' spaces surrounding ethnic residential territories. The research clearly demonstrates how such spaces become sectarianised through behaviour, despite a lack of outward territorial marking. Unwritten rules create geographical divisions on a micro-scale. Thus, public space surrounding segregated residential areas is not so much shared as divided along ever finer lines. Residential segregation is thus reproduced by people's spatial practices as they engage in a multitude of activities related to production and consumption. However, these behavioural patterns also entail a crucial ambivalence. While the minute carving up of 'neutral' space is motivated primarily by the desire to increase safety, it simultaneously serves to increase the visibility and predictability of people's movements. An individual's identity can thus be read from her/his use of space.

Moreover, it emerges from the research that the rules for spatial practices in both types of area are gender- and age-specific. Fear of violence most severely curtails the activity spaces of young males. Beyond the social characteristics of individuals, likewise, temporal factors play an important role. However, any spatial movements are subject to the overall political climate. Residents feel obliged to renegotiate their spatial practices in times of heightened tensions.

Ultimately, however, the decisive factor is socio-economic: it is those who lack private transport whose lives are most severely affected by fear of violence.

Furthermore, it is important to note that the boundary rulebook crucially builds on the assumption of equivalence and reciprocity: that is to say, on the expectation that the members of the 'other' community follow identical rules. It thus constitutes a tacit agreement between communities.

The research leads to the conclusion that an unwritten rulebook impacts on spatial practices in local neighbourhoods in a twofold way: it prescribes which spaces an individual can use (and which are 'off limits'); and it dictates how an individual should adapt her/his behaviour when moving about in public space. It effectively defines 'appropriate' and 'inappropriate' spatial practices in terms of safety and danger.

The findings suggest that Darby's concept of two main strategies underlying behavioural patterns (avoidance of contact and selective interaction) can be refined as a result of shifting attention from relations between communities towards individual members of one or the other ethnic community in Northern Ireland and their specific spatial practices. Strategies of avoidance do not merely seek to curtail social interaction with members of the 'other' community. Individuals use coping strategies that are far more intricate. In situations where an individual's activities necessitate entering the neighbouring territory of the 'other' community or supposedly 'no man's' land, the imperative is to *avoid* drawing attention to one's presence, to *avoid* provoking the 'other', to *avoid* becoming a target for sectarian violence by managing the predictability of one's movements. In other words, the overall aim guiding spatial practices is to use space 'intelligently' and thereby to achieve an 'unremarkable', near-invisible presence.

Thus, the spatial practices of many residents in working-class areas of Belfast are highly conditioned. Although they may safeguard individuals from falling victim to sectarian attacks, they simultaneously inflict violence on people's everyday lives. The fact that individuals are forced to undertake these complex daily negotiations of their spatial movements ultimately represents a further manifestation of the violence of the Northern Ireland conflict, one that permeates into a much wider population than those who fall victim to the bombings and shootings with which the area is most commonly associated.

Notes

1 All geographical references have been anonymised to provide confidentiality to respondents.
2 These areas are distinct from other districts of Belfast (particularly in the west of the city), which are segregated on a larger scale, thus ensuring that residents have little need to enter 'hostile' territory.

References

Boal, F. (1969) 'Territoriality on the Shankill–Falls divide, Belfast', *Irish Geography* 6: 30–50.

Boal, F. (1978) 'Territoriality on the Shankill–Falls divide, Belfast: the perspective from 1976', in D. Lanegrin and R. Palm (eds) *An Invitation to Geography*. New York: McGraw-Hill.

Boal, F. (1981) 'Residential segregation and mixing in a situation of ethnic and national conflict: Belfast', in P. Compton (ed.) *The Contemporary Population of Northern Ireland and Population-related Issues*. Belfast: Queen's University, Institute of Irish Studies.

Boal, F. (1982) 'Segregating and mixing: space and residence in Belfast', in F. Boal and D. Neville (eds) *Integration and Division. Geographical Perspectives on the Northern Ireland Problem*. London: Academic Press.

Boal, F. (1987) 'Segregation', in M. Pacione (ed.) *Social Geography: Progress and Prospect*. London: Croom Helm.

Boal, F. (1993) 'Between too much and me', in B. Murtagh (ed.) *Planning and Ethnic Space in Belfast*. Coleraine: Centre for Policy Research, University of Ulster.

Boal, F. (1994) 'Encapsulation: urban dimensions of national conflict', in S. Dunn (ed.) *Managing Divided Cities*. Keele: Keele University Press.

Boal, F. and Livingstone, D. (1983) 'The international frontier in microcosm – the Shankill–Falls divide: Belfast', in N. Kliot and S. Waterman (eds) *Pluralism and Political Geography. People, Territory and State*. London: Croom Helm.

Boal, F., Murray, R. *et al.* (1976) 'Belfast: the urban encapsulation of a national conflict', in S. Clarke and J. Obler (eds) *Urban Ethnic Conflict*. University of North Carolina.

Cairns, E. (1987) *Caught in Crossfire. Children and the Northern Ireland Conflict*. London: Appletree Press.

Darby, J. (1971) *FLIGHT. A Report on Population Movement in Belfast during August 1971*. Belfast: Community Relations Commission.

Darby, J. (1986) *Intimidation and the Control of Conflict in Northern Ireland*. Dublin: Gill and Macmillan.

Darby, J. (1990) 'Intimidation and interaction in a small Belfast community: the water and the fish', in J. Darby, N. Dodge and A.C. Hepburn (eds) *Political Violence. Ireland in a Comparative Perspective*. Belfast: Appletree Press.

Darby, J. and Morris, G. (1974) *Intimidation in Housing*. Belfast: Northern Ireland Community Relations Commission.

Doherty, P. and Poole, M. (1995) *Ethnic Residential Segregation in Belfast*. Coleraine: Centre for the Study of Conflict, University of Ulster.

Fay, M.-T., Morrissey, M. *et al.* (1999) *Northern Ireland's Troubles. The Human Cost*. London: Pluto Press.

Murray, R. (1982) 'Political violence in Northern Ireland 1969–1977', in F. Boal and N. Douglas (eds) *Integration and Division. Geographical Perspectives on the Northern Ireland Problem*. London: Academic Press.

O'Duffy, B. (1995) 'Violence in Northern Ireland 1969–1994 – sectarian or ethno-national', *Ethnic and Racial Studies* 18(4): 740–72.

O'Duffy, B. and O'Leary, B. (1990) 'Violence in Northern Ireland 1969–June 1989', in J. McGarry and B. O'Leary (eds) *The Future of Northern Ireland*. Oxford: Clarendon Press.

Poole, M. (1983) 'The demography of violence', in J. Darby (ed.) *Northern Ireland. The Background to the Conflict*. Belfast: Appletree Press.

Poole, M. (1990) 'The geographical location of political violence in Northern Ireland', in J. Darby, N. Dodge and A.C. Hepburn (eds) *Political Violence: Northern Ireland in a Comparative Perspective*. Belfast: Appletree Press.

Poole, M.A. and Doherty, P. (1996) *Ethnic Residential Segregation in Northern Ireland.* Coleraine: Centre for the Study of Conflict, University of Ulster.

Smyth, M. (1998) *Half the Battle. Understanding the Impact of the Troubles on Children and Young People.* Derry: Incore.

Smyth, M. and Fay, M.-T. (2000) *Personal Accounts from Northern Ireland's Troubles. Public Conflict, Private Loss.* London: Pluto Press.

White, R.W. (1993) 'On measuring political violence: Northern Ireland 1969–1980', *American Sociological Review* 58(4): 575–85.

Index

Printed in the United States
33517LVS00001B/296

9 780415 301305